12.⁰⁰

D1280226

Guidance
of the Young Child

GUIDANCE OF THE YOUNG CHILD

SECOND EDITION

Louise M. Langford
Helene Y. Rand

JOHN WILEY & SONS, INC.
NEW YORK SYDNEY LONDON TORONTO

PHOTO CREDITS:
Anne Cousineau, Roxbury Child Care Center, New Jersey
Steve Eberhardt, Aida Burdrick Child Care Center, New Jersey
Maynard Frank Wolfe, Industrial Home for the Blind, Brooklyn, New York

Library of Congress Cataloging in Publication Data:

Langford, Louise M
  Guidance of the young child.

  Bibliography: p.
  1. Children—Management. I. Rand, Helene Y.,
1930—   Langford/Rand II. Guidance of the Young Child
HQ769.L24 1975   649.12'3   74-18339
ISBN 0-471-51646-5

Printed in the United States of America

10 9 8 7 6 5 4 3 2

Preface

The group care of children outside of their homes has become important for several reasons: research has strengthened the belief that the early years are the most crucial ones in the development of children; an ever-increasing number of mothers of young children are employed in the working force because of economic or self-fulfillment needs; and sociocultural pressures for adequate and equal opportunities for all children have become prevalent.

These circumstances have created an urgency for more proficient teachers and teaching assistants for young children and for more knowledgeable parents. It seems imperative that all adults who are in contact with preschoolers should try to understand how youngsters can be guided toward achieving their best potential.

Many child care centers in colleges, junior colleges, high schools, industrial complexes, and community settings provide field experiences for students who want to observe and learn about child development and guidance. However, despite the superabundance of written material, there appears to be almost no usable textbook for beginning students.

Excellent books have been published that comprehensively describe human development. Some of them stress evidence of growth patterns as shown by research studies, some discuss specific patterns of growth and development, and others deal with behavior responses at various maturational levels. Also there are laboratory manuals that stress methodology, space, equipment, procedures, and administration. Here, at the end of each chapter, we recommend many of these books and offer brief descriptions of them.

The purpose of the present volume is to present basic facts concerning child development and various points of view relative to child guidance in such a way that the student can formulate an individual and personal philosophy of guidance. Instead of a detailed account of human development and teaching theory, the book is intended as an introduction for students who will do further course work and research before they assume responsible positions in guiding groups of children. We have included information and suggestions that were considered helpful and important by several hundred students, teachers, and assistant teachers of young children in choosing patterns for their own behavior with youngsters.

The development of children in four general areas is described. We are aware that these areas are interrelated and overlapping, and we stress this fact. Physical and social development have been given specific chapter headings. Emotional development has been emphasized in Chapter 5 on personality growth and has not been defined as a separate topic because the pervasive nature of the child's feelings in all areas of his life is our main point of focus throughout this book. Indeed, we continuously emphasize the importance of how the child feels about himself and the world around him. We have included a new chapter about learning with applications of recent findings in the area of cognition but here, too, we have stressed the interrelatedness of all kinds of development. Modifications have been made that reflect the growth of knowledge about how children change as they mature, and materials concerning the guidance of the handicapped child have been expanded.

The examples relate to individual children. There is an increasing awareness that, if we are to avoid educating for mediocrity, we must consider the training of the individual person. Our focus is on the child, not children. Although child care centers deal with groups of children, the program of a good preschool is planned on the basis of the needs of individual children, and its purpose is the beneficial guidance of each child. Since children have similar feelings, needs, and desires whether they are at home or at school, this book will be of value to parents in their everyday dealings with young children and to public health and social workers who want to help parents guide their children.

We think that the material will be helpful to all adults who want to learn something about how children develop, and who want to recognize signs of progress toward maturity. They will gain an insight in understanding how children feel about themselves, other people, and their experiences. They will be able to recognize the importance of adult-child interaction during the process of growth and will learn important ways to evaluate child care centers. Finally, they will develop a philosophy of the kind of child guidance that will permit children to develop their individual potentialities and learn the controls that will be necessary in their future living.

We have worked professionally with young children, teachers, directors, paraprofessionals, students, and parents. Each of us has two children and, therefore, have an understanding of parents that has enriched our perceptions of the dynamics of adult-child relationships. This book is a synthesis of what we believe will help the potential child care worker to learn how children develop and how adults can best guide them physically, emotionally, intellectually, and socially, toward optimum growth.

We are grateful to our families, students, colleagues, and the children and parents with whom we have worked. They made this book possible. We especially thank Rose Mukerji, Chairman, Division of Early Childhood Education, Brooklyn College, City University of New York, for her valuable suggestions and Irene Davis, Group Care Specialist, Department of Social and Rehabilitation Services, State of Kansas, for her recommendations relating to the current concerns of group care personnel.

Louise M. Langford
Helene Yagoda Rand

Contents

ix

chapter 1

Introduction to the Laboratory Child Care Center

In the past few decades social scientists and psychologists have become progressively aware of the importance of self-attitudes, and of the relation of self-confidence to good emotional adjustment and happiness. It is certain that through our study of small children with their naivete in expressing their feelings, their short-time emotional responses, their trial-and-error methods of attaining physical, social, and mental skills, we are in a better position to understand ourselves, our feelings, and our actions. Self-insight is one of the finest rewards in the study of child development and behavior.

Probably we can all benefit from a better understanding of very young children. Most of us have lived in family groups with young children, are living with them, or will be in the future. Just as a better understanding of other people at any age level will make social contacts easier and more rewarding, so a knowledge of the preschool child should help us to live with him and guide him wisely.

There is no better way to understand the young child than to watch him in his reactions to his own feelings, to his physical world, and to other people. Assignments to observe in group-care centers will provide common bases so that students and instructors may have an opportunity to study and discuss school programs, specific incidents, and individual children.

PURPOSES OF PRESCHOOL EDUCATION

Some basic facts about the purposes of the group-care of children should enable students to more easily assume proper roles in the child care center and to feel assurance during their periods of assignment. Goals and purposes of preschool education will be emphasized throughout this book and only those that will be of the most help to students as they first become acquainted with the child care center are included at this point.

There has never before been a time in the history of our country when so many people are living in small apartments or mobile homes with so little space for children to move around or have the kinds of materials and equipment that they need for their optimum overall development. The large rural home of the past with its spacious yard far from traffic congestion and with the presence of adults whose work was usually done in or near the house provided many opportunities that do not exist for most children today.

At present many parents are enrolled in colleges or are in the military service. In these cases, if families are to be together, cramped housing often must be accepted. Small living quarters may make freedom of movement for young children impossible. In fact, with modern housing conditions, it often is necessary for parents to discourage their children from being active despite the fact that the need for vigorous activity is paramount.

Under good supervision, children respond beneficially to space and freedom. In order to learn to use his body effectively the child must have the opprotunity to practice motor skills, to try out his individual ways of action. In a good child care center, provision is made for space, equipment, and guidance that actually promote strenuous bodily activity.

A good preschool will provide not only space and equipment to encourage vigorous physical activity but also diverse materials that will offer an opportunity for the child to practice manipulative skills. Play materials and equipment are scaled to his size and abilities so he can carry on his activities in his own way. Low tables and chairs, low lavatories and toilets, low shelves and book racks make it possible for children to be more physically independent and to gain confidence in themselves. The young child must meet problems and his feelings about his successes and failures will set a pattern for his later responses. Adults who observe young children soon realize that many of their own attitudes were established early in life. Sometimes it is interesting to trace some of these beginnings. Insight of this kind may help us understand not only ourselves but also our friends.

A good preschool experience will help stimulate the child's independent thinking. A well-planned program offers many opportunities for experimentation, problem solving, and the use of imagination. Through materials, equipment, and careful planning by competent staff a child care center can contribute to the growth of ideas and stimulate curiosity that may provide the basis for learning at all later age levels. The way in which they may be accomplished will be described in later chapters.

The group-care center has a unique influence because it offers many children the first opportunities outside their homes to associate with children of similar chronological ages and to develop attitudes toward themselves and other people that will affect their future learnings. At the present time, many families are characteristically transient and may put forth little or no effort to make friends because of possible sadness in leavetaking when they move agian. This tendency to avoid close entanglements with other people in the community undoubtedly is damaging to transient children and their families.

Preschool attendance also can help the child learn to understand adults and may lay a foundation for acceptance or rejection of adult authority in future situations. A few decades ago, when families were less transient, grandmothers, grandfathers, aunts, uncles, and cousins were residents or frequent guests in the home. In those days, children often were included in the social invitations of their parents. They had many chances to observe adults and to learn to know them. The child of today seldom has these opportunities. Grandfather and grandmother often are strangers whom the children see only once a year at holiday time when adults are busy with their grown-up affairs or, at best, when the usual pattern of daily living is not followed. Uncles and aunts may seem to be fictional people who send mementos now and then from faraway places such as Puerto Rico, Europe, or South America.

In some cases, the child's contacts with adults other than his parents are almost nonexistent. Even when he is old enough for kindergarten, the size of classes makes it difficult for one teacher to lend support to each child at every moment of need. A good preschool teacher can encourage a good relationship between the child and future teachers just by being able to attend to the child's individual needs within the relatively small preschool group with which she works. Together with parents, she can aid in strengthening the child's concept that adults are people who act with understanding and helpfulness, who are affectionate, who like people and who, in general, are pretty nice folks.

At times it may be to the child's advantage to spend a part of his day with adults who are not emotionally bound by his every need, who are not responsible for his entire future as parents feel they are. It is obvious that the emotional tie between parent and child is much more intense than between teacher and child. Often emotional upsets are harder to handle at home than in the group situation, and sometimes the age differences in the home cause conflicts and emotional tensions.

Since young children spend much of their time at home, the home is where ways of living are learned, where the child must practice ways of doing things, and where he learns to understand his capabilities and what others expect from him as well as what he can expect from other people. In these early years, a good foundation for satisfying parent-teacher relations for the future may be established. This is a time when parents and teachers can discuss the details of a child's life, when his home life and his school life are more nearly alike than at any time in the future. Cooperation between parents and teachers will help to establish parental feelings of trust toward teachers as a professional group.

Through group meetings, parents gain the assurance that their child is similar to others of his age. It is comforting to know that problems that once seemed unique to their home are, in reality, typical of the age level of the child. A preschool teacher often can be helpful by means of individual parent conferences, reports to parents, supplying books and pamphlets, or offering counsel when day-by-day problems arise.

Staff members in a child care center can help children develop acceptable social techniques. In the preschool, it is possible to direct energies into socially acceptable activities, to allow plenty of time for the child to set his own pace in social contacts, to help the child establish his contacts in ways acceptable to his age mates, and to provide time, space, equipment, and activities as aids toward social interaction.

A good preschool provides an emotional climate conducive to the optimal development of children. Modern scientific study indicates that instances of poor academic progress, some juvenile delinquency, and many nervous disorders might have been prevented or corrected early in childhood. The flexible program of the preschool with its small groups of children and its freedom from the interruptions that occur in most homes makes it easier for children to develop a sense of personal worth. Because the chief interest of the adults in the child care center is the welfare of the children, it is easy for them to plan a program that provides a balance between quiet and vigorous activities. If young children are to remain free of tensions, they need this kind of flexible scheduling. Since preschools, unlike public schools, can deal with small groups of children it is obvious that the curriculum of a preschool can remain comparatively unstructured; that is, the program can remain flexible within broad limits.

BECOMING ACQUAINTED WITH THE CHILD CARE CENTER

The plan for your first assigned visit to the child care center probably will be unique to the specific program in which you are enrolled. Usually it is advantageous for students to make their first visit when the children are not present. At that time, the supervising teacher or the director of the preschool probably will describe the purposes of the specific program, the ages of the children, and the principal reasons for which most of the children's parents have placed them in the school. Hopefully, these remarks also will include a brief statement of a governing philosophy relating to child guidance.

If adults are to be assigned for observation periods, it is important that they know what procedures will be followed when they arrive at the time school is in session. A preliminary tour will provide an opportunity to learn the following: (1) the general nature of participation if they are to be working directly with the children, (2) where instructions for students will be posted, (3) by what route students should enter the building, (4) time schedules for students' assignments, (5) where outdoor clothing, books, and other personal effects should be stored while school is in session, and (6) the location and plan of child groups both inside and outdoors. Some schools provide printed or mimeographed sheets listing rules for visitors. Students should be familiar with these rules and follow them closely until they are assigned to participate.

Students also must know where various equipment and supplies are stored. If they are to assist with the children's activities, teachers probably will expect them to gather materials when a change of activities is imminent. Obviously, a teacher who is responsible for a group of active children cannot take time to give explicit directions when she makes a request of an assisting student.

Recommendations for Student Behavior

Do

1. Listen carefully to any instructions before your visit.
2. Remove outdoor clothing when observing indoors. Do not wear a hat or head scarf inside.
3. Sit on a low chair.
4. Make notes on questions you may have and discuss them later in class. Other students will have similar questions.

Do Not

1. Chat with other observers or teachers.
2. Engage the children in conversation. If a child addresses you, reply briefly and courteously.
3. Move around through the rooms or hover over the children.
4. Laugh at the children or their activities. You should reserve your comments for the classroom or for private conferences with teachers or fellow students.

THE IMPORTANCE OF THE CHILD CARE LABORATORY

Students should find the knowledge gained in the laboratory valuable; the experience is pleasant and impressions that are gained are lasting. Not a few students who enter beginning classes state that they are ill-at-ease with young children or that they consider them difficult to control. As they watch groups of children in their daily preschool activities, they learn to understand children's feelings and the resulting behavior. They recognize that children are not miniature adults but are dynamic creatures who are changing rapidly: physically, mentally, socially, and emotionally. By observing the overt behavior of children and learning to understand the reasons for that behavior, students become increasingly tolerant of all children. Methods of guidance based on principles of development become natural and this, in turn, promotes feelings of acceptance and ease in future contacts with children.

It is a privilege for students to have the opportunity to observe children in a preschool setting. Scientific child study is relatively new. Obviously, procuring human beings for laboratory purposes is difficult. Until the twentieth century, research studies usually included only a small number of subjects since professional workers had to rely on their own families or close friends for lending their children for observation. Recently, a crucial need for the care and guidance of young children outside their homes has promoted a wide range of opportunities for laboratory experiences, sometimes called "field experiences."

A field experience may be valuable in preparation for employment. There is an increasing need for preschool teachers and trained personnel is scarce. Supervisory positions are becoming more numerous. A knowledge of child development and guidance also provides a good basis for professional work in home economics, journalism, elementary school teaching, human nutrition, nursing, retailing, welfare work, and other fields. Often, students who have majored in these other areas find limited opportunities in their specific lines of training in the communities in which they live. Those with some organized training in child guidance can start cooperative play groups, private nursery schools, supervise Head Start programs, act as caregivers for community day care centers, or serve as consultants to parent groups. If their training has been sound, they will recognize their limitations and will not assume responsibilities beyond their knowledge. Students should obtain information concerning sources of current books and pamphlets that might be useful to them later as they live or work with preschoolers.

If students have assumed the care of younger siblings or their own children, emotional ties and family patterns of guidance may have tended to influence their conclusions about how children grow and behave. If they have taught in Sunday Schools or summer recreation programs, their experiences with children have been brief and informal. If students have been employed as baby sitters, they have been subject to momentary parental planning and their observations probably have been based on the behavior of only one to three or four children of various ages and from similar family backgrounds.

Frequently the student who has had no experience with young children finds objective observation easier than the person who has been accustomed to close emotional ties with preschoolers. For many people, feeling at ease during the first few laboratory periods seems difficult. However, at the conclusion of a series of field experiences, students usually are unanimous in stating that the assignments have been enjoyable.

OBSERVATION OF YOUNG CHILDREN

Some centers are equipped with one-way vision screens that permit laboratory visitors to observe children without the children knowing they are being observed. These areas may be soundproof so that groups of students, instructors, and parents can discuss individual children and situations. Loudspeakers that may be turned on and off enable those who are observing to hear conversations in the children's areas when they desire.

In other schools, students are faced with the problem of moving into play areas and yet attempting to be unobtrusive so that children will not be affected by their presence. The purpose is to observe children as they really are and situations become unnatural when the presence of adults influences the children's behavior. The ability to observe and record minute details while staying out of the way of the children is likely to be difficult and uncomfortable during the first one or two field assignments. Later, students probably will become aware of the satisfactions of being near the children and working with them.

In order to evaluate children accurately, some kind of written record is necessary. Sometimes it is difficult to write things down as they happen; the next best procedure is to write them down as quickly as possible after they happen. It is wise to carry a pad and pencil and to jot down notes in abbreviated form. Most children will be so accustomed to being watched that they seldom will be curious about note-taking. If curiosity is evident, these children will understand a brief, concise explanation about "school work."

Observations should be recorded as accuratley as possible. This means that each record should be dated precisely as to month, day, time of day, and duration of the observation. Obviously, if several records concerning a child's behavior have been made, knowledge of the sequence and timing of the behavior will be necessary if students are to recognize his progress or regression.

Anecdotal records are explicit notes based on the careful observation of behavior. These records can provide useful information, and are also valuable as a basis for classroom disucssion. If they are assembled as they have been accumulated over a period of time for one child or for a short time for several children, they will indicate patterns of development and behavior. The notes may furnish clues for good methods of guidance and they permit interpretation and evaluation of individual children and of groups of children.

Writing objective anecdotal records is not easy. There is always a tendency to record one's own reactions to the people involved or to the situation. Stereotyping children as "good," "bad," "timid," "aggressive," or "destructive" sometimes is difficult to avoid. Such generalities interfere with objective attitudes toward children and therefore with the wise choice of methods of guidance. To understand children, it is necessary to observe them from a number of points of view and evidence concerning their status must be collected carefully.

Notes describing children and their activities should be precise and detailed. Personal opinions or conjecture regarding the child's feelings should not be included except when requested. For example, instead of saying, "Mary's feelings were hurt and she wouldn't play with Becky for a long time," say "When Becky refused to let Mary have the doll, Mary left the doll corner and began to work on a puzzle. When she had completed one puzzle, she brought another one from the puzzle case." Although the difference in these records may seem trivial, a better understanding of Mary is possible when we consider the second record. We know something about the kind of behavior on the part of another child that makes Mary feel rejected and we know what type of activity she is likely to resort to when her feelings are hurt. If a student believes some personal interpretation is justifiable, it is good to place the statment of an opinion in parentheses. Thus, diverse opinions can be discussed in class. It is not always necessary to try to find the reasons for behavior. The multiple causes of behavior cannot be ascertained unless many other data are collected.

Always be definite. Instead of writing "some teacher" if the teacher's name is unknown, write "the teacher who played the piano" or "the teacher who served the fruit juice." As we shall see when guidance is discussed, teachers may affect the situation in various ways according to their individual personalities and how well they know the children. No record of a school situation is accurate unless the names of teachers and children can be included. It is imperative that students know the children's and adults' names if they are assigned to the laboratory regularly.

Children's exact ages in years and months are important also. Although this information is not always necessary, it is good to develop a habit of including it. The importance of recording slight changes in the chronological ages of children will become apparent when we consider the rapid rates of change in their behavior during the school term.

GENERAL INSTRUCTIONS FOR STUDENTS

1. Notebooks with stiff backs or clip boards are necessary. Notes should be taken as behavior occurs and a firm surface to write on is essential if your writing in the laboratory is to be legible.

2. Record notes at the time the observation takes place. Do not rely on memory. (Sometimes instructors will give permission for remembered incidents to be included if they are marked specifically.)

3. Do not take notes when you are working directly with the children on an assigned activity.

4. Be on time and do not be in too great a hurry to leave. Doing a few extra things may make a better day tomorrow for both children and adults. Always tell the group teacher when you are leaving. She may think you are watching the children.

5. Be alert and interested. Try not to interfere in a child's activity. Interference is necessary, of course, if such activity is endangering him or some other child.

6. Do not be afraid to go ahead. You may make mistakes, but that is better than not moving in when it is necessary.

7. Generally it is a good policy to withhold assistance from a child until he requests it or shows that he needs it. Often, a reassuring, "You can do it yourself," is all that is needed. Too much help hinders learning; too little help, when needed, discourages the child in his efforts. Be ready to help whether he asks for it or shows by other behavior that he needs it. There are times when he may be too tired to do things which he does readily on other days. Maintain a flexible attitude; adjust to the situation.

8. Do not be upset if some child does not cooperate or if he fails to respond to your approach. It could be for a variety of reasons. Try a different approach the next time. Study the child and discuss your problems with the instructor.

9. If you have not worked with young children, you will be surprised when you learn how interesting they are. Have a happy face and a pleasant voice, enjoy the children and they will respond to you.

10. Children should be allowed to settle small difficulties by themselves. A child should not be allowed to interfere unduly with the activities of others nor to endanger the safety of individuals or the group.

11. Be kind but firm in any instance where you step in to straighten out a difficulty. Report to the teachers what you have said or done in unusual situations.

12. Read your assignment carefully before going to class and have the things you want to look for clearly in mind.

13. As an observer, you must keep in the background. Use your eyes and ears and do not follow the child with your whole body.

14. Sometimes it will be necessary, when observing a specific child, to follow him as he goes about his activities. You should stay close enough to be able to hear clearly and to see his facial expressions but do not get so close that you interfere.

15. Guard against grouping with other adults. No more than two students should be in one place at one time. Adult conversations should be kept at a minimum and should never relate to the children or their activities.

16. Observe professional ethics. For students to understand children, it is necessary for teachers and students to discuss them frankly. It is important, however, that children never should be quoted outside the class.

Even in large towns, it is surprising how quickly Mrs. Jones will hear that a student was discussing some cute thing Mary Jones did at school. Laboratory work will be helpful and students will enjoy the clever actions and sayings of preschoolers but it is much better if they report to their friends that "a sweet three year old girl" or "a handsome four year old boy" did "this" or "that." However confident parents may be in the school program, it is disconcerting if they hear about their children through strangers.

In any community, it may be that students will know or will become acquainted with the relatives of preschoolers who attend the school. When questions are asked about the child or the school, it is good to be noncommittal, to state that the child is getting along "nicely" or, in case of a problem on the part of the parents, to give assurance that staff members are glad to schedule parent-teacher interviews or to visit with parents in person or by telephone.

Probably you will feel at home in a group-care center only after several visits. Frequently, students find their interest mounting only after assignments become definite and class discussions can be geared to specific activities.

SUGGESTED ASSIGNMENT

1. Learn the names of all staff members. Reports will be of value only if the teachers' names are recorded accurately.

2. Learn the names of the children in your group. It may be important for you to take notes on the individual children so that you will recognize them when they are dressed in different clothing when you make your next visit.

3. Learn the approximate ages of the children in the group to which you are assigned. This is important. The child you judge to be the youngest because of small physical size may prove to be one of the older members of the group.

4. Observe one child and write a detailed account of that child's activities for a ten-minute period. Make your record accurate and objective.

5. Choose a second child who is very different from the first child in appearance, actions, and activity interest. Write a detailed report of the second child's activities during a ten-minute period.

SUGGESTED READINGS

1. Breckenridge, Marian E., and Margaret Nesbitt, *Growth and Development of the Young Child,* 8th ed., W. B. Saunders, Philadelphia, 1969.

This book, with its numerous revisions, has become almost a classic in child development literature. The focus continues to be mainly biological although social and psychological aspects are also presented. For the student who plans to secure a college major in the field, it would be a good choice for basic information about children.

2. Dittman, Laura L., *Your Child From One to Six*, rev. ed., Award Books, N. Y., 1968.

This book first was published by the U. S. Children's Bureau in 1918 under the title, *Child Care—The Preschool Years,* and has been revised many times. It is an easily read, practical reference for parents. It would be good reading for the young person who wants to be a well-qualified baby sitter. The chapter, "When a Child is Sick," includes much practical information about communicable diseases and how to treat children when physical emergencies occur.

3. Host, Malcolm S., and Pearl B. Heller, *Day Care Administration,* Office of Child Development, U. S. Department of Health, Education, and Welfare, Washington, D. C., 1971.

This is an excellent source of information not only for those who plan to establish a day care center but also for students or parents. Part 2, "Components of Day Care Services," will be especially helpful. This section includes a discussion of the purposes of day care, the developmental needs of children in day care, and outlines for evaluation of programs and for the understanding of the children enrolled. For those who are working in preschool centers, good ideas are presented for evaluation of staff. Suggested forms for initial interviews with parents and for general administrative processes are included.

4. Association for Childhood Education, *Nursery School Teachers' Portfolio,* rev, ed, Washington, D. C., 1969.

These sixteen leaflets describe the aims of education for children under six and include suggested activities and methods of guidance. The form of publication makes division or addition of materials possible, Such a series is good for beginning teachers.

chapter 2

A Good Child-Care Center

A knowledge of the evolution of preschool education will promote an awareness of changes that are in progress and the reasons for them. The few historic facts that are given here are so brief that the student who is planning to major in areas closely related to child development and guidance is advised to refer to the more detailed accounts in the list of suggested readings at the end of this chapter.

ORIGINS OF THE PRESCHOOL MOVEMENT

More than two thousand years ago, Plato stressed the benefits of education for the very young child and since that time child care and guidance outside the home have taken many forms and have been undertaken for diverse reasons. Early in the eighteenth century, centers for preschool children in England stressed religious training and health protection. In Italy, England, and Germany, "infant schools" were established between 1810 and 1830.

In the latter part of the nineteenth century the kindergarten movement, instituted by Froebel, became popular in Germany. These schools, theoretically at least, were for the purpose of helping children develop their potentialities. We may consider them as true forerunners of our modern preschools since they represented the first early education that did not emphasize religious and moral discipline.

The nursery school, in name, is British in origin. The first nursery school was established in London in 1909 by two sisters. Margaret and Rachel McMillan. Its purpose was to care for the neglected children of poor parents and, therefore, the program was based on their health, cleanliness, and proper feeding. The school was largely custodial and the name, nursery school, as we think of it today was not truly descriptive.

At about the same time, Dr. Maria Montessori, a young woman physician in Italy, was appalled at the neglect of tenement children whose mothers were employed outside their homes. Dr. Montessori established schools where children were encouraged to use various materials for developing motor and mental skills. Her philosophy was that busy children were happy children. This belief has an important bearing on child guidance concepts at the present time.

Maria Montessori also hoped to aid mothers in learning proper methods of child care and this custom of working with parents is an important part of nursery education today. Montessori's venture in nursery education met with a great deal of criticism and her schools prospered far better in other European countries than in Italy. Finally, however, the merits of her plan were recognized throughout the world. In fact, several educators from the United States traveled to Europe to study the so-called *Montessori Method* and a number of schools using similar techniques were opened in this country. Adherence to specific Montessori techniques became less popular in the second decade of this century but many of the materials and some of the philosophy of the Montessori schools were inherent in the programs of all group-care centers. In the late fifties and early sixties, a recurrence of interest in more highly structured child care programs evolved and Montessori schools again became popular. Many training programs for teachers were available under the instruction of Maria Montessori's former students.

In the United States, the day care of young children has been so widespread and diverse that it is difficult to trace its origins accurately. The influence of the McMillan sisters was significant and impetus was gained, also, from a variety of organizations with similar interests in child welfare. Day care centers have existed in urban areas in the United States since late in the last century. Some of these could be described as group baby sitting situations offering only custodial care.

TYPES OF CHILD CARE CENTERS

An accurate listing of centers for young children in operation at the present time would be impossible to secure. So many diverse types of loosely structured preschool centers are in existence that categorizing them cannot be done. Some information about various types of schools, however, seems appropriate. Although methods and philosophies will vary from place to place and from center to center, some broad definitions and conditions are basic.

One kind of preshool exists solely for the purpose of scientific study of young children. These research centers sometimes are established as part of large universities and may be most closely allied with departments of medicine, home economics, psychology, sociology, physiology, anthropology, or education. From the study of individual children and group interaction among children in these centers has come much of our knowledge concerning good techniques of guidance. Their main purpose is not teacher training but rather the provision of better understanding as a basis for other professional work. These research centers contribute invaluable information about principles of human development.

Rather closely related to the research center type of preschools are the teacher training laboratories existing in many of our colleges and universities and in a few of our junior colleges and high schools. Usually, these centers are operated by departments of home economics, education, or psychology for the purpose of teacher training but, frequently, students from classes in other areas are assigned to them for observing. Sometimes, limited research also is conducted in these laboratory schools.

It is difficult to state how many privately operated preschools exist in any state but there are many of them in most of the cities in the United States. These schools are conducted for the purpose of money making by the operators, and fees often are so high that only parents from high socioeconomic levels can afford to enroll their children. Recently, several franchise companies have entered the day care field of private preschool education. Discriminating parents who carefully study the particular school usually can find a good private school for their child.

Recent changes in the field of education for the young child include a greater emphasis on parent education and participation. Cooperative day care centers fill a special need in that they may provide definite parent education if a well-qualified director is hired. As the name implies, the cooperative preschool classification may include any center that is staffed principally by the children's parents. Since an increasing number of mothers as well as fathers are employed, however, an alternate plan to involve them may be to require attendance of parents at meetings that are scheduled periodically. This system will be referred to later in this chapter.

Philanthropic child care centers are numerous in the United States. Many of these are operated by church groups or by such organizations as the Salvation Army, service clubs, or other community groups. These centers probably are increasing in number more rapidly than other types of schools. They often are organized by community leaders and governed by boards representative of as many different facets of the population as possible. Financial support is secured by private donations, through community money-making drives like the United

Fund programs, and sometimes is supplemented by state or federal grants. Rates are charged according to the parents' ability to pay.

Research in working with children in orphanages in 1939 indicated the importance of interpersonal relationships in stimulating cognitive functioning, but it was not until the 1960's that authorities began to report that disadvantaged children, when compared to middle-class children, were more likely to exhibit deficits in general intelligence, language development, fine motor coordination, time concepts, self-concepts, and motivation. This led to funding by the federal government of Head Start Programs throughout the United States. Criteria for admission to these preschools, according to the Office of Economic Opportunity, stated that any child was eligible to participate if he came from a family whose income was less than a specified amount, that amount depending on the number of family members.

In the past few years, another noticeable interest has appeared in the formation of a few centers for the children of migrant workers who are not eligible for other programs due to their brief residence in each community and because their parents' work often is located in nonurban settings. These programs usually have been financed by state funds.

Day care centers for exceptional children represent another kind of current concern. These schools sometimes are established by groups of parents of handicapped children, operated by churches, or sponsored by state governmental agencies. Additional information about their importance is provided in a later chapter.

Industry owned and operated centers for the care of young children were expanded because of World War II. During that war, several large war industries established special centers for the care of children whose parents worked in their plants. In most instances, these were well planned by professional personnel and operated by trained supervisors. At the present time, interest in such schools has gained impetus because (1) our country has 4.6 million working mothers of children under six years of age and that number is increasing, (2) these centers appear to reduce costly absenteeism, tardiness, and turnover of employees, and (3) many of these centers have been evaluated as a help to both employers and working parents.

HOW TO EVALUATE A CHILD CARE CENTER

Some states have passed laws that control the operation of preschool centers. The plan, however, for licensing preschool teachers has been delayed in many states, probably because of the need for more trained teachers than have been available. Most states have jurisdiction over group-care centers only insofar as whether or not the physical plant meets sanitary and fire prevention standards. In a few cities, facilities are provided by the public schools for prekindergarten groups and in still fewer cities teachers are hired by boards of education.

Licensing standards for each state can be obtained from state departments of health, education, or welfare.

Any preschool can be judged on the basis of whether it is providing for the optimal development of individual children. Attitudes and equipment that will help meet the child's needs cannot be specifically recommended and schools may be justified despite unique methods and program plans. It is important, however, that students who are to have field experiences know some of the ways in which centers can be evaluated.

A good preschool program is one that stresses four broad areas of care and guidance.

1. The child care center should provide for the child's physical well-being by protecting his health and safety; by providing nutritious food; by setting aside time for toileting and washing; by allowing space in which to move and practice body control; and by giving time for rest and relaxation.

2. The child care center should satisfy the educational needs of the child by providing equipment and materials that are interesting and stimulating; by encouraging each child to express his interests through materials, language, and music; by furnishing new experiences closely related to the child's day-by-day living; by providing experiences geared to the ability and readiness of each child; and by providing a group setting that will promote cooperative stimulation for learning.

3. The child care center should provide for social learning by recognizing the child's need to get along with other children and adults; by providing materials that enable children to enjoy playing together; and by helping the child to devleop techniques that will make him an acceptable member of a group.

4. The child care center should provide for the child's emotional growth by making him feel needed and wanted; by helping him to become independent; by accepting him and his feelings; and by guiding him toward releasing his feelings in acceptable ways.

The following check list should be helpful in deciding how well a program meets criteria in the four areas described.

1. Is a good variety of activity possible so that the child may have diverse and well-balanced learning experiences?

2. Are children given time to complete an activity they are interested in or does "keeping on schedule" seem more important?

3. Is there a good mixture of active and quiet play as well as outdoor and indoor play?

4. Is there opportunity for music, looking at books, and for conversation?

5. Does the teacher help the children learn about nature, basic science, and so forth?

6. Are experiences planned at the child's level of understanding and accomplishment?

7. Are experiences provided that help children get acquainted, learn to get along well together, and learn to share?

8. Are children helped to learn to use language for communication? Does the adult really listen to what the children say, does the teacher set a good example for them?

9. Are the children given time and encouragement to learn to dress and undress themselves, to hang up their wraps, to take care of play equipment, help set tables, serve food, and so forth?

10. Are health routines a definite part of the program so that children may learn to assume good habits and attitudes toward them?

11. Are the children encouraged to feel true kindness and courtesy toward other people?

No other factor, of course, is as important as the kind of teacher who will work with the child. Professional periodicals, newspapers, and popular magazines have published many articles in the past few years stressing the importance of early childhood experiences and there is a growing awareness of the value of good teachers for young children, but some people still believe that "just anyone" can care for the preschool child. Parents who have a sincere interest in their children's welfare will be thorough in investigating the training and personal characteristics of preschool teachers. The following points are especially significant.

1. Do teachers have warm friendly personalities?

2. Are teachers trained in child development and allied fields of study?

3. Are frequent parent-teacher interviews encouraged?

4. Are parents permitted to visit the school often?

5. Do teachers show respect for children and their parents?

6. Do teachers show pleasure in learning and in helping children learn?

Although many personal characteristics could be listed that would be important for a teacher of preschool children, the most important is a genuine liking and respect for children. If a teacher enjoys children, many other beneficial characteristics will be a part of her personal philosophy also. In keeping with a liking and respect for the young child, the good teacher will be a person who is patient, accepting, and eager to help him toward feelings of independence, self-confidence, and worthiness. It is evident that a sound knowledge of the ways in which children develop and how stages of development can be evaluated will be important if the teacher is to know when the child is ready for certain experiences.

A good teacher must experience joy in learning and in watching others learn. If the teacher takes pleasure in learning and enjoys the stimulation of increasing her own knowledge, she naturally will impart these characteristics to the child. Moreover, she will recognize his needs and decide on a proper curriculum or program to enhance his life. She will be alert to his needs for new activities and equipment, but accepting of his possible hesitancy to try too many new things at one time.

That the person who works with young children must be adaptable and flexible in her thinking and behavior is apparent. The ability to meet the crises of a day in the preschool is not easy to attain. If the teacher's philosophy is based on a liking for the children, their parents, and her work, it will be relatively easy for her to assume the relaxed, accepting attitudes that are so valuable in dealing with young children. This is not to imply that children must be allowed free rein in all their actions. In fact, limits and controls, if well chosen, give children feelings of security and are the basis for good techniques of guidance. A good teacher must be firm and consistent. Children should learn that their activities will always be governed by purposeful rules.

A teacher's philosophy of guidance must be built on knowledge of how the child feels, what have been the reasons for his behavior, and what his level of readiness is for future activities. Her thorough knowledge of the individual child will depend, too, on her ability to cooperate with the parents and to work with them toward the common goals that may be established by home and school. If the mother is free to work in the center on a regular basis, mutual understanding will be easier but, since most mothers are employed, contacts usually are planned by regularly scheduled parent meetings.

Since parents' feelings cannot help being reflected in the child, an understanding of those attitudes is as important as parental knowledge of the teacher's attitudes. Mutual reassurance, respect, and understanding reinforce the ways in which children benefit from school participation. It is always important for teachers and assistants in day care centers to remember that parents are well-meaning people. That high praise and admiration are due them is obvious in their seeking good care for their children.

Parent-teacher interviews before the child's admittance are imperative. At this time, parents often need reassurance. If there has been a family emergency, physical, emotional, or economic, that has made it necessary to enroll the child, there may be feelings of guilt on the part of the parents because they have been unable to protect the child from what the parent is afraid may seem like rejection. Parents may remember articles they have read about unfortunate children whose parents work. In this case, they may not be prepared to make the transition to the school easy for the child. Reassurance by the teacher will help both the child and the parents.

Parents that enroll a child only because they feel that he needs group associations or an enriched environment may also have mixed feelings about their decision to send the child away from home. Even if the decision has been made because it seems wise to place the responsibility of the child on someone else for a part of the time, parents may feel that they have failed because their parental responsibilities have been difficult to endure. These people may need to be assured that it is not abnormal to become irritated and annoyed in daily living with young children.

The personal characteristics and levels of responsibility of preschool staff and teachers are reflected not only in the program of the school but also in the physical facilities. If the building and playground areas meet certain specifications, parents can feel reasonably certain that, with sufficient supervision, their children will be even safer than in their own homes. Of course, types of buildings will vary widely depending on whether facilities are located in urban, suburban, or rural areas and whether the housing is rented, remodeled, or was built specifically for preschool purposes. Some features will depend on standards set by local or state health, fire, and insurance regulations.

Some general critieria by which buildings and playgrounds can be evaluated are:

Building

1. Is the building in good physical condition so there are few accident hazards?

2. Are the rooms large enough to permit vigorous activity (at least 35 square feet per child)?

3. Is the building well ventilated?

4. Are the playrooms bright and cheerful?

5. Are steps and low windows equipped with gates and locks?

6. Are toileting and washing facilities adequate for group size?

7. Are all areas clean and sanitary?

8. Is space provided for isolation in case of sudden illness?

9. Are telephones accessible for adult use?

10. Are rooms arranged so supervision of play is possible at all times?

11. Does the building have adequate fire exits?

Playground

1. Is the playground large enough for vigorous play (100 square feet per child)?

2. Is the playground free from rocks, ditches, and other accident hazards?

3. Is the playground well fenced for safety?

4. Is equipment in good repair?

5. Is the arrangement of equipment conducive to safe play?

6. Is there a good balance of sun, shade, and wind protection?

7. Is there a sheltered area for play in stormy weather?

SUGGESTED ASSIGNMENT

1. Make a list of questions that you think a parent should ask in a preadmission interview.

2. Make a list of questions that you think a teacher should ask in a preadmission interview.

3. If possible, visit another group-care center and write a paragraph comparing the facilities with those in the center to which you are assigned.

SELECTED READINGS

1. Assoc. for Childhood International, *Housing for Early Childhood Education,* Washington, D. C., 1968.

This pamphlet presents current ideas about a beneficial physical environment for young children. It will be useful for those who are planning to construct or to remodel a facility or for those who plan to rearrange and equip an area for children.

2. Day Care and Child Development Council of America, *Special Migrant Issue of Voice for Children,* Washington, D. C., 1971.

This leaflet was written in consultation with the Colorado Migrant Council. It describes the need for day care centers to care for this group of children and describes briefly the few programs that were in operation at the time of writing.

3. Fein, Greta G., and Alison Clark-Stewart, *Day Care in Context,* John Wiley, New York, 1973.

Chapter 1 of this book will provide information for the person who is interested in the evolution of day care in the U. S. from its inception for the purpose of the health and safety of neglected infants through the "nursery school movement." Parent education and types of programming are shown in an historical framework.

Pages 232 to 246 refer to the personal characteristics of caregivers that appear to be beneficial to young children. College instructors and day care supervisors will find comments about the training of day care personnel, professional and paraprofessional, helpful.

4. Frost, Joe L., and Glenn R. Hawkes, eds., *The Disadvantaged Child: Issues and Innovations,* 2nd ed., Houghton-Mifflin, Boston, 1970.

The dehumanizing effects of poverty in the U. S. as it affects children are presented in this well-organized collection of articles. An appendix provides information about how to obtain other information concerning this problem.

5. Gordon, Ira J., ed., *Early Childhood Education: Seventy-First Yearbook of the National Society for the Study of Education,* Part II, University of Chicago Press, Chicago, 1972.

This compilation of articles relating to preschool education will be useful to the serious student who desires knowledge about how experts view all aspects of the field. Descriptions of recent developments include a comparison of six Head Start models, findings about Project Follow Through, and contemporary trends in early childhood education in other countries.

6. LeMasters, E. E., *Parents in Modern America*, The Dorsey Press, Homewood, Illinois, 1970.

The author states that this book attempts to focus on what happens to parents during the child-rearing process. The emphasis is sociological, not psychological. This reading would be helpful for students who desire a deeper understanding as to how to work with parents. It would also be a good choice for a day care center lending library or for staff members involved in parent counseling.

7. Montessori, Maria, *The Secret of Childhood,* 7th ed., Garzanti, Milan Italy, 1960.

For the student who would like to read from actual source material written by Dr. Montessori, a translation by M. Joseph Costelloe is available from Ballentine Books, N. Y., 1972. In this writing, Montessori described the child in detail and discussed the kinds of materials and methods of teaching that would release his learning potential.

8. Parker, Ronald K., ed., *The Preschool in Action,* Allyn and Bacon, Rockleigh, New Jersey, 1972.

The selections in this book describe twelve of the best known kinds of programs in preschool education. The book includes current ideas about teaching the culturally and ethnically different children as well as the disadvantaged. Ways to use instructional materials are suggested.

9. Stanley, Julian C., ed., *Preschool Programs for the Disadvantaged: Five Experimental Approaches to Early Childhood Education,* Johns Hopkins Press, Baltimore, 1972.

This book should be of interest to those who plan to work with disadvantaged children. Articles present some controversial issues dealing with the worth of various programs.

chapter 3

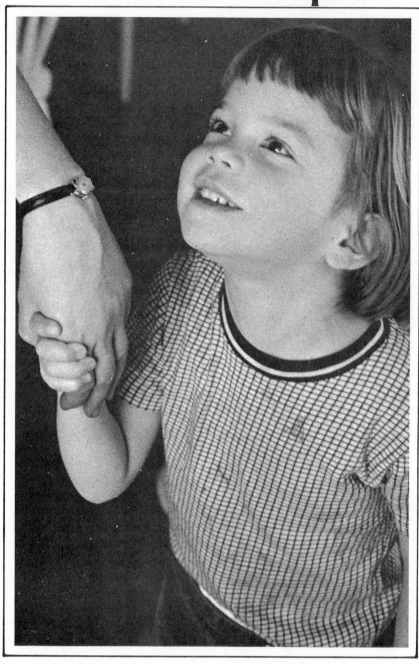

Types and Techniques of Guidance

People often speak of the way adults discipline children. Learning about good principles governing guidance, not discipline, of the young child is the purpose of this study. Therefore, it seems wothwhile to compare the connotations of the words, "discipline" and "guidance." Discipline usually indicates some action directed toward children, and guidance more often refers to actions with or for children. Guidance, then, represents every way in which the adult influences the child whereas discipline is merely a small part of the whole guidance scheme.

Guidance is applicable to all areas of child behavior and cannot be set apart, but when students are to observe children during a field experience some questions about general guidance practices arise as soon as observation periods are assigned. For that reason, a description of the purposes of methods of guidance is necessary before specific patterns of development and behavior are studied. Further discussion of the broad scope of guidance is included in all subsequent chapters.

PURPOSES OF GUIDANCE

Before guidance is described, its purposes must be considered. An immediate purpose of child guidance is the optimal and happy adjustment of children to the present demands of their environment. This is a twofold problem because guidance obviously must depend not only on what behavior is expected of the child but also on his individual ability to meet these demands.

A long-range view of the purposes of child guidance is also necessary. What is the ultimate goal in guiding children? It seems evident that the eventual result should be a happy, well-adjusted adult who is capable of self control and self direction and who functions to his maximum potential in his adult world. How then can we best fulfill immediate needs and eventual goals?

Since the beginning of the twentieth century, concepts of child guidance have been somewhat controversial. Before that time, authoritarian family patterns of living were the basis for child-rearing practices. Adults issued orders to children in an autocratic manner and the following expressions were prevalent, "Father knows best," "Children should be seen and not heard," and "Spare the rod and spoil the child." Children were expected to be "little ladies and gentlemen" and their feelings were seldom considered. For example, at large family dinners, children usually were expected to wait to be served until their elders had eaten.

To understand why such a heartless system of child guidance did not result in generations of thwarted and unhappy adults, it is necessary to consider other aspects of family life in those times. The home was largely an economic institution. Most of the family's needs were met within the boundaries of the home. The kitchen was the setting for many cooperative activities. Father or the older children helped with drawing and carrying water for washing the clothes, growing food-stuffs and preserving them was a whole-family enterprise, and most clothing was produced under the family roof.

In this setting, children had a working relationship with their parents and siblings so that there was a basis for interpersonal understanding and respect. Furthermore, as each child grew, he was expected to shoulder some part of the family responsibility according to his individual ability. His later role was clear to him and he could have a sense of pride in the place he would fill. This plan of family living obviously created feelings of achievement, recognition, and security in children. By playing a productive role in the family, children knew they "belonged." Because they were so wholeheartedly accepted in other ways, they could withstand the stronger controls that were the core of parent-child relationships.

At about the beginning of this century, technological progress and resulting industrialization brought amazing changes in family life. The functions of the family were altered because of greater concentrations of population in urban areas, smaller living quarters, and because less goods were produced by family members. Children became less important since it was no longer necessary nor even possible for them to help in vital family work.

Simultaneously, there was an increasing awareness of the worth of the individual personality. Sociologists and psychologists were beginning to stress the importance of the welfare of the individual and the significance of early childhood experiences. A widespread mental hygiene movement originated. Thus, a second concept of child rearing was formed. Extreme permissiveness in child guidance almost became a cult. Parents were warned on all sides that the frustrations of young children would have long-lasting effects. Mothers and fathers often believed that children's impulsive behavior should never be stifled and "Junior ruled the roost." In addition, children no longer had the secure feelings fostered by a united family group. Father often commuted and the children's waking and eating hours seldom coincided with his time at home. Mothers spent less time in preserving foodstuffs and in household tasks. Not only were there less tasks with which children could help, but children as they grew did not have the feelings of stability that were possible earlier when they were needed to assist with family chores.

Families were smaller and children did not have the opportunity to learn acceptable social behavior by practicing in their association with siblings. The fact that there usually were fewer children in the family probably caused parents to be more intent concerning their responsibilities; their interests were concentrated on one or two children.

During this century, recurrent economic turmoil and several periods of military involvement overseas have affected the serenity of adult reactions to life. Since we all are influenced by the feelings of those around us, and especially by those of our parents, the emotional upheaval of many parents no doubt has served further to make children feel insecure. Emotional maladjustments have been more prevalent at all age levels and children have not had the advantage of definite expectations from adults that might have provided emotional support.

Now, a third type of child guidance has evolved. It is the middle position between the rigid and the permissive types, a process by which demands are scaled according to the abilities of the child. Adult expectations are commensurate with the child's level of development. Our premise is that feelings need to be expressed and that good methods of guidance channel the expression of children's feelings into ways that do no harm to them or to others. Authoritarian guidance often made children feel humiliated because they could not meet the expected standards. Extreme permissiveness gave them no standards for which to strive. The new way indicates that children are respected for their efforts to act independently but insists that they find acceptable ways in which to express their independence.

Because our desire is for definite patterns of procedure in all we undertake to do, it is difficult to follow a scheme somewhere between two extremes. Most people who live and work with children, however, will agree that the present concept of good guidance for children is a far more sensible one than the authoritarian or the extremely permissive viewpoints. Its brief description would be "freedom within limits." That children need some definite limits or rules is apparent to anyone who knows them well. Modification of behavior can occur in simple everyday situations in any group-care center.

Jeffry had been rebuffed by several children in his group on the playground. He and Billy had quarreled over a tricycle and Billy had finally jumped on the trike and moved quickly away. A few minutes later, John and Danny had announced that Jeffry couldn't play "cowboys and Indians" with them. Jeffry walked to the sandpile and began pelting the younger children with sand and pebbles.

Miss Johnson reached for Jeffry's hand and said in a quiet, calm way, "You seem upset. Let's go over and sit on the bench and watch the weathervane." That Jeffry welcomed her intervention was apparent by the way in which he took her hand and accompanied her to the bench where they sat and talked about the weathervane, the bird house, and the large shade trees. Jeffry then got down and went to climb on the jungle gym with some other children.

Apparently Miss Johnson's pattern of guidance was well chosen because Jeffry followed her with his eyes as she moved about later in the playroom. Several times during the morning he approached her and made pleasant, happy comments about his activities.

Children's needs for rules are demonstrated at all age levels and at home as well as at school.

The Browns and their children, ages five and nine, lived in a neighborhood in which there were many children. Tommy and Becky Brown usually went to bed about eight o'clock. On warm spring evenings, when Mrs. Brown called to the children from the front porch, Jerry Stevens would often follow them to the front steps and say, "My mother doesn't make me go to bed."

This pattern continued night after night. One evening, however, Jerry's mother did call to him to come inside at about the time that Mrs. Brown went out to summon her children. Before responding to his mother, Jerry bounded up the Browns' front steps and announced proudly, "Did you hear that? My mother says I have to come in now."

Too many rules are confusing but we must all live within a framework of limitations. Enforcing reasonable rules appears to reassure children that we love them, that we care what they do.

All adults will be able to think of families they know that veer toward authoritarian practices and other families that tend toward extreme permissiveness. It seems certain that no specific child guidance pattern exists in families in general. That the personalities of the adults, the personalities and developmental status of the children, the community customs, and many other factors dictate what general patterns may be best is explained later in the discussion.

When we keep the true purposes of guidance in mind, our attitudes toward children are likely to be altered. If we desire good adjustment for children both now and in the future, we soon realize that when guidance is needed it must be planned thoughtfully, that it is not the child's behavior alone that we guide but, more important, his feelings about his behavior. We know that behavior patterns will be altered as the child grows toward adulthood, but his feelings about himself, his environment, and other people may become deep-seated attitudes. It is easy for students to recall some of their own feelings that have carried over from childhood.

If we put ourselves in the child's place, we can understand his frequently occurring frustrations. It is always worthwhile to try to see the world as children see it, to try to understand how the child feels when he meets his world. It is good for adults to consider what their own actions are when the world seems topsy-turvy. Adults have many emotional outlets. Eating candy, taking a walk outdoors, smoking a cigarette, reading a mystery story, or picking a quarrel with a friend will often relieve inner tensions. It is apparent that few of these safety valves are possible for the young child and that children should be helped to find acceptable outlets.

Moreover, the child often is confronted with desires for achievement that is beyond his abilities. Poorly coordinated motor skills, a lack of verbal ability, a lack of judgment because of his limited background of experience all serve to erect barriers in his attempts to meet the demands of his environment. If we are to understand how the child feels, we must have a knowledge of his level of development in four general areas: physical, emotional, social, and mental. These areas of growth overlap and each area affects every other area.

PATTERNS OF GROWTH

If we are to understand children, we must know something about what happens as they grow and we must be cognizant of factors that inhibit or promote growth of all kinds. According to some dictionaries, growth consists only of increase in size. Since we sometimes hear such expressions as "social growth" or "emotional growth," however, it may be worthwhile to consider the terms, growth and development, as synonymous.

Some specific signs that growth is occurring are obvious: (1) increase in size, (2) change in proportion and structure, and (3) the casting off of old patterns or features and the taking on of new ones. We can recognize these signs in all areas of growth. Since physical growth is the most obvious to those who observe children, this area will offer the most convenient examples. As the child grows, (1) his size increases in height and weight, (2) his body proportions become different, and (3) his bones, tissues, and the organs within his body change in structure. Although the third factor cannot be visually observed nor measured, it is an important process of growth that makes the child ready for a higher level of performance. This is maturation.

Comparable changes take place in other aspects of the child's growth: (1) his social contacts increase, (2) the proportions of his social contacts change from being mostly with adults to an increasing preponderance with his age mates, and (3) his social techniques change from nonverbal to verbal and from egocentric to cooperative.

There are other facts concerning human development that we must recognize if we are to guide children wisely: (1) growth is continuous, (2) growth follows a pattern, (3) growth is not uniform, and (4) growth consists of interrelated parts.

First, we can be assured that the process of growth or development is a continuous one and that, although there may not always be outward signs, the child is growing every day. For example, even with no appreciable change in height or weight, arms may be growing longer, feet and hands larger, bones harder, and muscles firmer. Motor skills and body coordination may be improving largely as a result of physical change.

Second, growth is not only continuous, it also follows a pattern. Most children grow in about the same way. That is, children sit up before they stand up, they crawl or creep before they walk, they grasp with their fists before they grasp with their fingers. When we consider physical growth, we can be assured that children's arms will develop before their legs and that growth in size will be more rapid during early infancy with a decelerating rate until puberty. When children grow socially, they play alone before they play alongside other children and they play near other children before they play with them.

The fact that growth is according to a pattern makes it easier for us to predict the next step and to decide on appropriate forms of guidance. This knowledge also enables us to understand that there is a time at which it is best to introduce or to expect new activities. This timing is the most important element in the guidance of children. Until the child has reached a certain developmental level, training in any area is without result and its pressures may be detrimental to future development.

The third fact about growth is that it is not uniform within the same child. Again, it is easy to recognize this fact when we consider physical growth. The pattern, as has been stated, proceeds by spurts; there are periods of rapid growth followed by periods of comparatively slow growth. Moreover, the various kinds of growth occur at different rates, so we cannot be certain that a child who is physiologically ready for a certain activity will be mentally or emotionally ready for it.

Students can recall the lack of uniformity of growth rates in their own experiences. Some will remember that their individual physical growth spurts in preadolescence made them feel awkward and clumsy in comparison with their later-maturing schoolmates; others will remember having feelings of inferiority when they associated with those who matured sooner. Many students also will have experienced unevenness of growth patterns in some of their school learning. Those who have learned to type will remember that typing speed increased rapidly for awhile and then there was no improvement. There might even have been a slight regression in speed which was followed by another spurt of progress. This lack of uniformity in rates of growth explains what sometimes are called "plateaus." These occur in all areas of development and if we know what is happening when the child shows little change, or even some regression in an area of development, we can guide him more wisely.

A fourth fact about growth is that it proceeds as a whole but that it is made up of interrelated parts. In order to guide children, we must remember that one kind of growth affects all other kinds.

Stephen was a very active child. He began walking when he was twelve months old and he was agile in all his movements. His verbal skills, however, seemed to lag. In fact, Stephen's parents were worried because he did not use even simple sentences when he was two years old. His verbal expressions consisted of merely naming things.

Conversely, Edith was slower in perfecting motor skills. She was content to sit on a blanket or to pull herself up to furniture until she was more than eighteen months of age. She chatted incessantly, however, and she was using complex sentences before she was two.

We might postulate that Stepan had little need to verbalize because he was so busy exploring his environment, that his interests were centered on the practice of motor skills whereas Edith concentrated her attention on vocalizing. These speculations may be true but what if the agile Stephen had also been the more verbal of the children?Other kinds of growth were occurring, also, and these two children, at the same chronological age, probably were not at the same level of development mentally, emotionally, or socially.

It is interesting to speculate how one type of growth can affect another type and to recognize that a spurt in one area may have either a positive or a negative influence on some other area. When children learn to walk, their world is enlarged. They have many more opportunities to know the true nature of their surroundings. No doubt this means that they can learn more rapidly than when they had to sit in the same place most of the time. It could be that social growth is encouraged because walking will enable the child to have more contacts with his siblings or other people. Conversely, other people may make less effort to entertain the child who has reached the runabout stage. Or the child's concentration on the complicated procedures of walking might discourage his learning about other things.

What effect will learning to walk have on the child's emotional growth? Probably he will gain recognition so that he will have feelings of achievement and self-confidence. But he may have frequent falls and physical hurts and his walking may cause criticism and admonition from adults. We should try to imagine how he will feel about the whole situation.

It is not possible to understand all the complexities of these growth factors as they occur in individual children but, in order to understand children, it is well to recognize that the interactions of growth patterns are unique to the specific child. People who work with very young infants are aware that they differ greatly in temperament and thus each child will react in his own unique way to the impact of his growth patterns. The significance of understanding these patterns is obvious when the purposes of guidance are reviewed: (1) to plan a program of guidance for the child so demands made on him are commensurate with his present abilities and will permit his happy adjustment to his present world, and (2) to consider how he can be helped to grow toward a well-adjusted adult life in which he can perform to the maximum of his potentialities. This involves studied care in choosing the challenges he will meet.

It is difficult to express the full meaning of the phrase, "understanding the child." A knowledge of the complexities of development patterns proves that it is impossible to learn the facts and details of all that is happening to the child as he grows. It is evident, however, that if we do try to understand a child, he will know it just as we have insight concerning the attitudes of other people toward us. If we realize that all behavior has two facets, the action and the feelings behind the action, we will realize that stopping the action will not solve the child's problem. It is not always necessary to know the cause of the behavior. Sometimes, it is possible for us to recognize the cause as well as the effect, but at other times there may have been sequential and multiple causes. Something unpleasant may have happened earlier in the day, the child may be approaching the onset of an illness, or there may have been contributing events yesterday or even last week. These complexities often make the wise choice of methods of guidance difficult.

METHODS OF GUIDANCE

Careful planning is important. Setting the stage for activities, choosing or buying appropriate toys and equipment, and planning a schedule that alternates vigorous with quiet behavior, action with rest, all are forms of good indirect guidance. This kind of guidance is aimed toward the environment, not direclty toward the child.

Young children, especially when they are away from home, need to know what to expect. A particular sequence of daily activities will make the child care center a happier place for everyone.

The preschool group usually came in from the playground, removed their outdoor clothing in the locker room, toileted, washed their hands, and then moved on into one of the playrooms for a mid-morning snack. The program was planned so one of the teachers came in a few minutes early, put napkins and juice or milk glasses on the table, and brought a plate of cookies or sandwiches from the kitchen.

One morning, the teacher with this responsibility was absent and the other adults had been detained in the locker room. The children moved quickly and quietly through the usual routines with wraps, toileting, and washing, and on to the playroom. When they found the table was not set for their snack, several kinds of undesirable behavior occurred. Billy and Jan pulled a lot of blocks out of the block cupboard and began skating around the floor on them; Nancy and Joe started crawling around on the floor, "meowing" in loud voices for their milk; and, after surveying the scene for a few seconds, Gregory grabbed a couple of jigsaw puzzles and threw them across the room.

This does not mean that everything needs to be done the same way every day, but it does show that children need to know when there will be changes. Their ability to accept change was shown in a similar situation.

The same group of children and their teacher usually sat on rugs in a circle on the floor at story time. One weekend, Miss Davis had not had time to unpack the clean laundry that included the rugs. While the children were eating, she said, "I have to go to another part of the building to get your clean rugs but I will read a story to you as soon as I get them. You can wait for me in the story corner."

As they finished eating, the children chose books from the book rack and moved to the story room where some of them sat on the bare floor and looked at their books and commented about them to their friends while others carried chairs from the snack table and sat quietly on them.

Usually, children will enter into a change in program as if they were embarking on an interesting adventure but they need to be told what is to happen. Probably many crises in home situations could be averted if parents could plan ahead and make these explanations to children. It is not unusual for preschool teachers to say, "We are going to do something different today. Let's talk about it for awhile." Sometimes it is worthwhile to see the misbehavior that is likely to result when careful and thoughtful planning is not carried out.

A group of two year old children probably needs a more definite time schedule than an older age group. Those who work with very young children know that they thrive on routines. For example, little children often insist that procedures be carried out in exactly the same way, time after time. During the dressing procedures, these children often insist that a certain order be followed, that one sock and then the other must be put on before hair is combed or that hair is combed before other details of dressing are started. This scheduling is important to the younger preschool child because he must learn the steps in various procedures by doing them. Only when children have learned how things should be done can we expect more flexibility to be acceptable to them.

Another aspect of indirect guidance requires careful thinking and frequent revision. Much undesirable activity can be forestalled if children do not become bored or tired. A program and materials that do not challenge the child's abilities are often boring. Children are doers and they need practice in developing the skills they are acquiring. It is important, however, to choose a program and materials with which the child can cope with some feelings of success. Otherwise he will become bored quickly and his feelings of failure may transfer to subsequent activities.

Changing the location of equipment is another good method of indirect guidance. This may promote new kinds of imaginative and dramatic play. For example, an attractive display of blocks arranged so that various shapes are accessible will encourage children to play at block building, whereas the same number of blocks thrown carelessly in the cupboard will not engender interest.

Most people become irritable when they are tired. Adults usually take time out for rest or a change of pace but the young child lacks the judgment to make these plans for himself. Scheduling so that story time follows vigorous play or creative activities follow a period of active group play indoors will help avoid fatigue and ensuing misbehavior. Parents of young children often remark concerning the difficult late afternoon hours. Some of these tensions probably could be eased if alternation of activity and rest could be planned in the home situation or if materials for the release of feelings could be available when children needed them. This planning is not always feasible with the many interruptions that occur in the home but its value often is demonstrated at the child care center.

Bobby was a quiet four year old boy. The other members of his group had been enrolled for several months before Bobby entered school. He was an outsider on the playground and at free play indoors. The other children chatted and planned their play but Bobby never was included. On several occasions, he moved quickly into the play area and snatched a block which the children were planning to use or a dish from the table where an imaginary meal was being eaten. The result was further rejection by the other children.

Finger painting was always an activity available to the children. The first few days, Bobby merely stood nearby and watched the other children. One day, however, he slipped his arms into a plastic apron and began to dab at the paint that had been placed on a sheet of wet paper. Bobby's arm movements became less tense as he worked and soon he was painting outside the boundaries of the paper. No comment was made by the teacher except to ask if he wanted a fresh piece of paper. Bobby shook his head and continued to scrub the entire table with large, sweeping arm motions. He would dab more paint from a jar nearby and he spent most of the morning at this project.

On many successive mornings, Bobby moved to the paint table as soon as he came indoors. On the third day, he started finger painting before the paper was provided. It seemed apparent that the only purpose of his painting was for release of feelings. It was pleasant to watch the happy expression on his face as he worked.

Soon, the other children became interested in the fact that Bobby was painting without paper and two or three of them joined him. Their activity encouraged conversation and the first steps toward social acceptance for Bobby had been taken.

Frequently, we can forestall undesirable behavior by finding substitute targets for children's aggressive feelings.

Sidney was a three-year-old boy who had grown very rapidly in physical size. He was larger than any of the other children in his group. As is sometimes true, Sidney's large body build was not accompanied by good motor coordination. His inability to control his movements was an incessant threat to his happy adjustment.

Frequently, Sidney released his feelings of frustration by pounding on the other children when they crossed his path. Sidney's teacher understood Sidney so well that she could tell when his aggressive feelings were on the upswing. When this happened, Miss Cain would see that a pounding board or the woodworking supplies were somewhere near. After a quiet suggestion for a change of activity, Sidney always seemed to enjoy the vigorous play. After a few minutes with these toys, he would appear to have released his aggressive feelings and he would return to happy play at the puzzle table or in the doll corner.

Of course, if indirect control of this type is not successful, direct intervention is warranted. Obviously, a child should not be allowed to hurt other children even if only because of his impatience with himself.

Good methods of direct guidance probably present a greater problem to students and parents than indirect. When guidance is direct toward the child, many people feel uncomfortable and uncertain. We must remember that the important thing is to let the child know that we like him even if we do not condone his behavior. Physical guidance of the child may be of three general types: (1) leading the child or showing him how to perform some action, (2) making him feel more secure or confident by means of physical contact, and (3) restraining his activity.

The effectiveness of guiding the child by demonstrating how to accomplish something will depend on his feelings about the task and his ability to understand and perform the action. Interest in the activity is as important at the preschool level as at later ages and the best clue to readiness is probably the child's desire for participation. As stated previously, if the child has not developed in all aspects to a stage at which he is ready for the activity, pressure toward performance is useless and may prove detrimental. For example, until a certain level of eye-hand coordination and mental reasoning is reached, a child cannot be expected to work a simple jigsaw puzzle and his unsuccessful efforts to do so can be frustrating.

Frequently, children will be demanding in their requests for adult help or demonstration. Suggestions concerning how much help should be given are more appropriate to specific descriptions of the child's mental, emotional, and physical rates of growth which are discussed later. We must know, however, the child's developmental level and his background of experience before we can judge how much help he should have. For example, if we know the child is mature enough to perform the task and yet he seems to be excessively demanding of help, we might ask (1) how much help is he accustomed to receiving at home, or (2) does he want me to show him or to help him simply because he wants my attention? The pertinent question is: How does this child feel about this situation?

When children seem worried, tired, or afraid, physical contact by an adult may forestall more accute unhappiness. Some students will remember that a competent swimming instructor, while giving no actual help, could by the touch of a hand create the difference between sinking or floating. Thus, the touch of a hand may give just enough guidance to enable the child to climb the jungle gym successfully.

Most of the pressures that adults impose on children are connected with restraining their activities but, of course, restrictive controls are necessary for the child's safety and happiness. Guidance cannot always be planned ahead of time and many situations require immediate physical action by the adult. When the safety of the child or of other children is involved, physical restraint is imperative. For this reason, it is best to assure students that any action is better than no action at all. Spur of the moment methods can be evaluated later in class. It may be comforting to remember that teachers and parents do not always choose the best methods when immediate action is necessary. The child's safety is of paramount importance in all situations and this can be especially true in a child care center. When parents entrust their children to other people, it seems obvious that the obligations of those in charge are great. Sometimes minor injuries are inescapable but it is unrealistic to imagine many injuries occurring if the ratio of adults to children is in keeping with good group-care planning.

In recent years the value of verbal guidance has been extolled. In our efforts to let children know we understand how they feel, adults are likely to resort to long winded explanations of the problem, how the child feels, what we think about those feelings and the child's actions. This technique often is appropriate for the older child but it can be very frustrating to the very young preschooler. For example, if he is emotionally upset, it is probable that our explanations will mean little to him, that he will not really hear them. Then, too, discussions are likely to be entirely useless if he has not developed concepts of cause and effect. Until he has this conceptual knowledge, it is better to make concise statements and to enforce them kindly and firmly rather than to indulge in meaningless harangues. Verbal orders to children should be kept to a minimum. When we are dealing with the very young child, a good method of guidance often is distraction. Most two year old children have not had enough experience to understand why certain behavior is not acceptable and there will be time for logical explanations when they are older.

Distraction is not as good for the older preschool child. It may only prolong his bad feelings. If the adult pretends to ignore the action, the child will be left with the responsibility of guilty feelings. Although such feelings are certain to occur in the process of growing up and are likely to aid in the child's understanding of right and wrong as he grows older, they may cause confusion in the mind of the preschooler. Again, before we decide on our method, we must know the developmental status of the individual child. Chronological age is a poor standard for judging how to plan verbal guidance. Personality traits of both the child and the adult are important in any situation. One teacher will find it easy to let the child know by short, meaningful sentences what is expected and at the same time to denote her acceptance of him as a worthy person. The same words used by another adult may be frightening and thus appear punitive from the child's viewpoint.

Certainly verbal guidance should be brief, firm, and positive. The following examples may be helpful.

SAY	DO NOT SAY
Sit down when you slide.	Don't stand up when you slide.
Dig in the sand.	Don't throw the sand.
Sit in the swing.	Don't stand in the swing.
Use both hands when you climb.	You'll fall if you don't watch out.
Climb down the ladder.	Don't jump off the box.
Throw the stick over the fence.	Don't play with the stick.
	You might hurt someone.
Keep the puzzle on the table.	Don't dump the puzzle pieces on the floor.
Turn the pages carefully.	Don't tear the book.
Talk in a quiet voice.	Don't shout.
Wipe your hands on the paper towel.	Don't put your hands on anything.
Be sure the ladder is safe.	Be careful. You might fall.
Sit on your chair.	Don't rock on your chair.
Move back on your rug.	Don't lean forward so that the other children can't see.
Walk around the swing.	Be careful. The swing might hit you.
Wipe your brush on the jar.	Don't drip paint on the floor.
Put an apron on.	Don't you want to put an apron on?
Time to go inside.	Shall we go inside?
Wash your hands.	Don't you want to wash your hands?
Drink your milk.	Don't you want your milk?
Drink out of your own glass.	Don't bother the other children.

An adult, in order to feel the ease that is beneficial in child guidance, will find it necessary to acquire techniques in keeping with his or her personality. However, the following general rules, which are appropriate to the foregoing examples of good verbal guidance, should be observed.

Do

1. Speak in a calm, kind voice.

2. Speak directly to the child; do not call to him across the playroom.

3. Speak in short, meaningful sentences which the child can understand.

4. Try to express your request in a positive way. This will help the child to learn a better or more acceptable way of doing things.

5. Get down to the child's physical level if possible. That is, stoop or sit on a low chair so that he can see your face.

6. Answer the child's questions, but do not monopolize his conversations; he needs to associate with his peers.

7. Keep your voice and facial expression pleasant.

Do Not

1. Make fun of the child.

2. Give the child a choice if he cannot have one.

3. Compare the child with another child by saying, "See how clean Jim's hands are." (This might make him dislike both Jim and you.)

4. Be dishonest with the child. Do not say, "Jerry didn't mean to hurt you." (He may be aware that Jerry did mean to hurt him.) Instead, say "Jerry didn't know how much it would hurt," or "Jerry didn't mean to hit you so hard."

5. Make a child feel guilty by saying something like, "Only bad boys do things like that." (Accept the child even though you do not condone his actions.)

6. Make a child feel inferior by saying, "You're a big boy now. You shouldn't act like a baby."

The following questions may be useful as a framework for observing guidance practices during your field experiences.

1. Are the children aware of the general schedule of the day?

2. Are children encouraged to work out their own problems whenever possible? Is adult support given when needed?

3. Is there consistency in handling situations within the group?

4. Does the adult appear to have "favorite" children? Does the adult ever "pick on" a particular child?

5. Does the adult show respect for and interest in the children as individuals? (Shown by the way she speaks to them and about them.)

6. Does the adult seem to understand constructive methods of guidance that help the child learn self-discipline? (Looking for specific examples will be especially helpful in this facet of guidance.)

7. Does the adult seem to work in a pleasant, relaxed fashion?

8. Does the adult "set the stage" by arranging equipment to catch the interest of the children and then give them the opportunity to develop their own interests?

9. Is the adult alert to keep children in view at all times?

10. Are directions given to the children positive rather than negative? Are demands made on the children reasonable and understandable?

SUGGESTED ASSIGNMENT

Part I

Indirect Guidance

Record three incidents at the center in which the behavior of the child or children was affected by manipulating the environment, by setting the stage, or by changing the setting of the stage.

Part II

Direct Guidance

1. Record one incident showing the use of physical guidance in which the adult

    a. demonstrated or illustrated how to do something.

    b. used physical contact to reassure the child.

    c. used physical contact to restrain child activity.

    d. modified the child's behavior by rewarding him in some way.

2. Give an example of each of the following types of verbal guidance in which the adult

    a. used positive expressions.

    b. used clear, short, meaningful sentences.

    c. made a request where the child had a choice.

    d. made a request where the child had no choice.

    e. helped the child become more independent through encouragement or through recognition of success.

SELECTED READINGS

1. Baker, Katherine Read, ed., *Ideas That Work With Young Children,* Association for the Education of Young Children, Washington, D. C., 1972.

This small book presents practical information for teachers who are developing child care programs. It includes thirty seven selected articles from issues of *Young Children.* These articles deal with understanding children, enhancing a learning environment, how teachers and parents can work together, and ways in which people in other professions can help the day care staff.

2. Dittman, Laura L., ed., *Early Child Care,* Atherton Press, N. Y., 1968.

This book is the result of four conferences sponsored by the National Institute of Mental Health, the Children's Hospital in Washington, D. C., and the Committee on Day Care of the Maternal and Child Health Section of the

American Public Health Association. Students working with economically disadvantaged children will be especially interested in Chapter 9, "Poor Families and Their Patterns of Child Care." Part IV, "New Research in the Prevention of Culturally Determined Retardation," will be valuable to the serious student.

3. Hartup, Willard W., and Nancy L. Smothergill, eds., *The Young Child: Reviews of Research,* Vol. 1 National Association for the Education of Young Children, Washington, D. C., 1967.

The eighteen articles in this volume will provide supplementary reading for the serious student in child development who wants a comprehensive knowledge of current research about the development and behavior of young children.

4. Hurlock, Elizabeth B., *Child Development,* 5th ed., McGraw-Hill, N. Y., 1972.

Hurlock's book can be considered a classic in child development literature. It was first published in 1942. New materials relate to (1) traditional beliefs that can be damaging to children, (2) methods of scientific research in child study, and (3) the growing interest in understanding growth and development.

5. Kritchevsky, Sybil, and Elizabeth Prescott, *Planning Environments for Young Children: Physical Space,* National Association for the Education of Young Children, Washington, D. C., 1969.

This pamphlet describes the importance of the physical environment and shows how space and the arrangement of equipment can help or hinder guidance of the young child. The authors include suggested methods for analyzing the physical environment of the center in which you work.

6. Munsinger, Harry, *Fundamentals of Child Development,* Holt, Rinehart and Winston, N. Y., 1971.

Munsinger has provided a comprehensive reference book for students of child growth and development. Chapter summaries are particularly helpful. The inclusive glossary is valuable in interpreting terminology if reading research reports is to be expected.

7. Staffieri, J. Robert, *What Do We Believe About Child-Rearing?,* Day care and Child Development Council of America, Washington, D. C., 1973.

This author offers materials that can be used in staff meetings to help staff members assess child guidance philosophies and promote their effectiveness in dealing with children.

8. Weber, Evelyn, *Early Childhood Education,* Charles A. Jones, Worthington, Ohio, 1970.

Descriptions of innovative teaching procedures employed in specific group-care centers in the U. S. are presented. This book will help teachers, supervisors, and parents understand how various programs differ and how to strengthen their own programs.

chapter 4

Physical and Motor Development

The child's body and the way he uses it are of primary importane in understanding him because its structure and functions denote the framework in which other kinds of development are encased. It has been said that everyone notices preschool children but that few people really see them. Too often we are likely to try to look beneath the surface and to describe the child as being secure or insecure, aggressive or shy, noisy or quiet with little thought as to how his body may affect those behavior patterns. When we consider physical and motor development, we recognize that growth is continuous, that it follows a pattern, that it is not uniform, and that the various kinds of growth are interrelated. Only the characteristics of physical growth that seem most important for purposes of child guidance are included in this chapter.

WAYS OF ASSESSING PHYSICAL SIZE

Until recent years, cross-sectional studies of growth and the height and weight standards that resulted from those studies were our only means of evaluating the

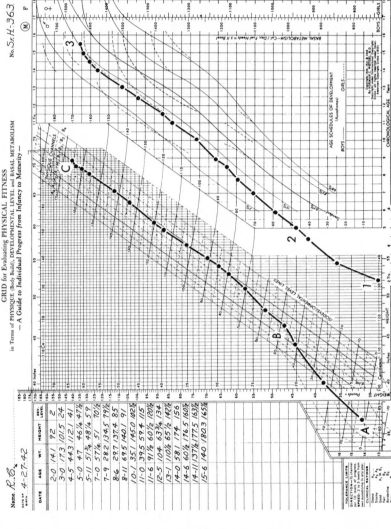

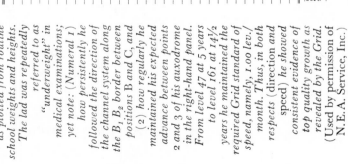

Fig. 1. A long-term Grid record of a slender boy as plotted from routine school weights and heights. The lad was repeatedly referred to as "underweight" in medical examinations; yet note: (Numeral 1) how persistently he followed the direction of the channel system along the B₁, B₂ border between positions B and C; and (2) how regularly he maintained his expected advance between points 2 and 3 of his auxodrome in the right-hand panel. From level 47 at 5 years to level 161 at 14½ years he maintained the required Grid standard of speed, namely, 1.00 lev./ month. Thus, in both respects (direction and speed) he showed consistent evidence of top quality growth as revealed by the Grid. (Used by permission of N. E. A. Service, Inc.)

physical development of children. Large numbers of children of the same chronological age were measured and weighed, and averages or standard norms were ascertained. In most instances, separate tables were constructed for boys and girls since it was evident that their patterns of physical growth differed. Boys usually weigh a little more and may be a few inches longer at birth, these differences become less marked during middle childhood; then girls reach the pubertal spurt of more rapid physical growth somewhat sooner than boys.

These cross-sectional studies resulted in physical growth standards for nonexistent children, the average ones. Their lack of value can be recognized by those of us who have compared our own height and weight measurements with those listed in similar tables. We are aware that differences in individual body build are far more important than norms or standards. Two people of identical height will recognize that the weight that is best for one of them may be several pounds too much or several pounds too little for the other. It is not difficult to understand that a stocky child normally weighs more than a slender one of the same height. Furthermore, it is apparent that there are greater differences within the sexes than there are between boys and girls.

However, some standards by which good physical growth can be evaluated are important. Otherwise, how are we to know whether children are developing as they should? If simple height and weight tables are the sole bases for reference, it is easy to imagine the apprehension of parents whose child is far below the standards for his age or whose child is far above them.

Longitudinal studies of children have provided scientific evidence that individual children develop in unique ways. In these studies, children are weighed and measured periodically during their entire cycles of growth, and changes in rates of increment are carefully noted. Obviously, the best way to evaluate the child's physical growth is to learn whether he is developing in keeping with his own specific pattern. Children who are heavier at birth tend to remain heavier throughout early childhood. A child may not be of a size similar to others of his chronological age but he will tend to maintain the same relative position in comparison with his age group unless circumstances interfere with his growth. Research has provided many scales, profiles, and tables to illustrate the individuality of growth patterns. Among these is the Wetzel Growth Grid.

Parents need to know when medical help should be sought. A good method by which parents and teachers can judge whether a child is growing normally is to keep a record of his height and weight regularly. These measurements should be taken at specific times during the day and as accurately as possible. That is, if the child is weighed and measured in the early morning, subsequent recordings should be made at the same time in the day. If he is gaining steadily in both measures, he probably is gaining as he should. If the child is weighed and measured often, some deceleration should be of no concern. It is the steady increase over a long period of time that signifies satisfactory development. The comparison of a child with his own previous height and weight is more important than comparing him with other children.

RATE AND PATTERN OF PHYSICAL GROWTH

The continuity of physical growth is certain and its signs are evident as we watch children increase in size, change in proportion, and assume differences in appearance. The most rapid rate of physical growth, of course, is during the prenatal period. Growth continues to be fast from birth until about the age of two years, then continues at a diminishing rate until shortly before puberty at which time there is another acceleration. Most children are somewhere between eighteen and twenty-two inches long at birth, and during the first year of life will show almost a fifty per cent increase in height. After the first year, the child's growth in height will decelerate to an average gain of three to five inches a year.

Increases in weight are even greater than those in height during preschool years. The majority of babies weigh between seven and eight pounds at birth. By the time they are five or six months old, they will have doubled their birth weights, and by the time they are a year old they will usually weigh three times as much as they did at birth. In accordance with the orderly pattern of growth, increments in weight then decrease and most children gain only four or five pounds each year. Although weight is important as an index to health, increase in weight does not always mean healthy growth. A fat child is not necessarily a healthy child. The important factor, of course, is not the quantity of growth but the quality of growth.

That physical health has a great influence on physical growth deserves recognition. Adults who are interested in the welfare of children will be alert to their dietary needs, will see that they eliminate regularly, will plan a proper balance of activity and rest during the day, and will provide beneficial conditions for good sleeping habits. Of course, temporary illnesses and their complications usually can be recognized and medical attention can be sought. However, when it seems that children are not showing signs of good physical growth, it is probable that professional advice is needed. Surely, periodic physical examinations should be planned during preschool years.

Knowledge concerning physical growth patterns is important in child guidance because it enables us to realize what dramatic changes are taking place. Since we know that all kinds of growth are interrelated, it is often good to specualte as to how children must feel during these fast-growing years and to try to put ourselves in their places. The child is faced not only with the problems resulting from rapid rates of growth but also by the fact that the various parts of his body are growing at different rates. It is easy to recognize that children are not miniature adults.

The child's body grows in accordance with two patterns: cephalocaudal, from the head downward; and proximo-distal, from the center outward. At birth, the circumference of the head usually exceeds that of the chest; at age two, it is about the same; and at age five, it approaches a two-to-three ratio. The upper part of the baby's head is proportionately large for the small face and the very small mouth. Head height in the newborn infant is about one-fourth of his total height, whereas at maturity it will be approximately one-eighth. This top-heaviness makes it difficult for the small child to control his body and is somewhat responsible for the long period of infancy and dependency in children. It is wise to try to imagine how adults would function if their proportions were similar.

The absence of a neck during babyhood also demonstrates a contrast to adult proportions. The comparative narrowness of the shoulders is obvious. The baby's arms are poorly developed and will increase in length between three and four times before he reaches mature size. Since points of sequential development are from the head downward, the lower extremities are very poorly developed early in life. The tiny baby has small, spindly, crooked legs and his feet are extremely narrow at the heels and have no appearance of arching. His legs will increase in length between four and five times as he matures.

It is important, also, that consideration be given to the process of maturation—that aspect of physical growth that is occurring but that cannot be seen. At birth, the brain is approximatley one-half its eventual size and by the time the child is about six years of age it will have reached mature size. As is evident in recognizing body functions, the heart is well developed at birth. Pulse rate is much more rapid than it will be later, however, and this fact is important in the guidance of children since rapid pulse rates sometimes are alarming to those who care for children. It is not unusual to hear a parent or teacher remark, "His heart is beating at a terrible rate." It is desirable to know that a rapid pulse is entirely normal in young children.

At birth, the child has about two hundred and fifty bones. These bones are gristlelike in structure. Gradually, throughout childhood, bones harden or ossify. The softness of children's bones is especially apparent in the six soft spots or fontanelles on a baby's skull. These soft spots in the bones of the head allow for the rapid growth of the brain during the early months of life. By the age of about eighteen months, these fontanelles have closed. Throughout the body new bones form as bits of bristlelike cartilage appear and then ossify during childhood. Thus, there are many more bones by the time the child reaches puberty. Fusion of bone parts then occurs so that there are fewer bones at maturity than at birth.

The softness of the bones of young children is significant in child guidance because it indicates the ease with which the child's body can become misshapen by pressure. Thus, a flatness on the back of the head will result sometimes if the child is always placed on the back of his head; or shoes that are too short will usually affect the shape of his feet. The pliability of the child's skeletal structure is apparent when we consider how easily he can place his foot to his mouth.

A knowledge of the flexibility of children's bones has an aspect of reassurance, however, since it indicates that the child can withstand many falls and that when breaks do occur they are likely to heal rapidly. The importance of skeletal growth is obvious since we know that the bones must carry the weight of the body, support the organs, and act as levers for muscular action.

The stage of physical growth that an individual child has attained can be ascertained more accurately by studying his skeletal development than by any other means. A knowledge of his level of skeletal maturation indicates how far he has proceeded toward maturity, but most people who guide young children are unable to measure the growth of the child's bones. Therefore, a thorough knowledge concerning the child's status in other areas of physical growth is especially helpful. Only by knowing how children develop is it possible to plan activities and experiences commensurate with their present abilities and beneficial to their future growth patterns. It is apparent, also, that the ways in which children behave are dependent in part on the manner in which they are growing. Periods of rapid growth or uneven growth dictate specific types of behavior that frequently are assumed to be misbehavior. We cannot understand children unless we are aware of how they grow.

SEQUENCE OF LOCOMOTOR AND
MANIPULATIVE SKILLS

Crawling or creeping, walking, jumping, and running are functions that all children master in a somewhat orderly sequence. At birth, the infant has almost no specificity of movement. His muscular activities are general reactions. His arms and legs twitch and jerk independently, and his head rolls from side to side. When you touch any part of his body, his whole body responds.

The development of locomotor skills occurs gradually. By about one month of age most children, when placed on their stomachs, can hold their chins up for brief periods of time. In other words, the first stage of purposeful locomotion consists in gaining control of the muscles of the head and neck. During the second month of life, the majority of children will be able to raise themselves on their arms so their chests will be raised and by four months of age they usually can sit in an upright position if supported. Most children can sit up independently when they are about seven months old, and this skill leads to the ability to stand with help a few weeks later. After a period of creeping or crawling has been experienced, walking with some help is possible.

Individual differences in locomoter skills are apparent and this individuation is especially noticeable during the creeping or crawling stage. At about five months of age, most children can roll over from a recumbent position by rotating the upper portions of their bodies and then throwing their legs to one side. This represents the first purposeful whole-body locomoter movement. A few weeks later, children can support the weight of the upper portions of their bodies by one or both arms. Sequentially, the child can bring one knee forward so he assumes a crawling position. Diverse methods of creeping or crawling can be observed. These methods appear to be unique to individual children.

Some children who appear to be precocious in their skills of creeping or crawling move on quickly to attempt standing and walking. Other children seem so satified with their efficiency in getting around that they show little interest in walking until past the time at which this skill might be expected. Most infants can pull themselves to a standing position by the time they are about ten months old. When the young child first stands without support, his legs are far apart and his feet are turned out in order to keep his body in balance. His abdomen is prominent not only because of the weakness of its muscles but also because of the comparatively large size of the liver and other organs.

Usually, those children who have just learned to stand can sit down only by relaxing and tumbling back upon their hips. Children of this age begin to be interested in stairs and, before they can walk independently, many children can climb two or three steps although descending is impossible for them. Some children walk as early as nine months of age and others who are prefectly normal do not walk until they are eighteen months or even older.

It seems evident that normal children will walk when they are ready, that encouraging children to walk is not only a waste of time but may be emotionally upsetting to the child. In time there is a definite urge to maintain an upright position although often children who are capable of walking resort to creeping as an easier means of locomotion. It is only necessary to consider the top-heavy proportions of the very young child to wonder at his ability to maintain his equilibrium as early as he does. This is an important basis for the understanding that is necessary for those who assume his guidance. During observation of a group of two-year-old children in a school situation, it is wise to remember how recently they have acquired their simple locomotor skills.

Between the ages of two and three years, walking becomes almost automatic. Improvement in the child's sense of balance is noticeable and it is possible for him to attempt physical feats that require nimbleness and daring. By the time the child is three, he can usually climb stairs with support, alternating feet. By this age most children can ride tricycles satisfactorily, also.

Although most of these skills have been attained before the child is eligible for preschool attendance, we need to be aware of their recency. The younger children probably have only recently begun to display fairly good body balance. Also, it is important to remember that children learn by doing. Many of the activities of young preschoolers demonstrate that simple motor skills require their rapt attention. For example, the two and a half year old child who climbs on the jungle gym will usually concentrate his entire attention on the mechanics of climbing whereas the older child will appear to climb almost automatically and can incorporate that activity with some kind of cooperative play. The same characteristics will be evident when one watches these children as they ride on tricycles on the playground. Similar traits are apparent when children are performing manipulative skills.

By careful observation, the child's level of development can be evaluated and, on this basis, his activities can be planned and equipment can be chosen that will aid him in his growth. It is good to remember that there are individual differences in motor performance at all ages.

The development of manipulative skills appears to be an even more intricate process than that of locomotor learning. This is logical when we consider the more precise eye-hand coordination on which manipulative skills are based. The small infant responds to stimuli by general body movements, and apparently eye fixation does not function until he is about three months old. It is impossible for children to be adept at reaching, grasping, and handling until they have had much practice in controlling their larger muscles. These facts are in accordance with the processes of physical growth. At birth, the child's arms and hands are poorly developed.

Before the infant is capable of turning his head to follow an object with his eyes, he will appear to be interested in a rattle that is hung in front of him. Later he will be able to turn his head and to focus his eyes on the rattle when it is moved. Already he is learning by doing and his eye muscles as well as those in his neck and shoulders are being exercised. Thus, children's first steps toward manipulation consist of showing an interest in objects without actually touching them. Soon there is whole body movement and the child's facial expression will exemplify a kind of reaching for an object. This movement becomes specific as the child begins to bring his hands together as he focuses his eyes on the rattle.

By the time children are about seven months old, they usually can sit up without support and they are capable of grasping a small object in each hand. A few weeks earlier, most children reach toward these as if by accident, they will lift the small object from the surface on which it rests. When children are first capable of focusing their eyes on their toys or other objects and of grasping them, their grasping motions are with their whole hands. Their fingers are extended and the manipulative movement is with the entire arm and hand. Soon, they will be able to transfer objects from one hand to another and to retrieve articles that they drop. Reaching movements change from diffuse circular motions to the forward reaching that is necessary to insure contact with the object.

By about nine months of age, the majority of children can make definite grasping movements with their thumbs and forefingers, and the basis for precision skills has been formed. They still are incapable of reaching forward with one arm alone, however. It is apparent that when the small child reaches forward his body balance is disturbed and thus the other hand and arm must act as a pivot for his activity. Some movement of the whole body still seems to be necessary. It is helpful to recall the top-heavy proportions of small children as their awkwardness in these motions is noted. Children will be more adept in handling objects that are placed very near to them. This is evident when the two-year-old places an object in front of himself at a small table. Students should pay close attention to his manipulative skill.

Toys that will help young children in practicing these developing skills are discussed in a later chapter. Children enjoy activities that lend opportunities for practicing the skills that they are perfecting. Thus, simple color towers or form boards are of special value for the young child.

Since the various areas of growth are interrelated, a plan of activities for children cannot be based on motor development alone. Although eye-hand coordination is an important factor in many activities, the child's mental and emotional progress are also important. For example, the youngest children will probably enjoy one of the simple form boards or jigsaw puzzles if the pieces are large enough to handle without great manual dexterity, yet other similar puzzles may be too difficult. Their failures may not always be due to poor eye-hand coordination but often to the child's lack of spatial concepts or to his brief span of attention. However, the child's level of manipulative skill surely should comprise a major criterion in choosing his experiences. It is in the area of eye-hand coordination and manipulative skills that adults are most likely to expect unattainable activities from children. Resulting frustrations by both children and adults are common.

At Christmas time, Mr. Davis visited the toy department in a store near their home and decided to buy a simple model airplane kit for Ricky, his five-year-old son. Ricky did not seem especially interested in the kit when he received it, but this was not surprising since his new sled and doctor set had been his expressed desires. When the newness of his other toys had worn off, however, Ricky seemed bored one Saturday afternoon and Mr. Davis decided it was a good time for the two of them to sit down and work at assembling an airplane.

At first, Ricky seemed interested as his father explained the picture that was included in the kit. Mr. Davis believed that children learn by doing, so he began to tell Ricky where each piece belonged and the order in which the assembling should be done. Ricky was careful as he began to put the plane together, but he started to show impatience when the pieces would not fit when he first tried them. He would attempt to force the pieces into place but his hands appeared to be "all thumbs" and he began to cry because some of the small pieces of wood slipped out of place. Mr. Davis tried to comfort Ricky and began to do the more difficult steps for him.

Mrs. Davis called her husband to the telephone and when he returned Ricky was attempting to make the partially assembled plane soar across the room as he made appropriate noises during its flight. Ricky seemed happy with this game but some of the small pieces of the plane had already been broken.

It is not difficult to imagine the feelings of frustration that both Ricky and his father must have experienced. Since growth is a many-sided process, Ricky's level of manipulative skill probably was not the only cause of this crisis but it was an important factor. If adults know that children learn by doing, they will choose activities in which children can really take part. The adult role should consist mainly of offering encouragement and recognition of success. Simple activities for the preschool child are likely to be those that are helpful and satisfying, although toys that present no challenge to developing skills may cause frustration through boredom.

Practice in manipulative skill during preschool years takes place frequently during the daily routines: dressing and undressing, toileting, washing, and eating. Thus, methods of guidance in these areas can be chosen by considering the child's level of development in eye-hand coordination. It is helpful to attempt to understand how these everyday procedures must appear to the child. For example, adults are so accustomed to dressing as a step toward some occassion or activity that the process itself becomes almost automatic. They go through the motions of getting into garments without cognizance of the motor skills involved. If, however, adults view the task as it must appear to the young child, they will become aware of what a complicated and interesting procedure it is. When we remember that the child learns by doing and that a great deal of practice is necessary in order to perfect manipulative skills, we will be much more patient when children appear to dawdle.

It is good to try to recapture childish interest in buttoning and unbuttoning, in how zippers work, in buckles on boots, and in putting shoelaces through small eyelets in leather. When we realize that these activities are as good for small children and as interesting to them as anything that occurs in the playroom, we are more satisfied to make the school schedule flexible so that children's needs for experimentation and repetition in everyday routines can be experienced.

It is important to know just what the child can do when he is in the process of acquiring a new skill and he needs and wants to practice it. Feelings of confidence and satisfaction are imporant to all of us. Good indirect guidance would include such planning as placing large buttons and buttonholes in the clothing of children who are at this level of development. Adults should watch children closely in order to know at about what time they are capable of many simple tasks. For example, the majority of children cannot be expected to tie their own shoelaces until late in their preschool years. This is the most difficult manipulative skill in the process of their dressing. Relationships between adults and children can become strained when adults expect behavior that is simply not possible by the preschool child.

All infants seem to be ambidextrous. They use one arm and hand predominantly for awhile and then they are likely to change to major use of the other arm and hand. Authorities differ in their opinions as to the causes of being right-handed or left-handed. Some writers speculate that handedness may be culturally initiated. However, it is certain that many children by the age of two to three years have established definite practices in using one hand in preference to the other. It is important that teachers in the preschool recognize the hand preference of each child. Sometimes the activities of left-handed children may be hampered because equipment arrangements are planned for right-handed children. Among persons who guide children there seems to be agreement that no pressure should be exerted to influence the left-handed child to use his right hand.

Some children tend to lack proficiency in motor skills. Reference to these cases will be presented in the last chapter of this text.

THE INFLUENCE OF PHYSICAL SIZE ON MOTOR SKILLS

There seems to be a specificity in motor skills. This means that children who excel in some kinds of motor activities may be comparatively inept in other types. It is interesting to observe that children who are most successful at locomotor activity are frequently not interested in precision activities and vice versa. Probably there are many causes involved. Orderly patterns of development, of course, would indicate that children become proficient at large muscle activities at an earlier age than that at which they can master precision skills. As has been implied, also, personality factors will dictate those activities in which children will be most interested and, therefore, those at which they will practice and become competent. Then, too, the level of social development that the child has attained may denote which kinds of activities are the most enjoyable for him.

The influence of physical size on motor skills is interesting to contemplate.

Phillip, age three and one-half, was an extremely active child on the playground. He was much larger in size than the other children. Although he walked rather awkwardly, with his hands swinging wide at his sides, his body balance in climbing on the playground equipment seemed fairly good.

Phillip had many ideas for group play and he was always the center when the children played follow-the-leader on the slides or rode their tricycles around the perimeter of the yard. Indoors, Phillip seldom entered into creative activities. His handling of paints and crayons seemed awkward and his products were never pleasing to him. He stayed with these activities for only brief periods of time. He often moved to a nearby child, snatched some of the supplies with which the child was playing, and ran to another part of the playroom, verbally teasing the other child to follow him. The only prolonged interest Phillip displayed with creative media was when he played with modeling clay. He made no effort to create anything, but he would pound and roll the clay vigorously and carry on a detailed conversation with nearby children about what he was doing.

Possibly, Phillip's large physical size made many of his movements awkward and therefore caused him to be happier on the spacious playground than in the smaller areas inside the school. He was the type of child about which adults occasionally say, "He's just big and clumsy." It is important to note, however, that physical size was not Phillip's only characteristic. He was the kind of child who seemed eager to play with groups of children. He assumed leadership roles on the playground and he liked to play there, whereas he was not happy when playing with creative media. His lack of interest in the latter probably was partially because he was not successful in tasks requiring precision and also because social interaction was lacking during these activities. Obviously, children tend to perfect the skills in which they are most interested.

Jack, a three-and-one-half-year-old boy, was small and lithe and quite agile on all the outdoor equipment. He enjoyed group play on the playground, but he was equally happy at quiet play indoors. Jack liked especially to work with crayons that he held easily between his thumb and forefinger. He spent long periods of time working with crayons and paper. He joined in quiet conversation when children were nearby, but when they moved away he often was so intent on his work that he continued to sit at the table by himself.

The conclusion might be that small, nimble children are likely to be proficient at activities that require manual dexterity, but we should keep in mind that growth is interrelated and that individual children are unique. Although Jack was more adept with creative media than Phillip, it would be unwise to believe that physical size alone caused these differences. It is evident that Jack was not so dependent on the companionship of other children. Therefore, it could be that he had spent more time in practicing these solitary skills.

Sometimes, children who are large for their ages have somewhat poorer body balance and precision skills than those who are nearer the average in size. Growth is not uniform and spurts of growth often cause difficulty since children have to learn to handle themselves easily at the new stage and to spend long periods of time perfecting developing skills by practice. These transition periods are likely to be discouraging times for us in our work with young children.

Children who are small in size often become frustrated in motor activities.

Susan, a three year old child, was unusually short in comparison with other children in her group. She was agile in walking, running, and jumping, but she found climbing activities difficult because her short legs simply would not reach from one step to another on the jungle gym or the ladder boxes. Susan's whiney disposition and her incessant demands for adult attention outdoors seemed to be a reflection of these failures.

THE RELATION OF MOTOR SKILLS TO OTHER KINDS OF GROWTH

References and implications have indicated the close relationships between physical and motor growth and other kinds of development. Recent research has stressed the importance of these correlations to such an extent that it seems expedient to review them as a summary of this chapter.

Motor and mental activity are closely interrelated. Preschool children solve many of their problems by trial and error in motor activities, whereas, older children can consider and decide that many motor actions would be worthless. The sequential maturing of perceptual motor activities is inherent in standards set for intelligence testing. Moreover, portions of recent diagnostic tests used to assess reading problems in elementary schools require imitation of body movements, performing motor actions in response to verbal instructions, and demonstrating body movement and balance. It is evident that perceptual and neurological dysfunction usually are reflected in motor behavior. The observant adult can detect motor traits that indicate a child may need special help.

A skilled preschool teacher will be alert to the motor behavior of each child as a basis for choosing materials and equipment. Programs should include activities that require both large muscle activity and finer motor skills. Such activities will not only be beneficial to the health of youngsters but will stimulate their abilities and interests. The more competent children become in motor skills, the more they will enjoy their experiences and the more likely they will be to engage in them. Their emotional and social development obviously will be enhanced, too, because they will have a more positive self-concept. These cause and effect phenomena will be discussed in subsequent chapters.

The following facts should be noted.

1. Children who are growing rapidly need many oportunities to practice all kinds of motor skills. Adults should realize that there will be clumsiness and a tendency toward fatigue when the activities represent new experiences for the child.

2. Patience by adults is necessary as children experiment and practice developing skills.

3. Children who are learning locomotor skills need lots of space in which to play.

4. Providing clay or finger paints will offer the child an opportunity to practice manual dexterity that may lead to success with easel paints, crayons, and scissors that require more precision.

5. Since physical development does not occur except in conjunction with other kinds of growth, it is wise to choose activities for young children that satisfy their emotional needs, their intellectual interests, and their social strivings.

6. Equipment should be scaled so that even the smallest children in the group can have successful motor experiences.

7. It is important to try to imagine how the child must feel when his locomotor and manipulative skills are poorly developed.

SUGGESTED ASSIGNMENT

Part I

Physical Characteristics

Choose two children who seem very different in physical development and answer the following questions concerning each of them.

1. Is the child tall, short, medium tall? Is he slender or stocky? Is he small-boned or large-boned?

2. Is the child's manner alert, interested, enthusiastic, or listless? Describe the situation on which you base this judgment.

3. Is the child right-handed or left-handed? Describe the activity on which you base this judgment.

4. Does the child usually carry his head forward or erect? Do his feet turn forward, inward, or outward? Does he alternate feet on the stairs?

5. Are the child's teeth evenly spaced? Does he bite or suck his lips? Does he have a nasal discharge? Does he often pick at his nose?

Part II

Motor Ability

Answer the following questions about the two children you have chosen to study.

1. Does the child appear to have firm muscles and good posture or flabby muscles and poor posture?

2. Are the child's leg muscles more or less developed than his arm muscles? Describe the activity on which you base this judgment.

3. Are the child's movements awkward, graceful, light, heavy, quick, vigorous, slow, deliberate, careless, quiet, noisy, boisterous, steady, changeable from one activity to another? Describe.

4. When the child walks upstairs, does he alternate feet, hold the rail, or walk independently?

5. Is the child agile on climbing apparatus?

6. Is the child agile in running activities?

7. Is the child proficient in using the following materials: clay, finger paint, easel paint, crayons, and scissors? Describe.

8. Does the child handle utensils easily when eating?

9. Describe one of the child's favorite activities that you think depends on his manipulative skills.

SELECTED READINGS

1. Bayer, Leona M., and Nancy Bayley, *Growth Diagnosis,* University of Chicago Press, 1959.

The authors define normal growth and describe the range of individual variations in body build. This book will be of special interest to the reader who is interested in physical growth.

2. Connolly, K. J., ed., *Mechanisms of Motor Skill Development,* Academic press, N. Y., 1971.

This is a collection of writings by English authors. The emergence of motor skills, experimental analysis of skills, cognitive factors in skill development, and sensory-motor integration are among the topics included.

3. Cratty, Bryant J., *Some Educational Implications of Movements,* Bernie Straub, Seattle, 1971.

Cratty presents ways in which movement experiences may be used to help children who have mild to severe sensory-motor deficiencies. Some current theories concerning motor-neurological aspects of development are discussed and the research on which such theories are based is described.

4. Engstrom, Georgianna, ed., *The Significance of the Young Child's Motor Development,* National Association for the Education of Young Children, Washington, D. C., 1971.

This is a report of a conference jointly sponsored by the American Association of Health, Physical Education, and Recreation and NAEYC as a cooperative effort to examine the role of motor development in relation to the total development of young children. Ways of studying and evaluating development are emphasized.

5. Hopwood, Howard H., and Starr S. Van Iden, "Scholastic Underachievement as Related to Sub-Par Physical Growth," *The Journal of School Health,* October, 1965.

This research report covers a ten-year study of school children in Shaker Heights School District, Ohio. The Wetzel Grid was used as a measuring device to assess physical fitness. Students who plan to engage in research will find this study helpful.

6. Sinclair, Caroline B., *Movement and Movement Patterns of Early Childhood,* Division of Education Research and Statistics, State Department of Education Richmond, Va., 1971.

This research study establishes the correlation between motor skills and chronological age. For the student who is seeking standards of "normal" development and is interested in methodology for pertinent research, this will be a worthwhile reference.

7. Wetzel, Norman C., "Weight and Body Composition,"   *Pediatric News,* November, 1967.

Dr. Wetzel describes the dilemma of trying to evaluate growth by means of ordinary height and weight tables. He discusses the importance of evaluating the quality of growth and recognizing the individual child's unique physical endowments. This article will interest all those who are involved in working with young children.

chapter 5

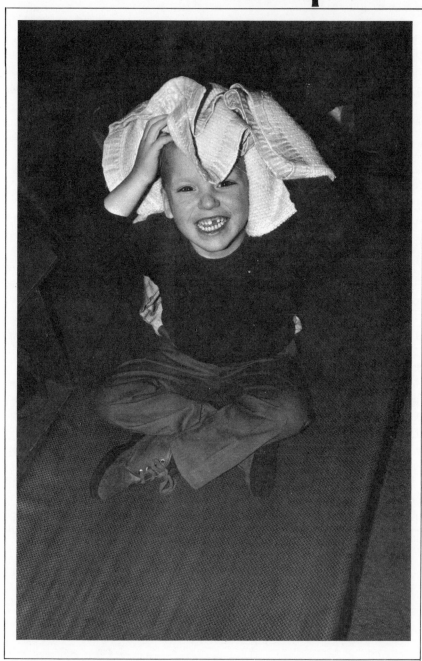

Personality Development

Men and women who are preparing to enter the field of early childhood education are confronted with many theories of personality development. It is evident that, to understand the personality of the individual child, we must have some knowledge of the variable components of growth and development in human beings.

Personality has its roots in the biogenetic chemistry of each individual. It can be affected by such factors as the mother's prenatal diet, her drug intake, illnesses during pregnancy, and any dietary deprivations she may incur during this period. The emerging personalities of infants are influenced by their diet, by how adults satisfy the infant's needs for warmth, food, and comfort, and by the emotional state of their caretakers. The cultural and ethnic mores under which a child is reared also influence which characteristics are preferred and will be nurtured by the adults who care for children. It is important that an adult who is guiding a developing personality be aware that knowledge of the specific child's background is a most helpful factor.

In the study of human development and interpersonal relationships, we become increasingly aware of the interwoven links between biological and sociological factors that make each human being unique. An individual frame of reference determines the way in which the child adapts to his society. Even identical twins, who have a commonly shared set of genetic components, encounter individualized experiences that can cause each child to react uniquely to a particular set of circumstances.

The person who works with young children must be aware that personality is a multidimensional factor, dynamic in concept. Personality is a word we use to describe the behavior that evolves in an individual as the result of the interaction of genetics, social environment, physical health, and chance happenings. Each of these factors influences how one relates to himself and to the world around him. This definition offers clues to the complex task of understanding how the personalities of individual children develop.

It is important to be aware that personality is dynamic and that the child's ability to adapt to a variety of circumstances is determined by how effectively he can cope with his environment. As young children grow, their personalities are affected by how they are perceived by the adults around them. It is essential that anyone who works with preschool children should be aware of (1) the nature of the uniqueness of individual development, (2) the continuity of growth, (3) common patterns of growth and development, and (4) the interrelationships of growth components. Adults who are involved with young children always should remember that the adults' own self-concepts and their value sets will influence the way in which they perceive others.

PERSONALITY AND SOCIETY

The circumstances that exist for each individual from conception on influence the emerging personality of every child. What are considered valuable traits to some groups of people, such as aggressiveness or passivity, are evaluated as negative traits by other groups. The emerging personality of the child is influenced by those around him who encourage some patterns of thought and behavior and discourage others. One school of thought concerning personality development and intellectual achievement is based on the acceptance or denial of a child's acts by structured, patterned responses of adults.

All adults have specific techniques that they consider useful in modifying the behavior of children to suit adults' concepts of desirable goals for emerging traits. The questions that we should ask are: (1) who should determine what a healthy personality is, and (2) how can one plan to work effectively with children if there is more than one framework for acceptable personality development in the environment? While theoreticians struggle with the problem of defining and evaluating behavior, the adult who is coping with the daily problems of working with children either as a parent or a professional needs some set of criteria for guiding the child so that the adult and child are comfortable with each other and can coexist in a common environment.

Research has offered some information as to how we influence personality development by the way we respond to the basic physiological and nurturing needs of the infant. The role of the primary nurturer can be assumed by one of several people: a parent, grandparents, nurse, "nanny," or day care worker. Who that person is may be determined by varying child-rearing practices in the culture as well as by varying nationalistic, economic, and social philosophies. Sociologists and psychologists currently are attempting to compare personality growth of children raised in collective settings in Israel, Russia, and Denmark to the personality development of children raised in other child care environments.

Societies demonstrate different degrees of concern for the infant even before he is born by the programs they have developed in offering prenatal care for the mother. When children have been born to mothers who have been unable to obtain proper nutritional and medical care, the children may have a range of problems related to this maternal deprivation. Poor health of the mother as well as drug-related problems lower the survival resources of the infant and establish a poor setting for healthy personality development. Problems of health, personality development, and intellectual growth have been evident in our own country as well as in many other countries.

Certain facts are apparent when the nurturer is establishing positive, secure relationships with infants. Babies make their needs for food, comfort, warmth, and security known by crying and by undifferentiated, gross body movements. The emotional tone for personality development is influenced by the way the adults who care for the child respond to or anticipate the infant's needs. If the baby does not receive response to attempts to contact helpers to meet those needs, research has shown that he can wither away because he stops seeking help. Even in circumstances of less severe deprivation, the emotional growth of the child may be damaged.

When infants' nurturing needs are met in a warm, accepting environment, they can begin to discriminate among the people around them and to respond to the caretaker who offers security. When this security is established, positive personality growth can occur. It may be harder for adults who are not secure within themselves to react in a positive, warm manner with children whose personalities may have been thwarted during infancy because of physical and emotional deprivation. These children may appear hostile, angry, withdrawn, or they may constantly test their relationships with adults. Caretakers often find it difficult to understand why their guidance is not accepted by a young child. Unless adults can understand the causes for the child's reactions, they may become angry because they are not accepted by the child and continue to sustain the negative feelings the child already has. In these instances, adults are unable to offer positive models for the child to seek to emulate.

The teacher who has been brought up in an environment that stressed such traits as independence or restraint of feelings may be very distressed when she encounters children who have been taught to depend on adults for direction and emotional sustenance. Students preparing to work with children should reflect carefully on the components of their own background environments and try to determine how their reactions to a particular child or group of children are influenced by a previously conceived set of rules. If you have lived in more than one area of the country, you may recall how you found the transition difficult because the way you were perceived in one environment differed from the way in which people responded to you in a new setting. You may have had to make some adjustments of your own before you felt comfortable and this undoubtedly affected your personal interaction with others. The person who works with young children in preschool centers should remember that these children often are encountering their first experiences in a large group setting and are attempting to formulate and define new strategies for coping with peers and vying for adult attention.

Initially, public child care services in the United States usually were designated for families who were not in a financial, physical, or emotional position to care for their own children. Parents often felt incapable of sharing in planning for the development of their child. Now, parents who use child care services span all socioeconomic levels and most parents are concerned, knowledgeable, and aware that they are the primary nurturers. The skilled child care worker is a partner with the family of the young child and is accountable to parents.

Many day care centers now are caring for children as young as six weeks. In these settings, it is imperative that parents and child care professionals become partners so they function as a team and maintain consistent patterns of responding to an infant's needs. If the baby must expend energy and time adjusting to conflicting patterns of child rearing, personality development may be hindered or inhibited. Gross inconsistencies in adult responses to an infant's needs can cause delays in the progression of events that are necessary for normal development.

PERSONALITY NEEDS

The knowledge that personality development occurs in an orderly pattern is not new. Discussions concerning this fact and the importance of early childhood years in the developing patterns have been included in most psychology books. The Midcentury White House Conference for Children and Youth was concerned particularly with personality development. From that conference, a consensus of opinion concerning the orderly development of personality became popular. The pattern of this development has been described by Erikson as a sequence that he called "The Eight Stages of Man."

Beginning students in child guidance need not endeavor to assess personality in the newborn infant, but it is important for them to know what facets of personality are evident early in the child's life. We cannot deal with the two-to-five-year-old child without reviewing what has happened in his development before those ages.

That the very young child thrives on and responds to affectionate care is certain. This is the chief reason for the increased popularity of the so-called rooming-in arrangement in maternity hospitals. It is an accepted opinion that the well-adjusted infant establishes a trust in his environment during the early months of life. This feeling that the world is a pretty good place is fostered, of course, by the satisfaction of his physical needs. The child's first feelings of security result from his being fed when he is hungry, changed to dry when he is wet, by his being warmed when he is uncomfortably cool and provided with suitable conditions for sleep. The importance of emotional tone is demonstrated in the first few months of life by the way in which a baby flourishes when he is cuddled and handled with affection.

During the first few weeks of life, of course, the people around the child are merely a part of his enveloping environment, but their roles in acceptance of him cannot be overemphasized. Within a short time, the child's social development begins to advance rapidly as he identifies the people around him as apart from the inanimate portions of his world, and his emotional satisfactions are correlated with the way in which they react to him.

Early in the second year the normal child begins to develop a specific sense of self. When we observe a young baby as he contemplates his kicking feet or waving fists, we become aware that his interest in his own body is an impersonal response, that his physical self is, to him, merely a part of his surroundings. As the child grows, however, he begins to realize that his head, his body, his arms, and legs respond to his dictation. He is establishing his first knowledge of himself as an individual.

Thus, gradually, the child becomes an egocentric creature. It is necessary that he test his importance in all areas. The child becomes proud of his somewhat clumsy motor skills. As a social being he is interested in his own pursuits and impervious to the wishes or property of others. It is during this time that adults are frequently irritated by some of the child's personality traits. Children who are in this stage appear to have an almost compulsive need for routine procedures. They are interested in doing everything in a certain way. It is important that the child should establish an acceptable self-concept before he will be ready to move outward to satisfy his future needs.

As the child's functioning as an individual improves, it is logical that he should begin to expand his interests and endeavors in all areas of behavior. This period is crucial in the life of the preschool child. Many types of experimentation are indicated. The child needs to find out about things, to touch and lift, to feel and test, to try and try again and again. Many aspects of this period in childhood are discussed later in appropriate chapters.

Those who guide children at this developmental level need to be alert to their interests, to provide equipment and materials that will be challenging and yet not too difficult in view of the child's skills, to be patient while he experiments. An enriched environment together with patience and understanding during his explorations are the best means for promoting his wholesome growth.

Personality growth is uneven in rate. As with other characteristics of the growth process, this pattern is unique to the individual. At times the child's personality adjustments seem to move rapidly toward meeting his problems, and these times seem to be followed by long periods during which he appears to be striving unsuccessfully for personal satisfactions. It is apparent that, as with other kinds of growth, rapid changes take place during the preschool years, that the following years are characterized by a lesser rate of increment, and that another rapid spurt comes at puberty. Often, when it appears that the child has satisfied his strivings for emotional satisfactions in a specific area, regressions occur which are baffling to those who live with him.

Jimmie entered the preschool at the age of three years and two months. His mother dropped by the school office when she was notified that there would be a place for Jimmie in the group during the following term. Good rapport was established between Mrs. Irwin and the school director. A few days later Jimmie and his parents came to the school and Jimmie seemed pleased with everything. Miss Edwards, the group teacher, visited with Jimmie and when she suggested that his mother and father wanted to talk to one of the other teachers Jimmie happily accompanied her to the playground.

When Mrs. Irwin brought Jimmie to school on the first day of school she made plans to remain for the entire morning. Jimmie paid little attention to his mother except to call her attention to some toy or situation now and then. He resisted their leaving at the end of the period but accepted reassurance that he could return on the following day.

On the second morning, Mrs. Irwin stayed for a few minutes and then told Jimmie that she had some shopping to do and would return for him at lunch time. Jimmie seemed to be unaware that his mother was gone. He played happily in group activities and followed the routines with ease. Jimmie's adjustment appeared to be excellent. During the first two weeks he resisted leaving when one of his parents called for him when the school day was over.

During the third week Jimmie began to cling to his mother when she brought him in the morning. He begged her to stay and was unhappy looking when she said she had to go to town on some errands. On successive mornings Jimmie became less willing for his mother to leave and he hung over the playground fence with a forlorn expression on his face. Mrs. Irwin was greatly disturbed by her son's unhappiness at school.

This situation is not at all unusual. We could speculate that the child is less happy after the newness wears off, that he may be jealous of his mother's activities during her periods of absence, that something might have happened at the school that has threatened his feelings of security. Frequently, what the underlying reasons or combination of reasons might be is not clarified. As in other problem areas with children, the child will usually readjust within a short time and it is unnecessary to probe into the underlying causes for his behavior. During his periods of unhappiness, however, he needs support in acceptance of his feelings. Perhaps the school situation should be made especially pleasant for him in some way until he feels better or perhaps his mother should remain at school for a few days until he is willing that she leave. Whatever the outcome, it appears that this child is having difficulty in personality adjustment at the present time.

It is obvious that staff members and parents must work as a team to insure the child's positive feelings about the child care center.

Samantha's mother had difficulty in parting with Samantha each morning and Samantha begged for "two more minutes" each time her mother prepared to leave her. Mrs. Ponds was ambivalent concerning her desire to permit Samantha to attend the preschool and her feelings were evident to the child. Once the break was made each morning, Mrs. Ponds was upset but Samantha had a wonderful time at school.

One morning Samantha hit her mother in the presence of the school director and Mrs. Ponds turned to the director for guidance. A teacher involved Samantha in easel painting so Mrs. Ponds and the director could confer. They decided that a prompt "Goodbye" and a "see-you-later" kiss would help resolve the problem.

At the start of the next session, a kiss, a "Goodbye," and "See you later," was issued lovingly and firmly and the mother left immediately. Samantha had a fine day and created a special project to give to her mother at "going-home" time. The problem did not recur and Samantha had a fine year at the preschool.

EMOTIONAL CONFLICTS IN PERSONALITY ADJUSTMENT

The interrelatedness of personality growth with other kinds of growth cannot be questioned. The definition of personality stated earlier in this chapter denoted that physical traits; current levels of motor, language, and social skills; intellectual status; and emotional tone are a part of personality.

As the child grows, it is necessary for him to satisfy the physical and psychological needs commensurate with his maturational level, but he also is confronted with the demands of his environment or "developmental tasks." At all ages, the degree of success with which the individual can meet these demands determines his happy or unhappy adjustment. For example, it is interesting if students consider their own situations regarding environmental demands. In our culture, at about the time when young people are ready for college or for job training, psychological weaning from the parental home should have occurred to some extent. If the individual is unable to meet this demand, if he is homesick in his separation from his family, if he finds it difficult to make his own decisions or to assume the task of self-direction, he is likely to be unhappy.

The inability to meet the demands made upon him is no less traumatic for the young child. If he is expected to share his toys and to respect the property rights of others before he has established a satisfactory feeling of self-importance and personal ownership, frustration is to be expected. Or, if the child has passed through this stage satisfactorily and, because of his level of development, needs to explore his world yet is reprimanded and restrained in this striving, we can again expect an unhappy child. Both these predicaments will result in what is misbehavior from an adult point of view. In the first instance, the child is likely to appear to be selfish, demanding, and jealous. In the second, he is likely to be destructive and aggressive. In both cases, there probably will be frequent outbursts of anger.

THE ANGRY CHILD

The most common cause for anger in the preschool child is frustration that is often induced by restriction of bodily movements. When the child's activities are curtailed, he usually responds with aggression. We should not get excited every time a child shows anger. Moreover, what appears to be aggression may not always be that. Children often hurt other people unintentionally. We must remember that they do not have good control over their bodily actions. Sometimes, too, they are merely experimenting to see what will happen. Children must learn by doing.

Gary was two years and four months old when he entered the school. As could be expected, most of his play was solitary, but he was an interested spectator during all the activities. Gary seemed to be especially interested in Carol who was about two months older than he. She was an active child and he would follow her from room to room with a happy expression on his face. Time after time, Gary would dart toward Carol, bite her arm or hand, and then stand back to see what the result would be. The teachers soon learned to foresee Gary's biting by watching his facial expression which seemed to say, "I believe I'll see what she'll do when I bite her today."

Obviously, Gary's behavior represented experimentation in social skills rather than actual aggression. Sometimes, adults are prompted to consider only the action and thus to think, "Gary is a bad boy. He incessantly bites Carol when she is not even playing with him."

Moreover, adults often resent any aggression, physical or verbal, which the child aims toward them. However, whatever the cause, it is probably better if aggression is aimed toward adults than toward other children. After all, adults are big enough to protect themselves. If an adult understands the reasons behind the aggressive act, a calm attitude is usually not difficult. Guidance methods can be more wisely chosen by an adult who is not emotionally upset. Impulsive adults often interpret aggressive behavior by children as being purposeful and pre-meditated. It is worth while to consider each incident from the child's point of view.

By being aggressive, children often indicate what they are unable to express in words. They may feel jealous, troubled, or frustrated. When children repeatedly attack other children, however, it is apparent that they deliberately intend to hurt. Since it is evident that something is wrong in the child's world, the first step is to try to learn what is troubling him. If there is no apparent cause, increased attention or affection may sometimes eradicate his unhappiness. This kind cf guidance may be difficult since it is not easy to respond to irritating behavior with increased affection. After all, adults have feelings, too, and parents in particular are likely to be embarrassed if their child is even mildly aggressive.

It is probable that an accepting attitude will help solve the problem. Usually, like most other problems of preschool children, this is a passing phase and can be handled well enough when specific situations arise. If the child persists in being aggressive over a long period of time, the parents should be helped to seek evaluative counseling. Sometimes a more specific diagnosis and special help are needed to prevent this child from feeling that the only way his needs can be met is through aggressive acts. By the time children reach elementary school years, they usually have learned to express their feelings without physical aggression unless this is the way in which they have been handled by adults.

Children, in releasing their pent-up anger, may try to hurt inanimate objects. This is proof of the impersonal attitudes that underlie many of their aggressive acts.

Jenny, age five, lacked good motor coordination. She could not climb as well as the more agile children, she found it difficult to complete the simple wooden puzzles at the school. Her impatience with her failures in many activities resulted in her stomping her feet and crying.

One night, Jenny's mother was cleaning the bathtub after Jenny had finished her bath. Nearby, Jenny was getting into her pajamas. Her left hand slipped out of a sleeve and hit the lavatory. She immediately turned, hit the lavatory with her right fist, paused a moment, and said to the lavatory, "Well, I hope you're happy. Now, you've hurt my other hand, too."

Seldom can children verbalize these feelings, but it seems certain that they must be hurt often by the inanimate objects in their environment. Similar responses of impatience and irritation with inanimate objects sometimes occur with adults. No doubt, students will be able to recall similar examples.

THE DESTRUCTIVE CHILD

The child who is destructive presents problems both at home and at school. As with the aggressive child, it is advantageous if the feelings behind the child's actions can be ascertained. That destruction is frequently unintentional is evident.

Tommy was an unusually large child for his chronological age. He was taller and heavier than any of the other children in his group. Moreover, Tommy had an exuberent attitude in all activities. When he entered the school at the beginning of the morning period, the slamming of the outer door accompanied by verbal "whooping" denoted to all present that Tommy had arrived.

Tommy's motor skills were not highly developed. He walked with a lumbering gait, his long arms flailing at his sides. His enunciation was poor, but he made up for this lack in verbal skill by the volume of his vocalizations. Many of Tommy's activities resulted in broken toys and equipment. It seemed difficult for him to walk past a table without dislodging some article. He was "all thumbs" during creative activities; delicate objects seemed simply to fall apart in his hands. It was hard for some of the teachers to refrain from criticizing Tommy's destructive ways.

Unintentional destruction often occurs, also, when children attempt to explore and experiment. Adult reactions to this type of destruction must seem puzzling to preschool children. Children must learn by doing and it is only natural for the older perschool child to want to take things apart. Parents often buy toys that are designed with this purpose in mind. Yet, if the child disassembles a toy not made for this use, many adults are likely to respond by scolding or some other form of punishment.

If a preschool child removes the clothing and pulls out the yarn hair of an old rag doll, there may be calm adult acceptance, but if the child gives the same treatment to a fragile doll that recently has been purchased, many adults will respond in a punitive way. True, children must learn in time that their ways must change according to the situation, but the preschool child has had little experience, he has much to learn concerning the demands of other people. Chalk may be used on chalkboards but not on walls, scissors may be used on some kinds of paper or even on some scraps of cloth but not on new magazines nor on table covers, and it is,permissible to tear old newspapers and magazines but unacceptable to tear those that adults have not read. Here again, adults should consider the situation as it must appear to the child.

As with the angry child, if a child is destructive in many ways and for long periods of time, two steps are logical: (1) we should endeavor to understand the feelings that underlie his actions and to eradicate those feelings, and (2) we should seek help if the destructive tendency is of any excessively long duration.

THE CHILD WHO IS AFRAID

Guiding children who are fearful is another important task of those who associate with preschoolers. The importance of good methods in this area is great. Obviously, it is necessary that children learn to be cautious of some objects and situations. The runabout child must be cautioned concerning a hot stove or radiator, electrical appliances, traffic, strange animals, and other things threatening his safety. Our problem is: How can we instill caution and not cause fear? If a child learns from his own experience that a certain object or situation may hurt him, he will react with a natural caution; yet it is not feasible to allow children to experience injury in order to learn many of the dangers that will confront them.

In the preschool child, interest precedes judgment. Therefore, it is logical that we should be alert to their actions so that accidents can be prevented. On the playground, it is not unusual to see a child prepare to jump from a high box or platform with no understanding that he will be hurt in doing so. If enough supervision is possible, a nearby adult can move quickly and ease his fall. If there are few adults on duty, the piece of equipment should be removed.

As noted in a previous chapter, long-drawn-out explanations are useless with the very young child. Consequently, in this area of guidance, definite and quickly enforced rules are imperative. Whenever a child's safety is threatened, adults should be adamant in enforcing rules. However, adult orders should not be so forceful nor occur so frequently that the result is the child's fear of the adult instead of his fear of the situation to be avoided. This will not happen, of course, if a warm relationship has been established.

Certain fears are likely to occur at specific periods in the child's development. During early infancy, fear of loss of support or of sudden, loud noises is common. Later, unfamiliar objects, persons, or situations cause fear. Separation from parents is a concurrent stimulus for fear. A common fear at about the time they enter preschool is that of being left alone in a strange place or in the dark. Other normal fears during preschool years are: fear of pain and injury, fear of animals, fear of crippled people, and the fear of death. All these fears, of course, depend to a great extent on their backgrounds of experience. Some of these fears can become long-lasting attitudes. Occasionally, students can trace their present fears to situations that occurred during their preschool years.

Many fears of childhood may seem foolish from an adult point of view, but it is incorrect to assume that they are not felt intensely by the young child. Sometimes, it is possible to trace their origin and to avoid their recurrence by manipulating the child's environment or experiences until he is older and better able to cope with the fear because of his ability to understand. For example, a painful experience with a playful kitten may cause the child to be afraid of all animals.

Fears are contagious. By example adults can help in reassuring the child. For instance, if a mother shows that she is afraid of storms, her small children will usually react the same way. The contagious nature of fears is apparent when one observes small children at play. There seems to be a thrill accompanying the group activities of older preschool children in which imaginary things are frightening. When we observe them in their play, we often hear remarks like

"There's a bad old tiger in the shed. He's waiting to eat you up," "There's an old man hiding in the garage," or "A big steam roller is going to run right across this yard and smash everybody." Infrequently, children can express the lack of reason for these fears even though their feelings are not changed.

Mary and Dick Evans slept in adjoining bedrooms that were adjacent to a screened porch. After the children had been put to bed, they called to each other and conversed about many things. These conversations often related to the bears who "lived on the porch outside the windows." Although Dick was six years old and Mary was only four, it was she who had started their thinking about the imaginary bears. One night Mary called her mother to her room and said, "I've been trying to scare Dick about the bears, but now I'm scared, too."

Such activities, of course, provide much of the fun in some Hallowe'en celebrations when children are older.

Adults frequently cause fears in children, also, because there are admonitions that must be made to the children whom they guide.

A supplementary playroom was equipped in the basement of the school. When inclement weather prevented play outdoors, the children often enjoyed going there to play. Kevin always refused to accompany the group to the basement. When he was encouraged to do so, it was evident that he was afraid; an expression of horror appeared on his face.

Since Kevin thoroughly enjoyed group play, he seemed unhappy when he was allowed to remain upstairs. At intervals of only a few minutes he would ask, "Will the children come up soon?" When the teacher would suggest that he join the group, he would shrink back and begin to sob.

Finally, an interview with Kevin's mother was planned. At first, she seemed unable to explain his reactions but after awhile both she and the school director were able to trace Kevin's reasons for fear. His father was a flower fancier and spent his leisure time in his beautiful flower garden. He stored his sprays and insecticides in a cupboard in the basement of their home. Although the cupboard was locked, both the cupboard and the lock were of inferior construction. Consequently, it was customary to demand that Kevin never should go to the basement unless his mother or father were with him.

Children have active imaginations. In this instance, it is impossible for us to recognize what dire things Kevin may have thought were lurking in all basements.

Occasionally, children's fears are related to their concepts of time. The lack of true understanding of time is exemplified when children ask such questions as "Is this tomorrow?" Many adult-child communications could be made easier if adults were aware of this fact. For example, when parents leave their children they often state that they will be back in three hours, or tomorrow, or in a few days. To the small child, tomorrow may be meaningless and any separation may be considered as a final one. This is unfair to the child if we consider the situation from his viewpoint. Although there may be little we can do to assuage his apprehensions, it will help if we can understand his feelings. When parents leave young children, they should see that the person with whom the children are to stay is in the home long enough to be accepted happily and that the liking of adult and child is mutual. Then a casual leave-taking will be less frightening.

As in other kinds of child guidance, the adult role should be one of quiet, calm understanding and reassurance. Only those emotional conflicts that are encountered daily in the preschool situation have been included here. Other emotional problems will also be discussed later in appropriate chapters.

INFLUENCE OF EARLY FEELINGS ON LATER DEVELOPMENT

Guiding children involves providing models for them to follow. As we have stated, an adult who is insecure about his own values often fails to provide a positive model for the child to imitate. Recent research has reenforced the belief that young children tend to model their behavior after adults who are meaningful to them. When adults act in a confused or inconsistent manner, it makes the task of growing up harder than is necessary.

Because there is a plethora of literature about child guidance, it is only the secure adult who can discriminate and realize that, if the overall set of experiences between the child and his surroundings has been positive, loving, and accepting, the nurturing adult need not be overly concerned about an occasional failure in meeting a child's immediate emotional needs. A child usually will offer an adult a second opportunity to rectify the error.

Nevertheless we can speculate about what may occur when children are unsuccessful in fulfilling their psychological needs (1) for feelings of trust in their environment, (2) for a satisfying acceptance of themselves, and (3) for a satisfactory testing of initiative. These needs are never completely satisfied and all of us are striving for thier fulfillment throughout our lives.

It is not appropriate to attempt to classify ourselves or our acquaintances as mature or immature emotionally. All people are more mature at some times than at other times and more mature in some ways than in other ways. However, it is interesting to imagine what characteristics an adult who has been emotionally deprived in childhood might display. For example, it might be that the person who did not derive a satisfying feeling of trust in his environment in his early childhood would be fearful in all his activities in adult life, that he might mistrust not only the physical environment but all people. This is entirely hypothetical, of course. Only the abnormal person is completely lacking in his feelings of security and trust. The hypothetical adult who was unsuccessful in developing a satisfying belief in himself in early childhood might continue to be egocentric in all his activities; he might be trying incessantly to satisfy this need. We could expect him to be unmindful of the needs and property rights of others.

The adult who did not have an opportunity in childhood to satisfy his need for exploring his world and testing his abilities might display an insatiable craving for new experiences or adventures. Or, conversely, he might be fearful of showing an initiative; he could be an individual who would never try any action nor propose any ideas.

It is more realistic, of course, to recognize that some children appear to display greater needs in these areas than other children and that parents and teachers can help in satisfying these normal strivings. As a basis for understanding the preschool child, we should make an effort to know how he must feel about himself, his world, and other people.

SUGGESTED ASSIGNMENT

Part I

1. List 10 personality characteristics that are used in describing people. Define these with positive and negative values. For example, "aggressive" means "pushes people around" or "meets other people easily in social situations."

2. Describe your own feelings when you enter a room full of strangers. How do these feelings reflect your sense of trust, your sense of self, your sense of initiative?

Part II

Observe one child for twenty minutes and record his behavior. Analyze your record for evidence of the following:

1. Do you think this child has a feeling of successful achievement and self-confidence expressed through constructive and creative activity? How did he show it?

2. Do you think this child has a feeling of security and belongingness expressed through free, spontaneous behavior and happy relations with others? How did he express it?

3. Did you observe examples of the child's emotions as expressed by aggression, destruction, or fear? Describe the situation in which you thought such behavior was shown.

Part III

After your class has been divided into committees of four members each, your individual assignment is to read a book on child rearing that has not been chosen by any other member of your group. Then, in group discussion, compare the theories of the various authors and answer the following questions.

1. How does the author offer to help the reader?

2. In general, what does the author expect from parents?

3 How does the author show that he or she is knowledgeable about children?

4. Would you recommend this book to a parent? Why?

5. What book that another member of your group read are you most interested in? Why?

Part IV

How have you developed your ideas as to what constitutes a healthy personality? Be explicit.

SELECTED READINGS

1. Bobson, Sarah, *Self Concept: An Annotated Bibliography of Selected ERIC References,* ERIC Information Retrieval Center on the Disadvantaged, Teachers College, Columbia University, N. Y., 1973.

This bibliography lists and describes sources of information concerning self-concept. It will be useful for research purposes.

2. Brody, Sylvia, *Theory and Research in Child Development,* Early Childhood Education Council of New York, 1972.

In pamphlet form, the author succinctly ties together the history of theories of personality and child development. Comments about observations and research in mental health and personality developemnt are included.

3. Cohen, Dorothy, and Virginia Stern, *Observing and Recording the Behavior of Young Children,* Teachers College, Columbia University, N. Y., 1972.

This excellent little book gives specific techniques for observing children. It would be most helpful for anyone who plans to use observation as a research tool.

4. Erikson, Erik H., *Childhood and Society,* W. W. Norton, N. Y., 1950.

The author describes and discusses personality development and psychological needs of persons of all ages. Students who are familiar with other references may desire to consult this important source for supplementary information.

5. Feshbach, Norma, and Seymour Feshbach, "Children's Aggression," *The Young Child,* Vol. 2, pp. 284-302, National Association Education of Young Children, Washington, D. C., 1972.

This presentation discusses research on causes of aggressive behavior and suggests directions for seeking solutions to modify behavior.

6. Gottesman, I. I., "Heredity and Intelligence," *The Young Child,* Vol. 2, pp. 24-53, National Association Education of Young Children, Washington, D. C., 1972.

This report on research will provide an example of methodology that involves interest in biogenetic and sociological traits. The serious student would find it interesting.

7. Jersild, Arthur, *When Teachers Face Themselves,* Teachers College, Columbia University, N. Y., 1955.

This text is directed toward teachers and future teachers who are led to reexamine their motives for seeking teaching careers. It is a good book for introspection.

8. Skeels, Harold M., *Adult Status of Children With Contrasting Early Life Experiences,* Monograph, Society for Research in Child Development, Vol. 31, no. 3, University of Chicago Press, 1966.

This is a follow-up study of children who were first studied as subjects of emotional deprivation during infancy. As original research, it should be of genuine interest to those who want to explore the area of personality development and adjustment.

chapter 6

Social Development

The process of interacting with other people begins early in the infant's life, continues throughout his lifetime, and influences the total developmental process. Laboratory schools and other settings where there are adequate personnel offer excellent opportunities for observation and research into the study of human social growth. Anyone who is interested in learning about children should be prepared to spend time observing and recording their social behavior in order to study the dynamics of social development. Before an observer attempts to become judgmental, the following questions should be considered: how do parents and child care personnel influence developmental patterns of social growth, (2) how do individual differences influence patterns of social development, (3) how does maturation affect social development, (4) what is the relationship between self-concept and social growth, and (5) why does the environment that surrounds a child influence his social development?

ADULTS AND THE CHILD

Parents and other caretakers directly influence social development of children since they constantly are guiding children's relationships as they reward one kind of behavior and restrict another. Many children have been guided toward healthy social growth because adults close to them have provided a sensitive and perceptive framework that has encouraged positive social relationships. In some cases, children who come from physically crowded homes or homes where the socioeconomic status of the family is uncertain appear to have less than satisfactory social growth patterns during their early years. In these situations, family pressures can interfere with the ability of the adults to afford adequate time and motivation to provide the young child with sufficient nurturing to give him diverse opportunities for social growth.

Some families encourage boys to have more varied opportunities for social growth than girls as they start from infancy to rear each sex with a specific set of social values that are related to the family's concept of male and female behavior. Parents often retard the social development of their child if they (1) have a poor self-image, (2) have come from a family where child rearing practices were harsh and abusive, or (3) are suffering from mental illness that prevents them from coping with social situations. Parents who feel comfortable with themselves and secure in their relationships with others provide a more secure social environment for a young child.

Children will be more likely to be accepting of other people if the environment is a happy one. A happy person of any age will employ more pleasant methods of approach toward other people. Consequently, the first requirement is a pleasant atmosphere. In child care centers, teachers and aides can provide this environment by being happy and relaxed people themselves. Fortunately, most people no longer believe that "anyone can take care of small children." The importance of early life experiences indicates that only well-adjusted adults should supervise the young.

When teachers enjoy being with children, children appear to feel the warmth of their presence. Although individual differences of both children and adults make it impossible to prescribe how we can help children to accept other children, some general rules seem appropriate. If children have pleasant social experiences, they gain in satisfaction and self-confidence so that future social contacts are more likely to be successful. Thus, if adult-child relationships have been pleasant, children are more likely to approach their peers in pleasant ways. As the child meets with success, he will tend to be happier and to maintain and improve wholesome social techniques.

As a first step in recognizing the complexity of the social process some hospitals have taken steps to permit the father to be present during the birth of an infant. Advocates of natural childbirth believe the bond between the infant and his family begins before birth and that the presence of the father at the time of birth establishes a special tie between the parents and the child and sets the tone for healthy social development. Hospital administrators often have conflicting concerns about the need for sterile conditions and the nurturing needs of the neonate. There is an awareness that infants in isolettes should be touched as much as is feasible to offer the child the opportunity to sense and feel the human touch.

Recent research indicates that premature neonates who have been considered extrauterine fetuses respond to physical and vocal nurturing. Other research is attempting to clarify just how early the infant is actively involved in social responses. Researchers have shown that social interaction begins at birth and is an ongoing process. Babies appear to display a minimal response to the nurturer except for the reduction of crying during physical comforting but studies indicate that early attention to neonates can foster long term cognitive gains. In other words, human sociability can influence the total development of children. The infant who is in close physical contact with his caretaker for feeding, fondling, bathing has a healthier start toward developing positive social patterns.

Individual differences in developmental patterns of social growth are apparent very early in life. Within the first few days after birth some children seem more aware than others of the presence of adults nearby. Colicky infants or those who experience physical discomfort and who are awake more than other infants are more vocal in their demands for assistance and are persistent in their demands for responses from adults. Possibly, differences in the early awareness of adult presence is the first indication of personality variations that are more obvious at later stages of development. Certainly some of us, regardless of age, enjoy association with people more than others do. Since there are so many variables to consider, the problem of evaluating social growth and planning for meeting children's needs is a complex task. It is certain, however, that as children gain trust in those who take care of them foundations for social development are established.

Bruce, a five-month-old infant was responding to adult attention with smiles and gross body movement. His mother, Phyllis, had an identical twin sister, Lila, who visited frequently with Bruce and usually was greeted with his usual smile. Suddenly Bruce began to cry whenever Lila was with him and the crying intensified when Phyllis and Lila were together. It became apparent that the similarity in appearance, tone of voice, and manner between the two sisters caused great confusion for the child and it was several weeks before Lila could be near Bruce without causing anxiety. Apparently Bruce needed time to establish precise criteria for distinguishing between two configurations that had much in common.

The environment around an infant should provide security and reasonable consistency. If he is confronted with constant confusion, his ability to make discriminating choices may be delayed. Infants need time to learn to know who cares for them; they are groping with the task of learning how to identify those people who can help. The child must also learn how he should respond to his caretakers so he can reduce his own internal stress. As a result, under normal circumstances, an infant's social interactions will remain focused around adults until he is about eighteen months old. The infant may respond to a young child but usually in an object sense, by touching, grabbing, or attempting to manipulate physically. As the child approaches the second year of life, he becomes aware of other children as physical beings and often will babble at them and initiate brief contacts or confrontations. However, during the formative years, social interactions revolve around adults in the nurturing unit either at home or in day care settings. Even at two years of age, children still spend most of their energies exploring the physical environment, developing locomotive skills and language as they reinforce their knowledge of themselves in relation to the world around them. Social contacts with peers are minimal but awareness of their presence usually is acknowledged in some way.

Two-year-olds like to be near other children. They spend a part of their time watching other children and they like to play near them and with similar materials. When a group of two-year-old children are observed in a preschool setting, they seem to be engrossed in their individual pursuits. Yet it is apparent that a type of social sharing has begun. These children are playing with similar toys, they are sharing adult attention, and they are broadening their own experiences by imitating a few of the activities that are occurring nearby.

Solitary play is necessary. Adults are likely to be too eager to push children into group activities before they are ready for them. It is imperative that the individual be allowed to set his own pace. In fact, it is probable that the privilege of playing alone should be more leniently allowed at all age levels. Certainly, the ability to play alone may be an asset to any child. Possibly, too many childhood activities are promoted by adults and result in fatigue and frustration. In a preschool group, it is not wise to accept the amount of social interaction and the level of adjustment as being analogous. Often, the facial expression of the onlooking child will indicate that he is deriving as much satisfaction from a social situation as the active participants. Certainly, he is learning how other people behave and that knowledge is basic to social adjustment.

Contacts between two-year-olds usually are spasmodic and of short duration.

Jimmy and Clara spent the entire outdoor play period in the sandpile. Both children were intent on shoveling sand into the small buckets and then dumping it. Now and then, each child would dig a hand down into the sand and let it trickle through fingers into the buckets. Once or twice, Jimmy scooped his shovel filled with sand into the bucket with which Clara was playing. When this occurred, both children would laugh and then return to playing with their separate utensils.

These children were almost entirely self-absorbed, but their brief periods of contact signified the beginnings of social reciprocity.

Simple social skills that are largely automatic in adult behavior are not possible for young children. If we understand the sequence of social learning and recognize the need for practice and experience, we will have patience and will allow these two-year-olds to set their own patterns. Few quarrels will develop if interesting materials are supplied. When two children of this age want the same toy, of course, grabbing and crying are usual responses. Anger is brief, however, and, as stated in a previous chapter, distraction is probably the best method for resolving arguments. These children are not ready to understand the values of sharing. They must first experience a sense of personal ownership or mastery. Possessiveness must be viewed as it appears to the child. Anything that he uses is considered as belonging to him and the meaning of ownership is beyond his understanding. The knowledge that sharing brings social approval will come later.

When children are nearing three years of age, playing together still is simple and seems almost incidental. Social interaction usually occurs during motor activities. Imitation of activities is common and, since motor activity requires less concentrated attention than at earlier ages, play of the follow-the-leader type often develops. When children first begin to play together, they usually play in pairs. By playing with first one child and then another, they begin to learn that each child is different and that different kinds of activity as well as different responses are necessary in associating with others. This knowledge is valuable all through life.

Doris entered school when she was three years old. She was smaller than the rest of the children in her group. Her complexion was pale and she did not appear to be robust. She did not enter into play with the other children. On the playground, she would crawl up on a bench near one of the teachers and observe the activities or, if the weather were warm, she would sometimes move to the sandpile and dig with one of the shovels.

Indoors, Doris continued to be an onlooker. When the children were in the doll corner, she stood nearby and watched them or sometimes moved to a table and worked with a puzzle. Her manipulative skills were good and often she would work several of the puzzles in succession. When the children were busy elsewhere, Doris infrequently went to the doll corner and sat quietly in one of the rocking chairs, holding a doll on her lap. During the story hour, Doris was an interested listener, but she seldom made any comment and did not enter into any of the group singing although her language skill was as good as that of her age mates.

The teachers always tried to encourage Doris to enter play situations with the rest of the group. Quiet verbal comments concerning the fact that her favorite doll was in the doll bed or questions asked of her when the other children were discussing some story or event brought no response. Doris appeared to enjoy school, however. Her parents reported that she talked a great deal about the other children and that she sang the nursery school songs often.

Onlooker and solitary play were continued by Doris during almost two terms of school. Then, rather quickly, she formed an apparent liking for Sara, one of the girls in her group. She took advantage of every opportunity to play near her. Since Sara was an active and sociable child, she soon met Doris' overtures with warmth and the two of them usually were together on the playground playing quietly in the swings or on the teeter-totters, chatting as they played. Indoors, Sara often played with two or three other children and at these times Doris would resume her solitude. For at least a part of each morning, however, the two girls would play busily in the doll corner.

About three weeks later, Doris began playing with Margaret in the same manner but, as with Sara, if another child entered the situation, Doris withdrew. She had not entered into group play at the close of the school year.

Apparently this was a normal pattern of social activity for this child at that time. School social experiences do not need to be in groups of children and the fact that, at preschool age, Doris became an active participant only when the situation involved one other child did not indicate that her social development was not proceeding as it should. As children grow, they become more aware of others. Although, at age three, solitary play still is dominant and social interaction is likely to be brief, children are becoming aware of the rights of others and there is evidence of taking turns and some sharing of toys.

Gloria was an active three-year-old. Her language skills were good and she was likely to call for adult attention as she engaged in play either indoors or outdoors. That she was self-centered was demonstrated time after time when she would call to the teacher, remarking that she was swinging higher than the other children or that she could climb to the very top of the jungle gym.

Jean was Gloria's favorite companion at school. The two girls played together on the swings or with tricycles on the playground or with doll buggies when the children moved indoors. In spite of Gloria's preoccupation with her own abilities, it was not unusual to hear her say to Jean, "Now I'll push you for a while," when the two children were playing at the swings, In the doll corner, Gloria always saw that Jean had a blanket for her doll when doll play began.

Adults involved with children in preschools frequently make the error of planning large-group activities for three year olds and thereby fostering unnecessary feelings of anger, frustration, and anxiety in the child who is not ready for group experiences. Good planning for young children offers many opportunities for small-group experiences, solitary play, and activities for developing oral language skills to help toward socialization. Preschool programs should offer settings for social interaction without demands for social herding.

Three-year-old Susan came from a crowded apartment in the heart of the city. Her play was restricted to association with siblings and her days usually were spent indoors unless her mother was able to maneuver Susan and her three siblings into a carriage arrangement and down the elevator. When Susan started attending the preschool, her play was solitary and she guarded any toy she was using. In response to a teacher's suggestion that she share her wooden pegs with another child, Susan's response was, "I want peace and quiet now. Just leave me alone with my things."

Susan apparently enjoyed school because it afforded her a place to have privacy. Her involvement with a small group evidently was satisfying during story time or outdoors, however. In those situations she responded to other children or to the gentle conversation of a teacher who might discuss something Susan was doing.

By four years of age most children can be cooperative in small-group settings. Motor development and language growth have contributed to social maturation and children demonstrate a desire to share their experiences with others. This increased rate of interactions often leads to aggressive behavior and verbal quarreling as four-year-old children begin to organize and structure their play. Fantasy and reality are interwoven in imaginative and perceptive dramatic play that can be carried through over several days or that can shift from one subject to another in a matter of moments. A kitchen scene in the playhouse can become a doctor's office when one persuasive youngster decides to play-act the role of nurse or doctor.

Social skills change as children begin to refine their use of language as a tool for social encounters. The adult who works with children must feel comfortable in letting children practice settling their own differences as long as physical or emotional harm to other children does not occur.

Since adults serve as models and are carefully watched and imitated by children, child care workers must be prepared to practice what they preach when they attempt to guide the social development of children.

Mrs. Killian, a teacher of four-year-olds, was made painfully aware of this when she interfered with two children who were having a tug of war over a toy. She suggested that Phil let Harry play with the toy until he was finished with it. Harry asked, "Why, Mrs. Killian? You took my toy yesterday at clean up time and I didn't finish with it."

In a positive, unharried, adequately-supplied environment, children usually can experiment with techniques of testing out behavior patterns and determine the success or failure of an approach with a minimum of adult interference. Whereas solitary or parallel play is the rule for most two-year-olds and many three-year-olds, the four-year-old is seldom observed in isolation unless he is absorbed in a task that is solitary by nature or unless he is uncomfortable in the situation. A new child entering a room where other children are playing often moves from solitary play to a parallel encounter before he makes his way into the group. The degree of social involvement often depends on the person's concept of his own skills for the group task. Children and adults often refrain from group encounters when they feel they cannot cope successfully.

Mike, a four-year-old was quite capable of working with blocks but his insecurity about appropriate social behavior caused him to leave the block area when other children attempted to involve him in group play. Even with the help of supportive teachers it was many months before Mike was able to become involved with other children.

A healthy sequence of social responses evolves as the child maneuvers his way from infancy into early childhood with a minimum of internal stress in an environment conducive to building positive frames-of-reference in situations involving other people. The child who spends much of his time playing alone in a fenced-in yard has little opportunity to test out social relationships and the child who spends many hours with a television set may acquire some language skills but not the concomitant social skills necessary for the growth of interpersonal relationships.

SELF—CONCEPTS

Self-awareness is a continually developing process that is based on how we feel we are perceived as we relate to others. The attitudes and reactions of adults are vital to children who depend on them for sustenance. Therefore, as we guide young children we must (1) help them form positive and reliable concepts about themselves, and (2) offer them appropriate opportunities for testing and evaluating their interpersonal experiences.

Establishing an awareness of self is a social process. Through learning about other people, discovering how they look and sound and feel and act, children develop an awareness of themselves. Recognition of successes will help them to evaluate their strengths, whereas exaggerated praise may create false self-images to which they cannot continue to aspire. What we think of ourselves influences what other people think of us. Most of us do not admire people who have no self-confidence or who have too much. Therefore, our task in guiding young children appears to be in helping them to form sound self-opinions and then to accept their evaluations of themselves.

The complexity of growth patterns is apparent in the midpreschool years: (1) emotionally, children are beginning to have intense feelings about their own abilities and to test the reactions of those around them; (2) physically, children have matured to the stage where motor skills are becoming more varied and vigorous play is needed for reinforcement and improvement of these skills; (3) mentally, children have begun to recognize the nature of the world about them and are curious to test and try a variety of equipment and materials; and (4) socially, children have established basic ideas concerning themselves and want to include others in their experiences.

We never outgrow our personal need for social acceptance and approval and realization of this fact should make us more understanding of the young child. What often appears to be misbehavior is merely a trial-and-error method of learning how to get along with other people.

Ralph, age four, had an active imagination that was helpful in initiating group play. He could always think of interesting situations that would be fun. In his eagerness to assign roles and to promote ideas, however, Ralph was likely to be bossy. His voice was loud and he would scream at other children if they did not respond to his directions such as, "We park the fire trucks (tricycles) here and drag the hose (rope) over here to fight the fire." Simetimes, one or two of the other boys would appear to be disgusted with Ralph's overbearing leadership and when his screaming continued they would retire to another part of the playground and start playing with other equipment. Being deserted by a part of the group was intolerable to Ralph and his frustration resulted in physical aggression. He would follow the boys, shouting at them. If his yelling were ignored, he was likely to begin hitting and calling names.

After several weeks, Ralph seldom was able to organize the group for play. His suggestions like, "Let's pretend we're cowboys and ride up to the canyon," usually met with silence. Ralph's aggressive behavior was ineffective and his facial expression indicated that he was hurt and puzzled. Eventually, Ralph again became a leader when he was able to resume more cooperative techniques with other children, when he was prepared to accept their ideas and to reorganize his play plans to include their wishes.

Several interesting facts are apparent in this descriptive example. Ralph had established a sense of self-acceptance as demonstrated in his confidence as he suggested ideas for play and directed the development of his ideas. That his concept of himself as a leader was accurate was shown when the children were willing to join in carrying out his plans.

Ralph's rejection by his playmates was caused by the methods he used in directing other people. The trial-and-error social learning process then was begun. When he learned that screaming was ineffective, he attempted to regain mastery of the situation by physical attack. Several weeks passed during which first one method, then another, or both, were attempted. It is not easy for adults to watch the unhappiness that social ostracism causes but, as already stated, children often have to learn by doing and it is best if adult guidance provides merely passive support. This does not mean, of course, that there are not many ways in which we can aid children in social learning. Verbal suggestion that other children would like to help in the planning or would like to enact certain roles in play is sometimes effective.

The observation of leadership and followership in the preschool provides an interesting study. Characteristics that promote leadership at the preschool level probably cannot be clearly defined, but we can assume that children who have had a variety of experiences and who have reached comparatively higher levels of development in all areas of growth will be most likely to be the leaders. Certain children seem to have the faculty for suggesting activities and of assuming the responsibility for planning. It has been stated that the majority of play during these years involves only two children. Almost always one of the pair will appear to be the leader and the other the follower.

Leadership sometimes seems to be situational, however. Children who are leaders in one type of activity are sometimes willing to follow the dictation of others when the type of play changes. As has been stated, skills in handling materials and equipment are important factors. Since children cannot always be leaders, it probably is beneficial if they can have practice in good techniques of followership as well. Ralph's initial self-concept appeared to be overpowering self-confidence, and it was only when he was able to modify his domineering role that he could associate satisfactorily with other children.

During the preschool years, children also form self-concepts concerning masculine and feminine roles. The child care center provides many opportunities to observe how children are learning to be men or to be women and how they feel about themselves in these roles. Children of this age are imitators and much of their play is composed of acting out situations that they have observed or that they imagine could happen. Current sociological and economic conditions have resulted in changes in the patterning of these sex roles. It is not uncommon to see children act our scenes of daddy cooking and taking care of the baby while mother is at work or to hear children from one-parent families play out a home life where one parent assumes all tasks necessary for family survival. Adults who work with children should not assume sexist attitudes in defining male-female interpersonal behavior.

> Several boys and girls were in the playhouse when Marci pretended to hammer a broken crib. David became angry and said, "You can't do that, that's a daddy job." Marci stamped her foot, placed her hands on her hips, and said, "Sometimes my mommy is a daddy because I have none and she is a good fixer!"

When adults state, "Boys don't cry," they are fostering unnatural patterns and depriving the child of a normal emotional release. To restrict or define a child's actions solely because of his or her sex places an unnecessary burden on the emerging social being and hinders the child in choosing future social goals. These goals should be regulated by interests and abilities, not by the imposition of existing social codes that currently are in transition.

ENVIRONMENTAL AIDS TO SOCIAL GROWTH

Physical, environmental, and social climates affect the process of socialization during the early years and, indeed, throughout our lives. Children and adults respond with more acceptable social behavior when the space around them is comfortable, inviting, and free of clutter. All human beings have healthier social encounters when the people around them are free from tension, hostility, and anger.

We influence how children relate to each other, also, by the way we arrange the space and materials we offer them. In recent years, play materials and equipment have been designed to foster specific social and intellectual goals determined to be desirable for society. There are some general guidelines that apply to most preschool programs that are worthy of consideration. A child needs body space, indoors and outdoors, room to move and manipulate without pushing or bumping others. The child needs play settings that place him in close proximity with other children, where opportunities exist for him to work alone or at a common task. Materials may include a sand box, a water table, a block corner, or a playhouse.

Blocks, wagons, bicycles, and climbing devices that are easily accessible, safe for children to use, and well-maintained provide encouragement for group play. A small table set with two or three place settings of doll dishes may be provocative. Several drums placed in the playroom will attract, as if by contagion, several children for rhythm activities. These are all good techniques of indirect guidance toward social growth.

Children also can be guided by helping them to understand the motives that underlie the behavior of other children. Physical aggression, which is frequent in a group of young children, is sometimes an attempt to establish social contact. Often, the adult reacts only to the behavior, not to the motives behind it. We can create a good social climate by understanding and by helping children understand the actions of other children.

Susan, age two-and-one-half, stood watching Becky who was playing at the toy sink. Soon she walked over and hit Becky on the back of the head. Becky began to cry. Miss Johnson, who was nearby, said, "Becky, I believe Susan would like to play with you. Perhaps you can wash the dishes and she can dry them."

Although the suggested activity did not occur, these children were made to feel more comfortable in the situation and the teacher's comment was helpful to both children. Becky was assured that Susan's attack was a friendly one and Susan had the satisfaction of having been noticed by both Becky and the teacher. With other similar suggestions, it is probable that Susan will gain the knowledge that some kind of cooperative play will promote social acceptance.

Even when children are very young, it is important that they recognize the liking and honesty of adults. If children are not injured physically, adult support for the child who is aggressive is often better than reassurance to the child who has been attacked.

Joe and Dick were four-year-olds. Joe became angry because Dick would not build a fence of blocks according to his ideas. He picked up a block and threw it, hitting Dick's arm. Dick placed his other hand on his arm and began to cry. Miss Weaver moved close to Joe and said, "People do not like to be hit by blocks. It hurts. It is better to ask Dick to build the fence a certain way. Perhaps he wanted it this way for a reason." Dick stopped crying immediately and listened attentively to what Miss Weaver was saying to Joe. The boys resumed their play amicably.

Many adults would have attempted to comfort Dick by saying something like, "Joe didn't mean to hurt you. He was just unhappy because of the way you were building the fence." The teacher might have placed a comforting hand on Dick's head. Obviously, this would not promote social learning by either child. Dick probably would realize that the teacher's statement was untrue and would continue to believe that Joe had meant to hurt him. Also, the injury might be magnified in his estimation since it brought adult sympathy. Joe, who already felt frustrated because Dick was not playing as he wanted, would be even more unhappy because Miss Weaver gave attention to Dick and ignored him. Therefore, he might feel hostile toward both Dick and Miss Weaver. Moreover, Joe probably would experience guilt feelings about his behavior and these feelings would make him less confident in future social experiences. Poor foundations for social reciprocity between these two children would be certain.

When children are well matched and start hitting and poking at each other, instead of stopping them, adults probably are wise to stand by and let them settle their own difficulties. Grownups in a preschool are frequently amazed at how quickly these children will be playing happily again. Mothers will testify that brothers and sisters are likely to be fighting one minute and to be extremely affectionate the next. Issues may become overemphasized by adult interference. Of course, under no circumstances, should one child be permitted to continuously attack another nor should sticks, stones, or other dangerous articles ever be allowed. If no injury is impending, probably it is better to consider what the effects of intervention will be as they influence the children's social learnings.

In order to judge how much help is needed to encourage a good social climate, we must know the children involved, their backgrounds of experiences, and their usual behavior patterns. Since this knowledge can be gained only by daily observation, it will not be easy for students to decide when intervention is advisable. Therefore, they should leave these decisions to the children's teachers. If injury is likely, of course, action is imperative and students will have to step in if no teacher is present. Students should not feel they have erred if they occasionally attempt to intervene and later decide this action was unnecessary. Not even the most experienced teacher can always time her actions wisely. Group discussion in the classroom will often provide ideas for improved techniques or judgments.

Obviously, if a small child is attacked by a bigger one, the teacher should assume immediate control of the situation. These conflicts are likely to be caused by the lack of social success by the larger child with others of his age. If groups are composed of children of similar chronological age, size, and ability, few incidents of this kind will occur.

Usually, grouping of children in preschool centers is most effective when some criterion for social and physical maturation is used as a guide. When very young children are placed with four and five-year-olds they may feel inadequate and overwhelmed by children who seem to have so much more power and control than they do. As we stated earlier in this chapter, socialization as a process is decelerated when a child feels he cannot join in play because he cannot cope with the level of functioning of the group.

Ahmed, age four-and-one-half years, had recently arrived from India and had no command of the English language. Although he was physically the size of a four-year-old, when he was placed with his age-mates, he was withdrawn and wistful. He could not seem to establish himself as a member of the group on a nonverbal basis. After a parent-staff conference he was placed with the three-year-olds where the play was less structured, less verbal, and more manipulative. In this social situation, Ahmed began to experiment with his new language, gained the respect of his new peer group because of his physical competencies, and in a short time became a recognized leader. When his command of English developed and he had acclimated himself to the language and rules of social interaction at school, he was moved back to the initial placement. By this time he was able to adjust comfortably to the demands of play involvement with four-year-olds.

Children change rapidly and evaluation of the composition of a group of children must be a continuous process. Flexibility of groupings is an excellent technique for aiding the adjustment of children. Observant adults are constantly evaluating the relationship of a child to his peers. Their task in guiding social growth is to offer many opportunities for each child to maintain and develop the physical and verbal skills that are commensurate with his developmental level.

As illustrated in the discussion of qualities of leadership at the preschool level, skills are important factors in social acceptance. Adults can help children become more welcome in group activities by helping them become adept in using their bodies. The child who has poor body balance is likely to be rejected by groups engaged in running and jumping play. He cannot keep up with them. Although we cannot help a child develop agility until his physical growth has reached a certain level, we can help him perfect his skills when that level of growth is reached. This can be done by providing equipment, opportunities for practice, and by encouraging him in his feelings of self-confidence. Children can be helped, too, if teachers understand the ways in which status in the group can be improved.

David was a timid child. He seldom was included in group activities and he became a participant only during story hour at which time he was eager to comment concerning the stories. Miss Brown was alert to every opportunity to allow David to talk about something that would be of interest to the other children. One day, when the story concerned a toy top that had been a favorite Christmas gift to a little boy, David commented that he had a top at home. Miss Brown was aware that the possession of a toy that other children desire is a social advantage, so she asked David to bring his top on the following day.

In demonstrating the toy, David lost his usual self-conscious manner and two of the other boys were unusually attentive to him that day. This incident marked the beginning of comparatively greater social experiences for David.

Since the child care center can offer an easier type of practice in sharing toys than the home can, children are seldom encouraged to bring their own possessions unless a certain time is specified for showing them. Obviously, it is easier for children to share toys that are the property of the school than their own treasured belongings. When a child at school has finished playing with some object, he is likely to accept the fact that someone else can use it. Verbal direction by the teacher in this situation may be, "You were not using the wagon so now you must wait until Jack has finished playing with it." The majority of children will be willing to accept this rule.

Because of adult influence, children sometimes are concerned with the misbehavior of other children, not because it is threatening to them but because they believe it to be wrong.

Jerry, a four-and-a-half year old, lived with his parents in a student housing area. He had no brothers or sisters. Both of his parents attended college and Jerry was often included in their activities with their college friends.

Social manners, as practiced by adults, were important to Jerry. When other children at the school were possessive in the handling of toys or responded to other children by hitting or poking, Jerry became unhappy. Often he would say, "It is not nice to hit other children," or "You are a bad boy." If his words were unheeded, Jerry was likely to report to students or teachers that some child was not behaving as he should. Jerry needed frequent reassurance that undesirable behavior was not "bad." Miss Anderson would say to him, "Perhaps Don did not know how to ask Martha for the book," or "Perhaps Jean has some angry feelings today."

These situations are difficult for adults outside the home since these preschoolers must learn to accept their peers and yet their home practices should also be respected.

Since children act as they feel and are imitators of adult behavior, guidance toward using good manners can be accomplished by indirect methods. Happy children who are accepted socially will naturally employ pleasant ways of acting in most situations. Then, too, adults who are polite to other adults and to children are setting good examples that young children will imitate. Many people who are thoughtful and considerate in their treatment of other adults are likely to be rude and inconsiderate when they talk to children. This must be confusing to preschoolers. All learning is slow and premature insistence on good manners before children are aware of the reasons for them will exert detrimental emotional pressures on small children. "Thank you" and "please" are meaningless expressions unless they are based on sincere feelings. Children who are forced to use these words before they know their meaning may assume the habit of the use, but they will not be prepared in many cases to cultivate the casual and natural diplomacy that good social adaptation demands.

Sometimes children will become so stimulated by group activities that they lose control of their emotions and resort to undesirable behavior. When this happens, it is often desirable to remove the child from the situation. An understanding teacher may say, "Chana, come into the storeroom with me while I look for some new chalk." In some instances, the teacher may chat with Chana about the storeroom and, as they start back to the playroom, she may ask, "Do you feel better now?" or "Have you rested enough so you can play with the other children?" Children usually will welcome this kind of supported control and will recognize it as being helpful in avoiding unacceptable behavior.

Morris was a very active four-year-old. His energy seemed boundless and he played with great gusto in all group activities. Frequently, he would become excited and would strike at the other children. Since there was no apparent cause for his hostility, he was losing popularity in the group.

Miss Seevers knew that Morris was likely to become tired and irritable and she could recognize the onset of a crisis in his behavior. Occasionally, she would take his hand and suggest a walk with her or an errand to another room. Sometimes she would take Morris on her lap and read one of his favorite stories. Soon, he would return to group play with a happy expression on his face.

That this curtailment of activity was welcomed by Morris was proved because when some aggressive act seemed imminent Morris often began to move toward Miss Seevers. One day, when he seemed to be tiring, he grasped her hand and said, "I think I'd better go in the house for awhile."

Morris was learning the self-control that is necessary as a part of knowing how to get along with other people.

Obviously there are many ways in which child care personnel can guide children toward healthy social development. Several suggestions for creating a good social climate for preschool children are:

1. Since the preschool probably provides the child's first intensive social experience outside his home, it is especially important that his time there should be pleasant and satisfying.

2. Careful choices of materials and equipment appropriate to use by two or more children simultaneoulsy will give impetus to social interaction.

3. Children need to feel that adults are understanding people. Adults in the preschool can reinforce children's pleasures in adult associations.

4. Encouragement and help in relationships with other children can be accomplished in diverse ways.

5. Since children need to establish good social relationships with their peers and can do this only by experience, adults should interfere as little as possible.

6. Sensible limits of behavior should be defined so that children will feel secure in knowing what kinds of behavior are acceptable to other people.

7. Careful supervision by adults is necessary so injury and repeated social rejection can be prevented.

SUGGESTED ASSIGNMENT

Part I

Give an example of each of the following.

1. A child is engaged in solitary behavior.
2. A child plays an onlooker role.
3. Children engage in parallel activities.
4. Children enter into cooperative play.

Part II

Give examples in which you observed the same child

1. as a leader.
2. as a follower.

Part III

Record incidents in which children demonstrated the following.

1. Respect for the rights or property of others.
2. Ability to maintain one's rights.
3. Sharing with one or more children.
4. Ability to cooperate.
5. Ability to initiate an activity.

Part IV

Give an example in which a teacher helped a child to

1. understand and accept the behavior of other children.
2. learn social techniques of entering a group.

Part V

Record an incident showing how a teacher

1. forestalled undesirable social activity.
2. gave just enough help so the child settled his own difficulty.
3. allowed children to settle their problem without help.

Part VI

List some of the materials and equipment in the preschool that encourage social experiences.

SELECTED READINGS

1. Bossard, James H. S., and E. S. Boll, *The Sociology of Child Development,* 4th ed., Parts I, II, Harper and Row, New York, 1966.

These sections focus on the effects of family patterns and cultural differences that influence social behavior.

2. Brody, Sylvia, *Theory and Research in Child Development,* Early Childhood Education Council of New York, 1972.

Pages 10 to 15 in this pamphlet stress the need for observation as a tool for learning and the author discusses significant factors that influence social development.

3. Landreth, Catherine, *Early Childhood,* Alfred A. Knopf, New York, 1969.

In Chapter 10, "Socialization," the author comments on socialization in different societies and discusses four main factors in the process of socialization.

4. Leeper, Sarah Hammond, Ruth J. Dales, Dora Sikes Skipper, and Ralph L. Witherspoon, *Good Schools for Young Children,* the Macmillan Company, New York, 1968.

Chapter 2 of this book is entitled, "The Young Child in His World Today." Social forces as they affect children are discussed. Descriptions of the importance of family relationships and conflicting educational theories are particularly interesting.

5. Lindgren, Henry Clay, and Robert I. Watson, *Psychology of the Child,* 3rd ed., John Wiley N. Y., 1973.

These authors explore factors that influence the perception of self and others during the preschool years. The book will be helpful for those readers seeking an overview of how research has helped us to understand personality development.

6. Yamamoto, Kaoru, ed., *The Child and His Image: Self-Concept in the Early Years,* Houghton-Mifflin, Boston, 1972.

Seven authors have examined the importance of fostering healthy self-concepts in young children. The role of the adult in helping children as they acquire feelings about themselves and their relationships with other people is a main emphasis of this book.

7. Weiner, Irvin B. and David Elkind, *Child Development: A Core Approach,* Parts II, III and pps. 235 to 237, John Wiley, New York, 1972.

The authors present an overview of the basic issues and facts in all stages of child development. The suggested pages can help readers codify their understanding of basic developmental patterns of infants and preschool children. The final chapter offers a succinct statement about our current knowledge of children and its implications for child rearing and education.

chapter 7

Language Development

Each child learns the language of his culture. A current problem in the United States is that, within our culture, there are various subcultural language groups. When standard language usage is employed as a measure of growth, we may distort our concepts of the mental status of children who are deficient in their use of the standard language but who are performing effectively in their own culture's language. How can we evaluate someone like Hernando, a six year old from the Puerto Rican community of New York when he says, "I can say it with my mind but not with my mouth?"

Nature and nurture are woven together throughout the process of growth. This occurs in the language development of children. As a society, we have become dependent on language clues for estimating the intelligence of children although research studies delineate many variables that affect language growth.

Adults who work with young children have the task of helping them identify sights, sounds, smells, and feelings of touch with verbal utterances. Moreover, caretakers must assume the responsibility for structuring the environment so a child can reenforce verbal learnings through exchanges of dialogue with adults and peers. Space and equipment in preschools should be designed to encourage dialogue between child and child and between child and adult. Responsible nurturers listen to children as speech develops. They encourage children to listen to sounds and voices around them and to reproduce these sounds as meaningful utterances.

We must be aware of the child's present level of functioning in order to plan for experiences that will promote organized, sequential growth. Language ensues only when there are encounters with people and when the learner produces and recreates sound patterns that others respond to. Eventually, the child's ability to express ideas tells us how he is perceiving, thinking, and planning. Adults often feel more comfortable when they can communicate verbally with the youngster, and the young child who develops speech early often meets with much approval from adults. This is only one of the ways that language influences social acceptance and the child's self-image. Contrary to the adage, "Children should be seen and not heard," in our American culture children are encouraged to be verbal and liguistically oriented if they are to be perceived as successfully maturing individuals. Therefore, the reader should have some knowledge of speech development in order to offer ample opportunities for language growth through thoughtful planning.

THE PATTERNS OF CHILDREN'S SPEECH

Speech is unique to man. In order to use verbal language, children must achieve a complex physiological level of functioning so that the neurological system can transmit messages to the brain that, in turn, can trigger a series of secondary reactions for parts of the body whose primary functions are structured for physical survival. The teeth that are meant principally for chewing, the tongue that is used primarily for eating and tasting, the lips the main purpose of which is for sucking and tasting, and the lungs and muscles of the chest that are necessary for breathing must all be synchronized in action before intelligible speech is possible.

Newborn babies are very vocal creatures but it is doubtful that their crying varies so that it could be classified as a recognizable response to specific feelings such as hunger, anger, pain, or fright. Within four to six weeks, however, adults who take care of infants probably can recognize the significance of intensity of tone in crying. Within a few weeks after birth, the majority of babies learn that crying is likely to attract attention. Certainly, children's vocalizations serve as a means of social communication long before they are capable of speaking words. Students who have had experience with young infants will realize that squeals of delight or grunts of displeasure are expressions of infants' responses to life.

The first sounds produced by children after the general crying sounds are nasal and often are heard when the child is uncomfortable. Later, we hear cooing and gurgling that appear to signify well-being. At about two-months-of-age a sort of babbling sound begins to occur and there are indications that vocal practice for vowel sounds is occurring. By about three-months-of-age the child who does not hear, or who is not responded to vocally, decreases his vocal utterances.

By about the sixth month, the infant begins to babble when he is spoken to or is near the sound of voices. He also may begin to babble to get attention. Within a short time the sounds probably will begin to develop intonation patterns that reflect the language pattern he hears. Normal infants begin to enjoy practicing sound patterns and, as astute adults repeat the sounds for the infant, he may laugh and repeat the sound. The infant who is interacting with someone as he practices derives acceptance and approval for his babbling. When he is encouraged to play the "sound game" he has more opportunities to practice vocal responses with varying tones, gradations of loudness, and rhythmic patterns.

The transition from vocal to verbal utterances can occur any time from as early as six or seven months when a few children babble the consonant sound, such as "mmmmm." Through adult inference and reinforcement, word forms result. The child who uses nonverbal sounds and body movements to order his world may delay speech until he is eighteen to twenty-eight months old.

Simultaneously with the initial stages of the child's vocal vocabulary, his understanding of the words of other people develops. Even the very young infant learns to identify his mother's voice. This is evidenced by his stretching, arching his back, waving his arms and legs, and gurgling. The comfort children receive from the pleasant tones of adults' voices contributes to the trust they feel in their environment and is important to emerging personalities. Infrequently, adults who care for infants do little talking because they think language is unnecessary since babies cannot comprehend meanings. This reasoning is entirely fallacious. The way in which a baby learns to interpret facial expressions and speech inflections is very important in his learning to talk. Possibly the retarded development of institutionalized children is related not only to their lack of handling but also to their lack of other kinds of communication with adults.

Within a few months, children demonstrate an awareness of the differences between pleasant and unpleasant tones of voice. This recognition of various tonal inflections may be the child's first experience with verbal guidance. Subsequently, passive or understanding vocabularies continue to expand more rapidly than the ability to use words. Very young children are aware of the meanings of many words before they can articulate. In fact, at any age level, the ability to understand words exceeds the ability to use them.

Before children can talk, their awareness of word meanings is demonstrated by their gestures. These movements may or may not be accompanied by intelligible utterances.

Betty was nine months old. Her mother, Mrs. Evert, frequently took Betty for a walk in the afternoon. Whenever Mrs. Evert would remark, "I think we'll go for a walk now," Betty would begin waving her hand as if to say, "Bye-bye."

Young children often use gestures to indicate their desires and sometimes they continue to rely on these motions long after they are capable of using words.

Margo was two years and four months old. She seemed to enjoy school, but she did not talk. When she wanted a toy or a book that was beyond her reach, she would point to the object and usually a student or a teacher would procure it for her.

When it was time to put on her outdoor clothing, Margo would stand by her locker and her eyes would seem to beseech aid. If no adult approached, Margo would take her snowsuit out of the locker and tug at an adult while she extended the garment in front of her. That she was capable of talking was proved by her one-word sentences when she could elicit attention in no other way.

As stated previously, children's language responses change from undifferentiated to specific. Obviously, there also is an evolution from unintelligible speech to meaningful articulation. Without knowledge of the specific sequence of language development, we could foresee that the child's first words would be nouns. The child's emotional needs and the stages in his personality development were discussed in a previous chapter that indicated that young children are occupied with establishing an understanding of their environment. Consequently, first of all, they learn the names of things.

Children gain a sense of security and trust by being made comfortable and by being handled affectionately by adults. They extend this feeling of belonging by their increasing knowledge of people, themselves, and inanimate objects. As in other kinds of development, extensive practice is necessary. Sometimes, adults become bored or irritable when young children repeat the names of objects again and again. Patience is more easily attained when we realize that naming is an important foundation for the child's later adjustment. It is good to remember that in order to learn children need much practice. Repetition in this stage of language development parallels the ritualism of activity that children find so satisfying at about the same chronological age. Probably, the ability to name objects can be promoted by adults who are willing to provide the names of items that are of interest to children. Children comprehend slowly that everything has a name and their ability to name things appears to give them satisfaction and confidence.

Words tend to have a general meaning until a child is able to differentiate shape and form as related to more specific detail. All four-legged creatures can share one generic name such as "dog" until the child becomes familiar with structural configurations that identify animal subsets.

Charles, age two-and-one-half, was a city child whose concept of "dog" was his aunt's toy poodle. He learned about horses from picture book stories. When he saw a large, sleek German shepherd he called out, "Horsey." His mother immediately identified the creature as a dog. Charles refused to alter his perception and restated his view, "Horsey, Horsey, giddiap." It was apparent that Charles needed more time and experience with "dogness" before he would be able to adjust his thinking to accomodate this larger form.

During this process the youngster moves from gross labelling to more specific identification with the help of adults who audit the speech utterances of children.

Mrs. Ransom was taking Donna, who was eleven months old, for a walk and they stopped for a moment in front of a department store window in which there was a male form. Donna looked, pointed, and uttered, "Daddy," in a questioning tone that differed from the way "Daddy" was spoken when Mr. Ransom was present. Mrs. Ransom identified that object as "Man." Donna repeated, "Daddy, Man," in one tone and then stopped pointing and said, "Daddy, Daddy," in the tone she usually used to communicate with her father.

Occasionally, young children are fascinated by identifying themselves by name. Possibly this demonstrates their attempts to identify themselves as apart from other people and objects. Certainly, it indicates proof of the increasing egocentricity of late infancy. As stated previously, children need to develop good self-concepts, so it is not surprising that most preschool language is egocentric in nature. Throughout these years, children talk about themselves and to themselves. They are concerned primarily with their own thought and interests. Their sentences are likely to contain a predominance of their own names and, later, the pronouns, I, me, and mine are characteristic.

The interrelatedness of various kinds of development is especially apparent as children's linguistic abilities mature. When locomotor skills are being mastered, there usually occurs a period of slow gain in language skills as if learning to stand upright and to walk must be requiring the major portion of the child's interest and energy. As youngsters become more active and alert and as their experiences widen, however, more objects become important to them. Thus, not only are they capable of identifying more items by name but they begin to understand and express more than mere identification. Often, one spoken word signifies full sentence meaning. For example, the young child who says, "doll," may indicate by tonal inflection and actions one of two or more meanings: "There is a doll," "Give me the doll," or "You take the doll." To the adult who knows the child, this one word becomes a functionally complete sentence. Simple two-word sentences soon appear. Examples of these are: "Daddy sleep," "Mamma bye-bye," and "Dolly nice." Obviously, these sentences are structurally incomplete.

Verbs or action words naturally come into use as the child becomes more active and his experiences more varied. As children increase their vocabularies, their knowledge of things is increased and this lends impetus to further linguistic learning. Regardless of the time at which children first begin to talk, language skills are acquired rapidly. Vocabulary increases are sometimes amazing. As in other areas of development, the preschool years comprise a period of rapid change.

With increase in age, there is an increase in the length of sentences and in their structural complexity. Speech is influenced by language patterns in the home and children select words and patterns from adult speech that they find functional. Young children are not ready to worry with grammatical rules or verb conjugations even after repeated correction. The message is important to them, not the structure of the sentences they speak.

Individual differences in language development are evident at all age levels and it is important that those who guide young children are aware of the progression of the skills of each child. Periodic assessment of vocabulary and syntax development helps the teacher plan for each child's guidance. The adult must keep in mind that the child who speaks most often with adults initiates more contact and thus stimulates further growth. During the course of a day at the preschool, each child should have an opportunity for exchanging language in dialogue with an adult. This is particularly necessary for those children who seem to withdraw, overwhelmed by their more articulate peers. As a result of previous training, some children are reluctant to engage in conversation with adults.

Ellen, age four, enrolled at the preschool in March. She was English and the product of a traditional preschool in Brussels, Belgium. During the first few weeks she spoke to no children and responded to teachers with merely, a "yes" or "no" and accompanying nonverbal gestures. Her mother called one day to say that Ellen had wet herself on the school bus because the teacher had not sent her to the bathroom at school.

A conference was scheduled for Mrs. Sampson. During the interview, the teacher learned that Ellen's former school had stressed self-control and had required her to sit at her table until each task was completed and she was dismissed. Moreover, toileting had been scheduled for a specific time. It was also learned that Ellen had told her parents she thought her brisk, British speech sounded funny and that she preferred not to sound different so she chose not to talk at school.

After several weeks of careful nurturing by a teacher who guided and supported Ellen in small-group activities, the child began to share her thoughts and to move around the room independently. She showed satisfaction as she assumed more control over her new environment.

Children, at about three years of age, begin to besiege adults with questions regarding every conceivable object and event. Not all of these questions are for information, although the majority of them do reflect the child's desire to learn. Some questions are devices for attention getting. Of course, when a child really desires information, it should be given readily. It is important, however, that explanations are brief, simple, and in terms of the child's ability to understand. Complex explanations or the use of scientific terms can be either so boring to children or so meaningless that they may be discouraged in making future queries.

Dovid came home from the child care center very upset because he had not completed a special art experience he had been working on with the art curriculum specialist. When questioned about the situation, he exploded, "All that art lady does is speeches us so we didn't have time to finish."

Adults who know individual children soon become aware when questions are asked in order to gain attention. These usually can be decreased or eliminated when the child is made to feel sufficiently secure and loved or when other causes for his emotional need are eliminated. Sometimes, children ask questions in order to tease adults. Wise methods for handling this situation depend on the experiences and personalities of the adult and the child involved. If rapport is good and the child is an older preschooler, these occasions may create humorous fun. If hostility seems apparent in the teasing, it is advisable to look for the underlying causes.

Some children use questions repetivitely as if they are attempting to irritate the listener. "Can I?" and "Why not?" often are used in this manner. The artful listener responds to the intent of the question rather than to its content. Before adults succumb to arguing with a young child in response to constant questioning, they should, as we stated in a previous chapter, take time to observe the relationship between the child and his environment to determine what is causing this youngster to provoke others by argumentative questioning. A child who questions constantly may be (1) testing authority, (2) seeking more attention than he is receiving, (3) feeling insecure about himself or the situation so that he is requesting help, or (4) showing evidence of a hearing problem.

LANGUAGE AS A SOCIAL TOOL

Man is characteristically social and formal language is unique to him. Therefore, it would appear logical that language skill and sociability are closely related at all age levels. Because the majority of the language employed by very young children is egocentric, there might be a tendency to discount its social significance. However, since language is used as a means of communication and even the remarks of very young children usually are addressed to other people, its social nature is evident.

Very early in life, when infants cry in order to gain attention, they learn the value of vocalization as a means toward social experience and this learning is reinforced as they mature. The ability of older infants to differentiate between pleasant and unpleasant tones of voice used by adults probably denotes their first understanding of social acceptance or rejection. Thus, even the child's passive or comprehending vocabulary has a definite bearing on his social development.

Social intimacy in the adult-child relationship usually increases as the child becomes more verbal. Some adults remark that they do not really enjoy infants, that they feel more at ease with somewhat older children. Although other kinds of development contribute to this change in rapport, probably language and the understanding of words are the most influential factors.

Adults guide very young chidlren by using nonverbal gestures to support verbal statements. Normal children learn to respond to articulated guidance before they can speak. Some adults feel that until they can communicate with a child verbally only a crude level of social interaction exists. This is an incorrect premise as evidenced by current thinking about nonverbal communication and its role in establishing relationships between people of all ages. Infants respond to the sound pattern of a voice and to the accompanying nonverbal facial and body clues of the speaker before they understand the verbal component. When the adult uses speech without the appropriate body movement and tonal reinforcement, the sounds may be meaningless jabber to a very young child.

Adult language, from the child's viewpoint, seems to be predominantly composed of orders and directions. It is wise to remember that preschool children often are unable to express their feelings or the reasons that underlie their failure to conform to adult expectations. Understanding adults will try to imagine what children would say in their own defense. Too often, misbehavior and apparent rebellion may be caused by poor language skills. Adults who have experienced the temporary loss of their voices will find it easy to sympathize with children's frustrations in this respect. Also, it is certain that children frequently simply do not understand verbal directions.

The social value of language in children's groups cannot be overemphasized. Again, the complexity of growth must be acknowledged. Children's language and their behavior compose the overt expressions of their levels of development. We cannot conclude that these are the only causes of social acceptance or rejection, but we can be certain that performance in speech and activity denote the social status of children. Even young children who play in a solitary or parallel fashion seem happier and more acceptable to their peers if they are capable of expressing themselves verbally.

Carl, Dottie, and Jim who were members of a young school group were sitting near each other playing with pans, cups, and spoons in the sandpile. Infrequently, one of the children would pick up a spoon that one of the others had discarded, but there was no other evidence of associative play. As Carl played, he said, "I'm gonna make a pie," "Big pie," "Big pie." He smiled as he talked. Dottie stopped now and then to listen to Carl and to watch him.

Sometimes, she would repeat, "Pie, big pie." They would both laugh and then resume their play. Meanwhile, Jim sat nearby digging. He, too, would stop and smile as he watched them, but he did not speak and Dottie and Carl seemed unaware of his presence.

As children grow older, their social status seems increasingly dependent on language skills. When for some reason language development is retarded, social rejection can be especially difficult for a child to accpet.

Marilyn was a partially sighted child at the nursery school. She was robust, alert, and agile but decidedly retarded in language ability. Although she was four years old, most of her speech consisted of naming objects and toys. Marilyn was very eager to play with the other children. This desire was demonstrated when she followed them, saying, "Boy, boy," or calling to a child by name when others did so. Her language usage made it impossible for her to enter into the dramatic play in which the group was engaged. During each play period, her overtures were repulsed because of her lack of communicative skill. After awhile, she would retire to solitary play in a swing or in the sandpile with a sad expression on her face.

Marilyn was referred to a speech clinic and her progress in verbal expression was rapid. As a result, within a few months she was an accepted member of the group.

Had the teachers in this instance been less discerning, this child's visual handicap might have been blamed for her rejection by her peers. Whereas it might have been one of the reasons for her rejection, it is probable that her handicap was largely an indirect cause in that it had prevented her from having the complex audio-visual experiences of normal children. It is imperative that adults watch children carefully in order to understand them.

FACTORS THAT INFLUENCE LANGUAGE DEVELOPMENT

Among variables that have been described as influencing language development are: (1) physical growth, (2) hearing, (3) the quality of the verbal environment, and (4) self-image. Other factors are also worthy of consideration. For example, a child's position in the family relates to his verbal behavior. Some studies indicate that the first child in the family speaks at an earlier age than his siblings. Probably a parent has more time for sustained encounters with the first infant and, as a result, this child receives more individual attention. Moreover, the household has fewer distractions and the infant can focus his attention on the task at hand. A younger sibling can become the "me, too," child who tags along but does not have opportunities to gain experience in using language with a consistent adult model. Slightly older siblings may discourage children's speech experiences by monopolizing adult child conversations. Conversely, siblings several years older may encourage language development by providing more opportunities for children to talk simply because there are more people at home who are interested.

Frequently twins are somewhat delayed in language development. This is not surprising when we consider that the companionship that twins provide for each other may mean that there is less reason for trying to communicate with other people. In some cases, twins seem to communicate with each other through gestures or incomprehensible words that they have learned to understand in their close companionship.

Sometimes adults are surprised at children's inaccuracies of identification. We must be aware of the influence of early environment.

Gina and John lived in a crowded urban area of a city where sanitary conditions were poor. They both attended a day care center located in the housing development. One day, the teacher set a new pet gerbil in a large box on the floor in the science corner for the children to discover and discuss.

Gina and John saw the animal and recoiled in fear as they ran to the teacher shouting, "A rat! A rat is in school. He's bad! He's bad!" Several of the other children heard the word, "rat," dropped their playthings and headed for the door. The teacher immediately placed the gerbil in a cage and spent several anxious minutes quieting the class before she could begin to discuss their new guest. Even after the discussion, the teacher sensed such a high level of anxiety that the gerbil was removed and a new pet was substituted.

This incident demonstrates that a teacher should be aware of the child's background and attuned to the experiential vocabulary of children. Had she been alert to playhouse conversations, she would have heard Gina at play there, meticulously cleaning the kitchen stove and chanting, "No food for the rats, no food for the rats."

Adults should listen to what children say as well as to what they say to children. Let us consider the sentence, "I saw," as if it were stated without any situational context. Depending on a child's experience and pronunciation pattern it could mean: (1) I saw Jane hit David, (2) I want to saw wood at the carpentry area, (3) I am sore or I hurt myself, (4) my eye is sore, or (5) I am angry.

Sometimes, we are so eager to hurry on to other things that we do not allow children time to speak. Frequently, also, adults fail to encourage talking by children because they interpret their gestures and supply their needs, and speech becomes unnecessary.

Betty was two-and-one-half years old. She lived with her parents and two older siblings, Barbara, age five, and Harry, age seven. Betty did not talk. She was a happy child, interested in her surroundings, but it was not necessary for her to speak because all of her wishes were anticipated. Possibly Barbara and Harry, who were both vociferous, presented such keen competition that it seemed uselss from Betty's point of view to interrupt.

Betty's parents became worried about her lack of language ability and, although she was not enrolled in the school, they consulted the director. Mrs. Evans suggested that Betty's mother set aside certain times in each day when Betty and she could be alone and that she talk to Betty about a variety of things. She cautioned Betty's mother that she should not become impatient nor show signs of disappointment if Betty continued her silence.

In addition, Mrs. Evans stated her belief that Betty might be encouraged to talk if her wants were not fulfilled so quickly. For example, she suggested that, if Betty wanted help with her boots, her parents should pretend not to understand what she desired. Mrs. Evans believed that as Betty became impatient and was asked to say what she wanted she would begin to have reason for speaking. The school director again warned Betty's parents that progress might be slow.

The outcome of the plan of guidance described in this example was gratifying. Before many weeks, Betty, although not loquacious, was beginning to find words useful. Motivation is important in the acquisition of verbal skill. Why should children bother to talk when parents, siblings, and teachers anticipate their wishes and understand their gestures?

Although children need to learn that sometimes adult conversations are not to be interrupted, there should be many opportunities for casual conversation between adults and children. Too often, people who would never think of refusing to answer another adult will ignore children's efforts at conversation or will even indicate that refraining from speech is virtuous. Here again, we should realize that children need practice and we can make the learning of communicative skills pleasurable. Frequently, children talk to themsleves or chant as they play with their toys. These monologues should not be discouraged. Such freedom of expression normally will be transferred to social occasions.

Children learn language best when the speaker is clear, concise, unhurried, and genuinely interested in talking with the child. In order for effective language growth to take place, open communication is essential and time to practice is necessary. Children often can be heard in monologues as they practice language in preparation for the appropriate social situation. This is apparent as we listen to a child talking on a toy telephone or at a doll.

Adults can use play situations to encourage language without pressuring children.

Janet, age two years and three months, was playing in the sandpile with a pan and a spoon. As she played, she repeated in a sing-song voice, "Dig, dig, dig the sand, Dig, dig, dig the sand." Miss Clayton, who stood nearby, quietly said, "Dig, dig, dig the sand. Pour, pour, pour the sand. Scoop, scoop, scoop the sand." Soon Janet was accompaning her teacher in these utterances.

This two-year-old not only heard new symbols used for her activity but she had the opportunity to use them herself.

The acquisition of language skills occurs on many levels and enunciation depends on physiological maturation of the mouth, tongue, teeth, and the refinement of audiological awareness. A child often is upset when he is not understood because of enunciation difficulties. Yet, when pressure is put on him in an attempt to correct his enunciation, negative feelings about his own ability can cause him to limit his efforts in communication and speech.

Lawrence, two years and four months old, substituted incorrect sounds for several consonants. Often, when he and his mother were shopping, someone would say to him, "What is your name, little boy?" Lawrence would look up, smiling, and say, "Wawunz." Usually the adult would repeat the question once or twice and Lawrence's mother finally would state his name.

One day, when Lawrence was almost three, he and his mother met a man who was a distinguished citizen of the community. The man stroked Lawrence's hair and asked the usual question. Lawrence looked up at him and said nothing. When the question was repeated, Lawrence remained silent. As they walked on, Mrs. Simmons was embarrassed and angry. She said, "Why didn't you tell the man your name?" Lawrence replied, "He wouldn't unnastan me."

During the natural course of speech development, precisely enunciated sound patterns for certain consonant letters and blends as well as correct grammar can be delayed by maturational variations until a child is as old as seven years. Adults can help and encourage proper enunciation and grammar by providing correct language models as they speak with children. While it is valuable to reproduce and reinforce the babbling sounds of the infant, reproducing infantile speech by repeating baby talk to the learning child serves only to provide poor and inappropriate language for the child to copy.

LANGUAGE PROBLEMS

Since language skill is influential in promoting social acceptance and feelings of adequacy, it is important that good speech pattern should be established before children enter elementary school. The majority of serious speech disorders begin between the ages of two and four. Those who work with young children must be alert to signs of trouble, but specific correction is likely to make children conscious of their deficiencies. Therefore, it is inadvisable to attempt training the child by having him correct certain sounds of enunciation. Training should be done in a casual, natural way. If the adult and child have good rapport, it may be possible to repeat words in a playful manner. Sometimes, incorrect enunciation will prove to be merely a matter of habit.

If there is reason to suspect that faulty enunciation will be difficult to correct, it is best to assign the child to a professional speech clinician, a person who is trained in the ability to introduce words casually that include sounds with which the child is having difficulty. It is not unusual for parents and others who are with the child most of the time to become so accustomed to his peculiarities of speech that they are unaware that problems exist. Then, too, sometimes families or the children in specific families have developed certain inaccuracies of pronunciation that are unnoticed. The teacher who is experienced with the speech patterns of preschool children can usually detect these and, by aiding in their correction, can spare the child the ridicule of children later when he is in elementary school.

The teacher who is aware of the uniqueness of each child can offer guidance and support for language growth without causing conflicting situations between the home and school environments. The adult who develops good relationships with the child and his family can help the child who lives in two language environments by providing effective language through daily opportunities for natural conversation with the child and by accepting any unique patterns that he may have acquired through modeling behavior.

Specific disorders such as impaired hearing, autism, mental retardation, and others affect language development. The observant adult should be alert for the child who has a short attention span, poor speech or no speech, usually is engaged in solitary play, fails to understand directions, sits or stands and engages in sustained periods of rocking, or generally appears to be antisocial or relatively infantile in his behavior. When a combination of these problems seem to occur in a child, careful observation may indicate the need for additional professional consultation with a physician or a psychologist to determine whether organic or emotional problems may be causing the retardation of language.

Refusing to talk, shouting and yelling, stuttering, and even excessive question asking may be symptoms of emotional tensions in children. Obviously, calm appraisal of the child and his environment is indicated. Parents of preschoolers usually are reassured when they know that such characteristics are at times normal in children. Parent meetings, sponsored by preschools have therapeutic value when some of these normal patterns are discussed.

Profane language often causes undue concern for some parents and teachers. Children model meaningful expressions they hear without understanding the precise meaning of the words. A child repeats language he hears, especially emotionally loaded words, with great enthusiasm because of the shock value to adults and peers. The intensity of the language as well as the degree of shock it elicits often is related to particular social and ethnic environments and crosses all economic lines. Ignoring the remark usually is the best way of curbing such language with young children. Punitive measures, for example, washing a child's mouth with soap, can cause severe damage to internal body tissue because soap is an irritant. Moreover, punitive measures magnify the importance of profane language.

If profanity persists in school, a child can be offered a private place to use his private language. Bathroom words often hold special pleasure for young children and often result in giggly responses from the peer group. In most instances, verbal diversions can offer distraction. On occasion, direct confrontation with the word can clarify the issue and the joy of teasing and shocking is lost.

Dana, age three and one-half, and several other children were working at the table with wet clay. The assistant teacher sat down with them and asked Dana how the clay felt. "It's mushy like doody," she replied. The other children began to giggle and smirk as they looked from Dana to Mrs. Goodson. "Is it the same color?" asked Mrs. Goodson. "No," said Dana, "doody is brown." Once again, it was clear that the children thought Dana had made her point. "Did you make the clay, Dana, or did you get it from the crock?" Mrs. Goodson asked. Very soon, Bill chimed in, "I got my clay from the crock and I'm rolling a snake." In their eagerness to talk about their work, Dana's descriptive language was forgotten.

By the time children are three-and-one-half to four, they should have begun to realize that conforming to certain rules is expected of them. They are beginning to realize that what other people think of them is important and they are becoming eager to meet their expectations. These children are old enough to understand that some kinds of behavior are acceptable and some are not. They can be told simply that profane language is not to be used, that their parents or teachers do not enjoy hearing it. Obviously, these directions should be given by someone who knows the child well and has his respect. If they continue to use such words, we can be certain that there are reasons. We should look beyond the behavior and try to determine the feelings of the child. The behavior may be for the purpose of gaining attention or because of hostile feelings or both.

Adults who work with young children may be exposed to verbal expressions that are used in some subcultures more than in others. For this reason the adult who expresses shock and indignation may be reflecting derisive feelings toward some children. The adult who explains the rules and offers viable substitutes for explosive language will have an easier time guiding children toward social acceptability in the school environment.

Robert, who was almost five, lived with his family in an urban high-rise complex where many children of all ages played in a common playground. He came into his family's apartment on the twentieth floor with a special gleam in his eye one afternoon. "Mommy, I can spell a word but you won't let me 'cause it's bad, but I can really spell the letters." His mother braced herself and said, "O.K., Robert. Spell it." "Will you write it, Mommy? I don't write the letters good." Following his spelling his mother wrote the common street word. Then she asked, "What is the word? What do the letters spell?" Robert enunciated the word with glee. "Good, you can read a word. Now I'll take the "F" away and put a "B" like in bike. Can you tell me the new word?" Mother and son went through several initial consonant sounds before Robert looked at his mother and said, "You take the fun out of things, Mommy." He smiled as his shocking word failed to shock and one common street word served several learning purposes.

Name calling is another problem in the opinion of some adults. Derisive name calling certainly is preferable to physical aggression, however. As stated in a previous chapter, children need to release their emotional tensions and they have fewer opportunities for release than grownups have. Releasing feelings by talking is far better than the kicking, biting, and hitting that younger children employ. Sometimes, students are surprised at the calm manner in which experienced teachers can accept verbal attacks. The ability to tell how one feels and what he thinks is an important step in growing up. Later, happy children will learn to control their language and to find emotional release in more acceptable ways.

Nicknames that are unpleasant to adults are often acceptable or even complimentary to the children addressed.

Steven Kellogg was four years old. He had attended preschool for almost two terms. Mrs. Kellogg was very proud of Steven and his younger sister. She was a conscientious mother, eager to provide the best of everything for her children.

One day when a caller was visiting in their home, Mrs. Kellogg addressed some remark to Steven, calling him by name. In a loud voice, Steven said, "Don't call me Steven. The boys at school all call me Stinkey. Stinkey is my name."

Sometimes these signs of growth as signified by pride in being accepted and known by a peer group are difficult for parents to accept. A wise parent is a person with a hearty sense of humor.

Occasionally, parents become alarmed because they fear children are telling falsehoods. During the preschool years, children have vivid imaginations and fact and fancy are closely related.

Peter came home from the child care center and told his mother he had played basketball in his white underwear. His mother phoned the teacher in an attempt to clarify the story. It happened that Peter's group had gone for a walk and had stopped to watch high school students in physical education uniforms practicing various sports.

Children who recount incidents that could not possibly have happened need not be encouraged by adults but neither should they be punished nor ridiculed. Adults who are adept in conversing with children can temper this characteristic by the way they accept these stories.

Stuttering is a speech difficulty that is especially frightening to parents. Small children who stutter repeat and hesitate and prolong their utterances. Stuttering is usually not constant but is intermittent and is more likely to occur when children are tired or upset emotionally.

Gavin's stuttering was of short duration although it was a matter of concern to his parents and the teacher. Gavin was an extremely energetic child. He was actively interested in all the happenings at school. His attention span was comparatively brief when his age group was considered, but he was never without ideas for a change in activities.

On the playground, Gavin usually played with Gary. When Gavin tired of playing with the outdoor blocks, he would begin to suggest excitedly that they play on the slide or on the jungle gym. Frequently, he would begin to stutter and, often, as he started to run to the suggested equipment, he would stop and stand as he attempted to complete a sentence.

The teachers watched Gavin and listened to him intently but made no effort to correct his difficulty. Within a few months, he began to spend longer periods of time at various activities and his pace in all behavior seemed calmer and more controlled. His stuttering disappeared completely.

From a guidance viewpoint, the important thing is the brevity of Gavin's speech disorder. Surely, it was wise for the teachers and parents to be alert to the problem. Several causes for Gavin's difficulty appear possible. It might be that he simply was so full of ideas that he lacked the ability to get the words out as fast as he desired. In view of what appeared to be his excessive output of energy and his brief attention span, it could be that his growth patterns in several areas were undergoing a rapid change that caused unusual behavior in many of his reactions or that he became tired easily. No kind of growth is even in rate and many problems of childhood occur when periods of acceleration are in progress. It is possible, also, that unusual circumstances at home may have existed and that this created temporary emotional tensions in the child.

Usually, a calm adult who offers physical contact, such as placing a reassuring hand on a child's shoulder, can help him calm down. It is important that the youngster be observed closely and evaluated often in order to determine the frequency, length, and intensity of the stammering. An evaluation by a speech therapist is sometimes necessary to predict if prolonged stammering will result in habitual stuttering unless professional help is secured.

Jane, a four-year-old, was a favorite with other girls at the child care center. She was dainty in appearance and graceful in locomotor skills. Her language development seemed to be progressing normally. One week, however, Miss Carter noticed that Jane had a tendency to stutter toward the close of the day. A note to this effect was submitted to the school director. Knowing that children frequently display tensions in similar ways, Miss Carter took no immediate action except to suggest a second story period or some other quiet activity for Jane when she showed the slightest signs of fatigue.

Within a few days, the school director received a telephone call from Mrs. Ewing, Jane's mother. Mrs. Ewing asked if Jane had been stuttering at school. The infrequency of occurrence was described to her, and then she stated that she was terribly worried because Jane had been stuttering at home. She explained that Jane's father frequently stuttered and that she was afraid that Jane was imitating his speech pattern. The director referred Mrs. Ewing and Jane to a speech therapist.

As in other incidents, it is not necessary that we know the exact cause of Jane's problem. It may be that Mrs. Ewing's fears were correct, but since Jane's speech was normal except when she was weary at the center it is possible that her mother's worry was transmitted to Jane and that emotional tensions existed in the home as a result. Certainly, the reassurance of professional help would be the best thing for both parent and child.

The acquisition of language is a complex process. It is vital to social, emotional, and intellectual growth, particularly in a highly verbal society where great emphasis is placed on reading. As adults guide the young child they must offer him many opportunities to explore language and to use language at home and at the preschool. A child must be encouraged to listen and must be listened to if he is to learn.

SUGGESTED ASSIGNMENT

Part I

Choose one child and record fifty consecutive statements that the child makes. Do not ask him questions nor initiate conversation with him in order to stimulate him to talk. Analyze your record for the following:

1. Indicate in the margin of your record if the statement was addressed to (a) an adult, (b) another child, or (c) himself. To which of these categories were most of his remarks addressed? On the basis of your reading, what does this indicate for the brief period when you were recording?

2. Children use language for many purposes. What are some of the purposes that appear to be characteristic of the child you observed? Give examples.

3. Do you find repetition of words? What purpose was served by this repetition?

4. Do you find nonsense syllables or words? Why were they used?

5. Do you find any difficulties in speech? If so, describe them.

6. What suggestions would you offer to guide or improve the language of the child you studied?

Part II

Observe the group of children to which you are assigned. Record examples of at least four of the following:

1. Original or unusually interesting remarks.

2. Remarks showing a sense of humor.

3. Language used in thinking through or solving a problem.

4. Language used as a social tool.

5. Pleasure and interest in new words.

6. Words misused or inappropriate to the situation.

Part III

Give examples showing how adults influenced the use of language by

1. Encouraging children's experiences with language.

2. Discouraging a child when he employed language.

3. Presenting language a child could model.

4. Exerting pressure to direct a child's speech pattern.

Part IV

List and define five suggestions you would offer someone who was seeking information about guiding speech development.

SELECTED READINGS

1. Blank, Marion, "Some Philosophical Influences Underlying Preschool Intervention for the Disadvantaged Children," *Language and Poverty*, Frederick L. Williams, ed., Markham Publishing Company, Chicago, 1970.

This chapter presents a summary of specific research and the author presents conclusions based on intervention programs.

2. Hamlin, Ruth, Rose Mukerji, and Margaret Yonemura, *Schools for Young Disadvantaged Children*, Teachers College Press, Columbia University, N. Y., 1967.

Chapter 5 informs the reader about language development of the preschool child through his first years at school. Techniques suggested for guiding language development are valid for all children.

3. Moore, Shirley, and Sally Kilmer, *Contemporary Preschool Education*, John Wiley, N. Y., 1973.

The authors offer a terse overview of several programs in guiding language development and compare these programs to traditional nursery school procedures.

4. Olim, Gillis G., "Maternal Language Styles and Cognitive Development of Children," *Language and Poverty*, Frederick L. Williams, ed., Markham Publishing Company, Chicago, 1970.

This is an excellent presentation as to how the relationship between mother and child relates to language development and learning.

5. Yonemura, Margaret, *Developing Language Programs for Young Disadvantaged Children*, Teachers College Press, Columbia University, N. Y., 1969.

Chapters 2 and 3 discuss basic understandings concerning language development and offer direction for adults who are concerned about their role in relation to a preschool child's language development.

chapter 8

Learning

How children learn and what adults can do to guide them toward successful learning experiences and optimum intelligence are questions of special interest to educators and parents. Adults concerned about teaching young children need information that will guide them to prepare each child for a lifetime of successful learning. There are many educational programs that focus on the infant and preschool child as a learner. We know that learning behavior is determined by biological development, neurological maturation, social interaction, and environmental influences. The primary purpose of this chapter is to provide the reader with insight about some factors that influence the learning process.

HOW LEARNING OCCURS

Who we are is the sum total of our physical development, our genetic limits, and our social environment as well as how and what we learn. What we know and understand establishes how we adapt to our environment and what our roles in society are. Knowledge and communication are key factors for successful coping with our physicsal environment as well as for coping with our social needs. This quest for knowing is linked to the earliest attempts an infant makes for ordering his world by getting his basic needs and drives satisfied.

Early in life, infants react instinctively and are dependent on their reflexes. Soon, however, they develop sensorimotor responses that are action oriented and when these actions are repetitive and sustaining they become habits or patterns. In turn, these habits or patterns become the basis for thinking as the young child eventually predetermines what actions or processes he must use to obtain satisfaction of his needs and drives from the environment in which he lives.

The developmental growth process that leads to learned behavior is dependent not only on the infant's reflexes and sensory abilities but also on the quality of the environment. If the environment lacks people and objects to which the child can respond, he cannot develop the sensorimotor responses necessary for patterning. Research has provided information about infants who have never been nurtured nor stimulated. These babies become apathetic and, in extreme cases, they actually have died because they have not been given opportunities to develop the skills they needed to survive. It is essential, therefore, that infants have a sufficiently warm, stimulating, responsive environment that offers many and varied opportunities to strengthen the sensorimotor development that forms the basis for learning behavior.

Not everyone who learns about the preschool child will conduct prolonged research or cope with the nuances of theoretical studies about learning and cognition. But everyone who works with children should understand that many kinds of learning experiences must occur as children explore their surroundings and attempt to control the environment.

What factors affect learning and what is important for a child to learn are subjects of scholarly and sociocultural concern. On occasion, conflicting views on learning as a process and learning as a tool have triggered serious disagreements among educators and parents. Governments of nations have become involved with' why and how children learn as they have come. to recognize the young as their greatest natural resources.

It is certain that early sensorimotor experiences form the framework for learning. Appropriate learning occurs when there is: (1) an adequate level of maturation of the nervous system, (2) a series of experiences to reinforce what has been learned, (3) interaction with human beings during the learning process, and (4) a self-regulating capacity to initiate growth. Communication is a critical tool for growth because children must be able to communicate and comprehend if they are to learn about their world.

Although there are many ideas about when children learn what, certain understandings are basic: (1) infants learn when there are adults who provide a social and physical environment that induces opportunities for habit forming responses, (2) all children need many opportunities for repetitive sensorimotor responses with increasing challenges, (3) the basis for understanding depends on opportunities for experiencing general maturation and self-concepts, and (4) learning is a complex task involving every aspect of a child's growth.

Stephanie was a three-month-old infant who remained awake for periods of time between feedings. She kicked and thrashed frequently and cried for sustained periods of time. She seemed to quiet down occasionally when she observed the motion of the bird mobile hanging from her crib. She would stare at it and follow its movements with her eyes for moments at a time. When the birds stopped, Stephanie would resume crying.

At the suggestion of a graduate student, Stephanie's mother tied a ribbon to the mobile and loosely looped it around Stephanie's ankle. When the mobile stopped, Stephanie began to kick and thrash as if in anger. When she kicked, she activated the mobile. As it moved, the infant observed it and stopped all movement in order to do so. When it stopped, she kicked and thrashed, again activating the mobile.

After many repetitions over a period of several days, her parents noticed that the thrashing and crying were reduced in several instances and they noticed that the infant had learned to kick both feet and then to focus on the mobile in motion. A few days later, much to the delight of the adults, Stephanie could be seen kicking just the foot that had the ribbon attached to it. She would coo at the birds in motion. In a few weeks, as Stephanie developed more involvements with adults around her, the game of the moving birds was forgotten.

Memory in infancy and early childhood often is illusive and of short duration because these youngsters lack the cognitive background that helps correlate information. Sensorimotor responses form the pattern for learning behavior that eventually is guided by verbal interaction. However, logical understanding and abstract reasoning depend on a more formalized system of relationships that does not occur until much later.

Mrs. Hart, a teacher for three-year-olds, worked with several children as they cut various fruits, tasted them, and discussed the seeds inside each fruit. She carefully explained the function of the seeds. As the conclusion to the learning experience, the children planted the seeds in containers of soil. Several hours later, John who had been an interested member of the group greeted his mother with the statement, "We ate fruit today and then God turned the pits into seeds and we planted them."

Logical thinking takes place when concepts have been learned through experience, communication, and social interaction so that a body of knowledge is formed that is consistent and structured. Adults probably can recall learning facts that were not fully understood. Learning to drive a car is primarily a mechanical task. Few of us are cognitively aware of the relationship between the task of driving, the complex human behavior necessary for good driving, and the mechanical functioning of the car.

Many studies have shown that children who learn most successfully come from families where the nurturer (1) has direct involvement with the child, (2) offers frequent praise for task completion, (3) encourages the child's experimentation, (4) respects the child's autonomy when he is performing a task, and (5) offers positive, frequent verbal support. Under these conditions, children are better prepared to acquire new skills and information. Learning behavior, therefore, is positively influenced by social interaction and by feelings of success.

FACTORS THAT INFLUENCE LEARNING

Several pertinent questions about the individual child must be considered by those adults who plan experiences and choose environmental conditions for young children.

1. How effectively does this child relate to others?

Evan was four-years-old when his mother, Mrs. Lyle, registered him at the child care center. Mrs. Lyle was forty-five years old and was going back to work on a full time basis. She expressed hope that Evan would learn to play with other children. She stated that the family lived in an area where there were no other small children and that Evan's only companion was his twelve-year-old brother. After a few days at school, it became evident that Evan did not know how to relate to his peers. His contacts with other children consisted of destroying their work, spilling their juice, grabbing their coats, and generally disrupting any group he happened to encounter during his aimless wandering around the room.

Evan's attention span was very short. He could not listen to a story, rest, nor share in a discussion. He was unable to cope with any learning experience occurring in the room. During a small-group cooking experience, Evan was observed carefully by a member of the staff. He was so involved with tactile experiences of touching children and he aroused so many angry feelings among the children that he gained nothing from the program in progress.

During a staff meeting, a plan for guiding Evan evolved. His teacher would spend fifteen minutes twice a day with Evan while they worked together and discussed whatever was of interest to the child. During the rest of the day he would be observed carefully and preventive guidance would be initiated by the staff. For example, if Evan happened to wander over to the block area, a staff member would suggest that he select several blocks so he could build his own structure. If the children were building cooperatively, she might suggest that Evan be shown where he could help with the structure. She would praise Evan when he followed directions, particularly when he was with the group. Soon the children began to imitate the staff and they praised Evan when he respected their rights.

After a period of about three months, Evan was able to play in the block corner and to follow the directions of his peers. He had begun to listen to them and to offer the correct size or shape block when it was requested. He was able to participate in small groups and he began to offer relevant remarks during discussion time. He demonstrated other signs of maturing socially and it became evident that Evan was ready to participate in all phases of classroom living. He was interested in working with many materials. His language and listening skills increased. By spring, Evan was absorbed in many facets of the program. Cognitive growth was apparent as was a much improved status in social relationships.

In this instance, the child needed to make up for a kind of development he had missed, social interaction, before he was able to direct his energies toward acquiring other skills.

2. Is the child receptive to new experiences?

Josh started nursery school at age two years and nine months. He spent the first day playing with a large toy truck. On following days he selected the truck as soon as he arrived and refused to play with anything else. When the truck was not available, he sat at a table and sucked his thumb. He became upset when anyone tried to divert his attention to another toy.

The teacher, Mr. Sanchez, and his assistant, Mr. Phillips, sought ways to help Josh in his dilemma. One day they brought in three trucks of different shapes and sizes and offered them to Josh. Mr. Phillips spent time with the youngster as they drove the trucks on an imaginary road. Mr. Phillips and Josh discussed the trucks and defined the differences in color, form, and size. Josh began to respond and the next day chose one of the other trucks to play with since the red one had been taken by another child.

A few days later, Mr. Sanchez brought some wood to school and suggested that Josh use the hammer and nails at the carpentry bench to make a truck. Josh responded to his suggestion and, when the task was completed to his satisfaction, Mr. Sanchez suggested that he might like to paint it. Josh accepted the idea and became very much interested in the process of painting. He was very proud of his finished product and when he showed it to his mother he said, "I paint truck. I hammer truck. I play."

With continued guidance, Josh began to use more equipment and each time he did so he learned new words and new skills. Before long, he was able to experience and describe many things. He began to integrate bits and peices of information and became an active learner in his group.

3. Does the child respond to language clues?

Mary, a five-year-old American Indian youngster, joined a Headstart class on the reservation in New Mexico. The staff of the school was drawn from outside the community. Mary was extremely reserved at school and displayed almost no interest in what was happening at the center. She did not follow directions and appeared to be apathetic about the activities of the other children. The staff members were likely to lead Mary from one place to another.

When an open-school night was held, the director learned that Mary was now living with her grandparents because both of her parents worked in a nearby town. Her grandparents spoke almost exclusively in their Indian dialect in their efforts to preserve their culture in rearing Mary. As a result of the situation, the director of the center decided to recruit a person on the reservation who was bilingual to help Mary and to help set a healthy social tone for the center.

A senior citizen volunteered to help with Mary. According to plan, as the teacher spoke, the volunteer translated the information for Mary. As a result, the child responded in her language and quickly demonstrated a body of knowledge commensurate with her age level. The teacher, in turn, learned the names of colors and how to give simple directions in Mary's dialect and tried to converse with Mary directly as often as possible. Mary was delighted with the teacher's halting efforts.

The child soon began to use the equipment at the school and, within a short time, began to speak English while sharing the climber with her peers. Subsequently, the volunteer helped Mary cope with verbal direction as the child began to want to do what the other children were doing. The volunteer also served as a catalyst between Mary and the other children. In a few weeks, it became evident that Mary was responding to the language of her peers as she participated in many activities. She was particularly involved during music time and often used the instruments as aides to pattern her English speech.

The volunteer remained at the center and was joined by others from the reservation community. Several were employed by the center because they provided a link between the staff, the children, and the tribal culture.

4. Does the child have a desire to demonstrate competency?

Illya was a sad-eyed three and a half year old child when she began coming to the center. She displayed no interest in the other children. Illya followed the teacher from place to place and was unable to perform even the simplest dressing task by herself. She could not wash her hands, take a toy off the shelf, nor put on a smock to paint. Her most common statement was, "I can't do it. You do it." During play time, she wandered or sat in a corner with a book. After careful observation, the teacher called Illya's mother in for a conference. Mrs. Janek, Illya's mother, said that she had little patience with the child and that she found it more efficient and easier to do for Illya than to let the child do for herself.

It was decided that the school staff should help Mrs. Janek understand that children need to feel independent and successful if they are to learn. The teachers then determined which tasks Illya could perform and established routine times for guiding her. Specific verbal directions were offered and repeated for hand washing, snack time, dressing, and undressing. Special praise was given for each effort that Illya made. When she felt successful and began to feel competent about her performance, more responsibilites were added. Soon she began to realize that she could do many things for herself and her reluctance to try new tasks gave way to greater self assurance. She began to say, "Show me. I do it." Each new competency led to a new discovery as Illya became an accepted member of the group and a willing participant in challenging learning situations. Several months later, Mrs. Janek reported that her daughter had become quite self-sufficient and was most eager to share her new feelings with her parents.

5. Is the child healthy and free from underlying physical or emotional disorders?

Billy Lomer, age five and one half, came to the preschool after two months of attending the public kindergarten. During the intake interview, Mrs. Lomer stated that the public school staff felt that Billy had few of the inner controls necessary for learning. They believed nursery school would help him prepare for kindergarten and that a year's delay would give Billy the opportunity to mature.

At school, Billy's behavior was similar to that of a two year old despite his adequate language skills. Even with special guidance, Billy could not seem to focus on a learning task for any length of time. His physical agility was good but he was a daredevil on the climbing equipment. He continually tested limits of guidance and seemed to have a short retention span when directions were given. He cried frequently and laughed raucously. He played with other children only for short periods of time.

Mr. and Mrs. Lomer were concerned about Billy. They thought he was difficult to handle at home as they compared him with their two younger children. Billy's teacher suggested that he be given a comprehensive physical examination at the local clinic and his parents were glad to make an appointment for this service.

The diagnostic study indicated that Billy had some minimal brain damage, probably contracted when he was an infant. It was subsequently disclosed that the family had purchased an old house when Billy was a baby. During the process of renovation, the child had come into contact with dust particles of lead paint that he had ingested in sufficient quantities to cause his handicap.

Special techniques for guiding Billy were recommended to teachers and parents, and the parents also were offered psychological help for coping with unique problems of child rearing that might arise. The child was given medication designed to help him become more calm. Eventually, Billy was placed in a special school where the staff was trained to work with special children.

The person who guides young children must understand that children learn what they experience and practice. They learn when there are materials that they can handle and to which they can react. Children learn as they interact with people who offer information about what the child is doing. Curiosity is necessary for learning. Children need freedom to explore and limits to insure their safety if inquiry and experimentation are to lead to new information.

In order for a young child to understand what is happening, he has to understand causal relationships so that he can evaluate his actions and the actions of others.

Melissa, age two and a half, was building a tower with blocks and when the tower collapsed, she began to cry. Mrs. Pines, her teacher, suggested that she try to balance the blocks again to see how high it could be built before it fell again. Melissa accepted the challenge as she proceeded to build several towers and to watch them fall. She carefully placed four blocks on top of each other, speaking as she worked, "you stay, be good." The tower blocks had been carefully placed and the structure was sturdy. Melissa turned to Mrs. Pines and said, "So big. All fixed." Attention was sustained by the adult and the child persevered.

Verbal support from the teacher and her own carefully controlled movement had helped this child cope with her feelings and she knew that she had done something important.

A child needs opportunities to imagine and to recreate the world and the behavior of people around him. Imagination permits him to succeed beyond his childhood limitations and offers him the chance to release his feelings as he orders his world.

Gene, age four, had been involved in many mischievous activities at school one morning. A student assistant saw him throwing blocks and she raised her voice as she demanded that he leave the group. Gene shouted, "When I be big, I put a pot on your head and bang you down and you be little and I will yell at you and make you go away!"

Through this emotional outburst, the child's concepts of size and power were evident. Moreover, it was apparent that he understood that he could verbalize his intentions but that he could not act out his feelings physically, His imaginative solution offered him an opportunity to explain his feelings and, at the same time, to avoid the consequences of his thought. Gene demonstrated that he was capable of creative thinking.

Children rely on concrete knowledge, not on abstract notions.

During a discussion about birthdays, a group of three year old children decided that Mrs. Stevens, who was fifty-five years old and wore size four shoes, was younger than Miss Young, who was twenty-two and wore size ten shoes, because Miss Young had bigger feet.

This conclusion is sensible to the child who knows that, as he gets older, he will get bigger. Young children are not experientially equipped to cope with abstract ideas.

Rachel, age five, lived in a high-rise apartment complex. One morning she looked out the window and saw a woman commit suicide by leaping off the roof. Mrs. Kiley, Rachael's mother, sought for a way to explain this to Rachael who wanted to know what the lady did. Mrs. Kiley said, "The lady went to meet God." Rachael then asked, "If I jump out the window, can I see God, too?"

Young children often try to cope with information they have learned but without precise information and sufficient maturation they fit what they learn into what they can understand.

During a class discussion about bridges, four-year-old James defined a bridge as "a sidewalk across the water."

The adult who is guiding young children needs to listen to what children discuss so she can (1) clarify meanings, (2) offer illustrations, (3) plan appropriate experiences, and (4) understand how children learn as they connect the bits of information they have gathered.

Jenny and Helen, two four-year-olds, were busy talking in the playhouse when Miss Gold, their teacher, overheard Jenny say, "Helen, you are so good I could eat you up." Helen looked seriously at Jenny and replied, "Don't do that, Jenny, you'll get sick. My mommy says I'm spoiled."

Young children may understand what you say but not what you are thinking. Learning occurs developmentally as a child becomes able to draw inferences from language and experience and when he begins to comprehend the relationship between events as well as people. Early perceptions children have pertain to what they see, hear, and experience.

The spontaneous interests of children should be enriched but not encumbered. As young children crunch autumn leaves, they can learn the colors, observe the different shapes, hear the crunching sound, and prepare to make a leaf collage. Lengthy explanations about the life cycle of leaves and detailed summaries of the four seasons fall on unprepared minds. It is possible for older preschoolers to watch a tree throughout a school year and, with the aid of pictures, frequent observations, and recollection, learn about trees and seasonal changes.

Children who discover that snow melts or changes to puddles of water when they take their boots indoors have a worthwhile experience that can be repeated many times and enriched with other experiences about snow and its properties. Listening to a lengthy explanation about how snow turns into drinking water the following spring is beyond the understanding of most preschool youngsters. Children who live outside of cities in northern areas see much clean, fresh snow and will understand more about what happens to snow than children from cities who see snow as dirty heaps piled on a sidewalk in preparation for a snow-removal machine. Experience and familiarity are important for learning.

A group of five-year-olds had been discussing a story book that described various houses for animals. The book misinformed children by stating that snails live in a shell house the same way birds live in a bird house and cows live in a barn. Miss Leland was a young teacher who believed in implementing the curriculum. Therefore, she brought some live snails to school for the children to examine. A group of children were looking at the snails and Miss Leland was called to another part of the room for a few moments. When she returned, she saw several pairs of scissors on the table and some very confused children. They had decided to see the inside of the house and had taken the soft substance out of the hard outer covering. Of course, they were upset to find that the snail did not go back into the house when they were finished with it.

Children need accurate, precise information if what they learn is to help them classify and conceptualize correctly.

CONCEPTS CHILDREN BUILD ON

A child needs to know names for things, properties of things, how he can use them or what they are for. He needs experiences about the size, shape, density, and forms of matter. He needs language and experience to determine relationships.

Mr. Clark, a college student, was thrilled with his position as a Headstart assistant. On his second day at the center, he decided to provide a tactile and language experience for a group of four-year-olds. He placed various kinds of fruit in a paper sack and told the children that they could take turns in putting a hand in the sack, feeling a piece of fruit, and saying the name of the fruit and describing its color. His inexperience was evident when some children were unable to name the fruits. In fact, he soon learned that several of the children were completely unfamiliar with some of the fruits he had chosen.

This experience led to an interesting disucssion two days later, however, when Mr. Clark placed the fruits in a basket and he and the children discussed each item, talking about its color, shape, and taste. The children were interested and seemed delighted with their new knowledge.

Language can be puzzling to the preschooler even after he has learned to use the words involved. How do we help a child understand the word, "on," since we put the book "on" the table and turn the light "on" in a dark room. The child learns the word, "on," before he understands the functional variations of word meanings.

Early in December, the older group in the child care center had been discussing their favorite story books. Each child, as they sat in a circle, mentioned the name of the book or described it in some way. Some of the children referred to books at the center, others spoke of books they had at home.

When Janet's turn came, she said, "My best book is the one about the girl that got sick on the ribbon." When Mr. Silva, the teacher, asked if she wanted to say anything more about the book, she said, "It's a poem." Mr. Silva was well acquainted with Janet's parents and curiosity led him to discover the name of the book. It was *'Twas the Night Before Christmas* and the lines to which Janet referred, were "Away to the window I flew like a flash, tore open the shutters and threw up the sash."

Many times, we offer experiences to children without evaluating how each child perceives the information he receives. Only constant monitoring of the information that is offered to children will help the teacher guide the child as he learns. Young children need practice in classifying or placing objects in appropriate categories. They can be helped to determine which things belong together and why.

Miss Ponds was a student teacher in a kindergarten class in a middle income area. She presented a lesson to the group on matching things that fit on each other. In discussion, the children matched hand to glove, shoe to sock, and several other pairs of objects. When she presented a cup, the children could find no answer. The saucer on the display table was apparently meaningless. A few minutes of conversation were necessary for her to discover that mugs were used at home and that, for this group of children, the saucer was not a part of their frame of reference.

Children should be guided toward ordering or seriation of objects. They need to encounter (1) comparative size such as big and little, (2) comparative quantity such as few and many, (3) comparative qualities such as hard and soft, and (4) visual stimuli differences such as bright and dull.

A child needs experiences that help him define space and spatial perception. He should be able to experience through movement and also through verbal encounters, spatial concepts such as up and down, above and below, in and out. The child who uses an elevator to go up to his apartment and down to the street will have a very different concept of himself in space than the child who goes up and down steps within his home to get from his room to the kitchen. Sometimes, when we listen to children, we are surprised at their limited spatial perception.

Nancy Sampson was a five-year-old girl who had been bedfast for almost a year due to a heart ailment. She and her family lived on a remote ranch and, prior to her illness, Nancy's experiences outside her home had been limited.

An appointment was scheduled with a heart specialist in a city two hundred miles from Nancy's home and an ambulance was sent from town to transport Nancy and her family to the city. When they arrived, an express elevator took the child, who was on a stretcher, and her parents directly to the twenty-fourth floor of the office building.

The heart specialist had been called away for an emergency and the Sampson's appointment was delayed. The doctor's staff propped Nancy up so she could pass the time looking out of the window and down at a large, grassy park with several roads crossing it. After awhile, Nancy said to her mother, "Mommy, there are lots of toy cars running around down there."

Children need guidance as they begin to conceptualize time and its relationship to their lives.

On Wednesday, Maria, age four, was told that tomorrow would be her birthday and that she could choose the story for listening time on that day. When she arrived at school on Thursday morning, she proudly offered the teacher a book and said, "Tomorrow is today, so please read this at story time."

Each level of intellectual maturation is interwoven with social, emotional, physiological, and developmental circumstances. In order to guide a youngster effectively as he grows in correlation with his unique pattern, the adult must help the child to understand his world. The proficient teacher is concerned about curriculum as it relates to specific children and their needs and goals. Adults may feel successful when they have taught young children to recite the names of the days of the week, but alert adults realize that a child is much more concerned about the relationship between yesterday, today, and tomorrow as they affect his life.

SUGGESTED ASSIGNMENT

Part I

Listen to children during their work time and record observations that illustrate:

1. How a child misuses a concept or word.
2. When a child is concerned about time.
3. When a learning situation is not suitable for a particular child.
4. How a child demonstrates mastery in a cognitive skill.
5. How a child handles new material.

Part II

Become familiar with the main contributions concerning cognition by the following people:

1. Jean Piaget
2. Jerome Bruner
3. David Elkind
4. Ira Gordon
5. D. P. Weikart
6. Susan Gray
7. Sigmund Bernreiter

Part III

Observe and record the behavior of an infant in his home once a week for five consecutive weeks. Describe the infant carefully and look for the following:

1. How does he respond to his nurturer?
2. Does he learn a new skill or only practice those he already knows?
3. What form of locomotion does he use?
4. How long can he concentrate on one action or toy?
5. What changes did you observe over the five week period? Be specific.

SELECTED READINGS

1. Almy, Millie, Edward Chittenden, and Paula Miller, *Young Children's Thinking,* Teachers College Press, Columbia University, N. Y., 1966.

The first section of this book explains and interprets some of Piaget's theories and prepares the reader for methods and procedures for an experiment that used Piaget's research pattern on conservation with a group of American children.

2. Chapman, A. H., *The Games Children Play,* G. P. Putnam, New York, 1971.

These selections offer insights into how personalities of children are influenced by early experiences in the home. The author presents an interesting approach of parenthood.

3. Furth, Hans G., *Piaget for Teachers,* Prentice-Hall, Englewood Cliffs, N. J., 1970.

The author presents Piaget's theories of learning in the form of letters to a teacher. He presents small segments in successive letters. Pages 1 through 43 can be most helpful if they are read carefully.

4. Lillard, Paula Polk, *Montessori, A Modern Approach,* Schoken Books, N. Y., 1972.

The author states that recent research in neurology and the works of Piaget and Bruner tend to confirm Montessori's theories about how children learn. Parents as well as professional workers are addressed.

5. Powledge, Fred, *To Change a Child,* Quadrangle Books, Chicago, 1967.

This book describes work done with disadvantaged children at the Institute for Developmental Studies under the direction of Dr. Martin Deutsch who views education as a tool for social change. This will be a valuable student reading.

6. Weikart, David P., Linda Rogers, Carolyn Adcock, and Donna McClellans, *The Cognitively Oriented Curriculum, ERIC-NAEYC,* University of Illinois, 1971.

Chapter 4 offers a sequential guide to teachers who want to use Piaget's theory of cognition as a base for program planning. Clear, specific directions for implementation are presented.

7. Yarrow, Leon J., and Frank A. Pedersen, "Attachment, Its Origin and Cause," *The Young Child*, W. H. Hartup, ed., Vol. 2, National Association Education of Young Children, Washington, D. C., 1972.

This is a presentation of the relationship of maternal nurturing to cognitive and social attainment. Trust is a key concept of this writing.

chapter 9

Toileting and Washing

In adherence to the belief that everything young children do is important in their future living, it is especially important to evaluate routine activities as they affect the child now and in the future. Too often, we overlook the importance of the routines in helping us to understand children and to promote their development.

WASHING AND ITS RELATION TO WATER PLAY

Water is important in ways other than that of procuring cleanliness. It has a therapeutic value to mankind. Physical therapy is a means by which tense muscles can be relaxed and some kinds of physical ills eased. In a lesser way, swimming as a recreational sport has a soporific effect on those who indulge in it. That water play is helpful in the relief of emotional tensions in children is shown whenever such play is permitted. Water play probably offers one of the best opportunities for preschools to provide an activity that is not often allowed at home. In the small apartment or attractive home it is difficult to furnish a spacious environment wherein splashing and dripping will not injure floors and furniture and, besides, most parents do not have the time to clean up after this kind of play. Since preschools are planned for children, however, and there are plenty of adults in attendance, young children should have opportunities to explore this medium. When creative activities are discussed, a variety of experiences with water will be described, but it is good to recognize that washing can offer similar pleasures.

Children vary in their enjoyment of water play. Some children seem to have the adult attitude that washing one's hands is a task to be completed quickly so that they can move on to more interesting pursuits. Others will dawdle for long periods of time at the lavatory. If we watch their faces and observe closely, it is apparent that they feel keen pleasure in the feel of the water. It is evident, also, that sometimes they are intrigued by the force with which the water comes through the faucets when they are turned.

Adults would be wise to consider the plumbing as it must appear to a child. It has a truly remarkable function. By turning a faucet, the child can have cold water; the other faucet will produce hot water, and the force of these streams of water can be regulated at will. The stopper in the bottom of the bowl is interesting, also. The feel of the water as fingers slosh through it is pleasant, and the increase in pressure caused when fingers are placed under faucets adds variety to the game.

Sometimes, it is comparatively easy for adults to imagine the feel of the soap as it slithers through wet fingers and to be patient as children rub soap vigorously into their hands. Wise adults will be indulgent, if possible, when soapsuds are not applied solely to faces and hands. Great fun can result when young children smear the suds over faucet handles and over mirrors that are hung in washrooms.

The furnishings and space in washrooms determine how much of this play can be permitted. If facilities are crowded, children cannot always be allowed to dawdle. Understanding adults will discern (1) which children engage in this water play in such a manner that it is not of great importance so that other types of play will satisfy them as well, (2) which children are dawdling in order to tease or to gain attention, and (3) which children are so serious in these pursuits that they seem to have a need for further exploration. As in other tactile experiences, usually the younger children enjoy this play, but it is not unusual for a child of middle preschool years to show interest.

Daisy, a three-year-old, seemed to have an inordinate desire to play in the washroom. When a request was made, she would move on with her group to the playroom but during free play periods she almost always returned to play in the lavatories. Since the washrooms were needed for practical purposes, Miss Comstock provided a large dishpan filled with water. The pan was placed on a low table and a plastic apron was provided for Daisy. A soap dish containing a bar of soap, an egg beater, a plastic sponge, and a rubber doll were placed nearby. Daisy spent hours playing with these objects in the water. Each morning she would move to that corner of the playroom when she came indoors. Occasionally, another child would ask for an apron and would play in the water and sometimes it was necessary to provide another pan of water. Other children, however, would soon go on to some other activity.

Every day for more than three weeks Daisy spent all of her indoor play period in water play. Then, one day when she came indoors, she went to the doll corner and began setting the table with the toy dishes. At no future time did she request the toys she had employed and her later water play experiences were only those that were planned for the entire group. It seemed that she finally had been satisfied.

It is regrettable that we cannot more often plan children's schedules at home and at school so that individuals can choose their own activities and set their own pace. Students with heavy classroom and social schedules can find vicarious pleasure in watching children who are free to linger when they are interested in a specific activity.

When we permit children to pursue an activity until they are satisfied, it seems we have helped contribute to their feelings of independence, adequacy, and security. We need not wonder nor try to determine why their interests in the activity appeared unusual at the time. Experiences should be planned for individual children and making many of their desired activities possible is a good form of indirect guidance. These experiences lead toward accomplishing the real purposes of guidance.

Water play has possibilities in the realm of dramatic interpretation. Washing rubber dolls as parents wash babies is an interesting activity for preschool children. Imaginative role playing frequently occurs in the doll corner when clothes or dishes are being "washed." Another favorite pastime of children is the scrubbing of equipment with water and sponges.

Children who have access to wading pools or seashore splashing are fortunate in being introduced to another interesting type of water play. The abandon with which children enter such activities is proof of the pleasure they derive from them. Parents can foster similar pleasures by allowing leisurely time for children's baths. Yet, bath time is likely to be as fraught with adult impatience as washing periods at school unless adults attempt to regard these experiences from children's points of view.

TOILETING HABITS

During infancy, urination and defecation are involuntary functions. Elimination is a pleasant sensation since the release and concurrent relaxation of muscular tensions provide bodily comfort. These sensations are related to children's first feelings of well being, so it is not surprising that emotional tone and toileting habits continue to be interrelated during preschool years. Moreover, toileting is related, in a child's thinking, to his intimate association with his mother and her care of him. His progress in toilet training is likely to signify approval or disapproval by those whom he loves most. His learning to control his eliminative functions probably has been accompanied by ambivalent feelings—the pleasures of bodily comfort and the imposition of adult interference with natural bodily rhythms.

A certain stage of physiological maturation must be reached before successful toilet training is possible. Since the body's mechanism is arranged for an automatic riddance of waste materials, only gradually can children substitute conscious control for their natural tendency to satisfy bladder and bowel urges. As in other kinds of learning, this is a complex function. A state of physical, mental, and emotional readiness should be present before training is attempted. Before control is possible, children must have developed sufficiently to recognize the pressures that occur in the bladder and bowel and to retain muscular tension.

Adults in our culture are almost ridiculous in the manner in which they regard toilet training as one of the most important accomplishments of children. This is foolish when we realize that all normal children eventually become self-directing in this routine. Most parents are likely to be embarrassed and sensitive if their children are not toilet trained as early as the neighbor's children. Often, a parent who is tired of washing diapers may seek to toilet train a child long before he is capable of control.

Since babies begin to have regular bowel movements at a comparatively early age, avoiding accidents of this type is often possible before children are little more than one year old. This can hardly be called training, however, since it is really a matter of the adult becoming aware of the child's individual rhythm of defecation and placing him on the toilet at that time. Frequently, young children's bowel movements occur at mealtime and it is not unusual for a teacher to find it necessary to leave the school lunch table to accompany a child to the toilet room. A more convenient time will be established as the child matures.

Children vary greatly as to the time at which they are capable of bladder control. Although some children achieve control by eighteen months, others may not be completely trained until they are past two-and-one-half years old. Thus, setting a definite age for expectancy in this area is as impossible as predicting at what age a child will begin to walk or to talk. Also, as in other kinds of guidance, the best sign is the indication of readiness on the part of the child. We can be assured that happy children will be eager to meet adult expectations when they are capable of doing so.

Several circumstances influence children's control of their eliminative functions. Usually, girls are trained earlier and urinate less often than boys of similar chronological ages. The amounts of liquids included in dietary intake are influential. The onset of physical illness or emotional tensions is likely to cause lapses or regressions in toileting behavior. Cold weather is a stimulant to urination at all age levels. Tight clothing often causes toileting accidents.

Certainly, we should expect and accept toileting accidents even after children have established satisfactory control. Lapses in bladder control are so common that they must be considered a normal characteristic of the preschool child. For sometimes after a child has attained daytime control of the bladder and bowels, an adult must assume the responsibility for complete control at night by taking the child to the toilet according to his individual need. Moreover, in daytime children concentrate on what they are doing and often they are not aware of their need to urinate until it is too late for them to refrain from wetting their clothing. This indicates the value of setting regular times when a lull in school activity provides an opportunity for toileting.

Techniques of guidance during these periods vary from one age group to another. The two-year-old needs to go to the toilet more often than the older child and it is wise to indicate that he is expected to urinate at regular intervals. As in other kinds of guidance, verbal requests should be expressed so the child has no choice. That is, instead of saying, "Do you want to go to the toilet?" it is better to say, "It is time to go to the toilet," or "You may use the toilet now." Later, less definite directions are possible.

Maurine entered school when she was two years and three months old. Her parents had reported that she had been toilet trained for the past five months and that she used a small toilet chair at home with no prompting.

Each morning, after the children had played outdoors for about an hour they went inside, removed their wraps, and went to the toilet. Maurine was resistant from the first day. She refused to go into the bathroom until the other children had finished and then she would enter only to wash and dry her hands. Verbal insistence that she "try to go to the toilet" met with emotional outbursts and further pleas were followed by her running quickly to another room and huddling in a corner.

Maurine had no toileting accidents at school, but toward the end of each session it was apparent that she was uncomfortable as she would stand first on one foot and then the other and would not engage in play of any kind. On the third day of the second week she went into the bathroom to wash and dry her hands when the other children were toileting.

One day during the third week, Maurine left the doll corner during free play, went into the bathroom used the toilet, and returned to her group. This self-directive pattern was her practice during the remainder of her school attendance.

The change from using a toileting chair to the regular toilets may have made Maurine hesitant. It is not unusual for very young children to fear the flushing suction of this equipment. It may have been the presence of so many people in the toilet rooms that bothered this child. Whatever the reason, this example illustrates that sometimes we underestimate the ability that children have toward independence.

By the time children are three to four years of age, they usually are capable of anticipating their toileting needs and of acting independently. Most children, however, will need to be reminded to go to the toilet for many months after they can take care of themselves. This is especially true at school where children become so interested in group activities that it is easy to forget.

The best criterion for what to expect of children and for the choice of methods of guidance is our knowledge of individual children. Toileting habits can become a major issue of emotional conflict between adults and children.

Kim entered school when he was three-years-old. Occasionally, he would become so engrossed in some activity that he was unable to get to the bathroom in time. A teacher or student would help him change his clothing without commenting about his accident.

Rather suddenly, Kim's toileting accidents became more frequent. Two changes of clothing during a school session were not uncommon. The teacher asked that students remind him more often of his need to go to the toilet, but this practice seemed to be of little help. Within a couple of weeks, the time spent in changing Kim's clothing and the clothing necessary for those changes were becoming a problem.

Kim's parents were unhappy, too, when two or three sets of wet clothing were given to them each day when they called for him. They mentioned that he had undergone a physical examination recently and it was plain that they were displeased with the school staff. Therefore, Kim's teacher made an appointment with the mother so they could talk when Kim was not present. His mother stated that she thought something at school was responsible for Kim's problem and that they were having frequent accidents at home, also.

A week later, a telephone call from Kim's father brought an apology for their suspicions. In some way, the parents had learned that a daily baby sitter who had been hired several weeks before had been spanking Kim whenever he had wet pants. Of course, the baby sitter was replaced. Within two weeks, Kim had regained control of his toileting activities.

Sometimes, then, the reasons for lack of bladder control can be corrected easily. When toileting accidents become frequent with an older preschool child, it is wise to try to find the cause. Often, the onset of an illness will be the reason. When lack of control is persistent and the cause cannot be determined, medical advice should be sought.

The mechanics of using a toilet can be interesting to young children. Some adults consider the processes of elimination shameful and it is difficult for them to recognize that these procedures are as interesting to children as the routines of eating, sleeping, washing, and resting. Children have no unwholesome attitudes toward going to the toilet until they have learned them from adults or from other children. The toilet seat, the roll of toilet tissue, and the flushing of the toilet can be fascinating to young children.

Family patterns vary and, since preschools supplement the home, procedures sometimes should be altered for certain children.

The school toilet rooms had no doors and most of the children seemed completely unaffected by the presence of other children using toilets nearby. Ruth, a three-year-old who was an only child, seemed reticent to enter the bathroom when other children were there. Frequently, she would be late for story time because she always waited until all the children were through in the toilet room. Miss Olson did not insist that Ruth alter this pattern. One day, she said to Ruth, "You may go across the hall and use that bathroom if you want to."

During the following months, Ruth would slip quietly away to use the other bathroom and then return to the group. Since Ruth was a shy child, her being granted this special privilege seemed pleasing in her general feeling of acceptance.

Family patterns and attitudes concerning eliminative habits are reflected in the preschool child's whole way of life since (1) they occupy a major part of his behavior learning at this period, (2) they receive much attention by his parents and, therefore, represent an important factor in his relationships with other people, and (3) they are the reason for blame and punishment that may be difficult for him to understand.

We must remember that children since early infancy have taken pleasure in the comforts of bowel and bladder release. These feelings of comfort are related to the love and affection of the adult who takes care of the child. Moreover, within a few months, adult expectations center on his progress toward controlling these releases. Thus, bladder and bowel activities continue to be one of the most vital channels of communication between adults and children. Guidance methods used by parents are probably indicative of their attitudes toward the child and signify their own levels of adjustment as well.

As stated previously, some people associate the idea of filth or shame with the processes of elimination. Their desire for cleanliness of body and mind give toilet training an almost moralistic impact. These adults have a compulsion toward the early training of children, they tend to consider a dry baby a good baby, then are repulsed by the child's attitudes of pleasure in his ability to eliminate, and emotions become particularly intense when toileting accidents occur. In view of our need to view the situation as a child sees it, these attitudes obviously are unfortunate.

The attitudes of parents toward elimination sometimes are reflected in the terms that children apply to these activities. Study of enrollment data in school files is enlightening as to the variety of words used by children to indicate a need to go to the toilet. Some of these terms are humorous when we consider their literal meanings. Teachers are faced with the necessity for quick thinking when very young children say these words and wet their clothing before they are guided toward the toilet. Occasionally, these substitute words are taught to a child so that parents will not be embarrassed when he indicates before other people that he needs to go to the toilet. Embarrassment of this type is false modesty when we consider that all people have identical needs. Moreover, by the time children reach elementary school age, they may be embarrassed by these inappropriate terms. It certainly would seem preferable that correct terminology be learned when toilet training is begun.

Although bed wetting does not usually occur frequently at school, an understanding of the problem is important. The manner in which bed wetting or enuresis is handled at home may dictate the child's general attitude toward all toileting procedures. Children usually have complete control during the day long before they are capable of remaining dry during sleeping hours. When parents are eager to eradicate bed wetting, one of the first steps necessary is to limit the intake of liquids near the bedtime hour. This plan is good only if the consumption of liquids is not curtailed but merely concentrated somewhat earlier in the day.

Another helpful technique is for parents to awaken the child and take him to the toilet before the time at which they previously have found him wet. Sometimes, parents will be hesitant to do this, fearing that it may result in a habit that will be difficult to break. If the child is thoroughly awake when he urinates, however, he may be conditioned so that he will awaken when he needs to go to the toilet. During middle preschool years, he probably will get up and go to the toilet by himself and, as control becomes more definite, he will withhold elimination throughout the night.

Some children continue to wet the bed at night long after control should have been accomplished. Here again, parents are likely to become upset by reason of their embarrassment or the extra laundry and bed changing that is necessary. However difficult it may be to assume a calm and accepting attitude, adults owe this to children because (1) a child does not continue to willfully wet his bed, and (2) increased emotional tensions may only serve to prolong the habit. Careful consideration of the child's life is necessary. If emotional pressures can be discovered, steps should be taken to eradicate them. In cases of persistent enuresis, a complete physical examination should be scheduled. Pediatricians are experienced in helping parents solve these difficulties.

QUESTIONS CONCERNING BODY AND SEX DIFFERENCES

Since the organs of excretion and the organs of sex lie so close together, toilet training and sex attitudes are probably closely related in the minds of some individuals. As has been stated, habits of elimination are an important part of the emotional well being of the child in early infancy and adult attitudes concerning body functions are influential in the early concepts of children. Long before sex instruction has begun, sex attitudes are being formed and adults' feelings are reflected in the learning patterns of children. If urination and defecation are considered by parents to be filthy functions, these feelings are transmitted to the children whom they guide.

Young children are curious about their bodies. As the child begins to realize that he is a specific entity, he is interested in his arms and legs. This is apparent when we watch babies enjoy the sight of their waving arms and their kicking legs. Later, these children explore their bodies with their eyes and hands. Soon after birth, infants derive pleasure in sucking on their fingers, a form of oral stimulation. Some adults are oblivious to the behavior of the child who explores his body with his hands as long as he does not touch his genitals, but they become upset and alarmed at his interest in body parts related to excretion or sex.

Handling of the sex organs should not cause the worry or embarrassment that often occur when parents discover their children in this kind of activity. Such exploration is the expression of perfectly natural curiosity by the young child. Sometimes it is difficult for us to realize that these actions do not denote sex consciousness by the child. We tend to interpret these actions in the line of our own experience and knowledge. These adult attitudes, although unexpressed, make an impression on young children and the child is led to believe that sex is something extraordinarily mysterious and unique.

Youngsters are likely to notice differences between children and adults and between boys and girls. If they have an opportunity to ask questions openly and to receive frank answers and a calm acceptance, a good foundation is laid for later guidance. Developing wholesome attitudes toward sex is essential to happy, self-directing adjustment, the real purpose of guidance.

The child's first information of sex differences may result when a baby of the opposite sex is bathed. These questions are likely to be: "What's that?" or "Why doesn't she have a penis?" In accordance with good methods of conversing with young children, replies should be brief, positive, and meaningful. For example, the mother might reply, "That's his penis. He urinates through it," or "A girl baby doesn't need a penis to urinate." Usually, a further explanation is unnecessary for very young preschoolers. As in other kinds of guidance, training is ineffective until readiness is established, but good rapport between adults and children will provide wholesome relationships so that further questions will occur and can be answered.

The casual way in which sex differences are accepted by children is demonstrated in preschool toilet rooms. Usually, children are at the school toilet when other children and adults are present, but evidences of sex curiousity are uncommon. Here again, we need to recognize that sex differences have no unwholesome connotations to small children. This is apparent even when some curiosity is evident.

Jennifer Gorman was almost four-years-old when she entered the child care center. During the initial interview, Mrs. Gorman stated that her husband had

died two years before. Jennifer's only sibling was eighteen and in military service. Jennifer and her mother had moved into the community recently in order to live with an elderly aunt of Mrs. Gorman.

Mrs. Gorman had been alarmed because she feared that Jennifer had an abnormal curiosity about sex differences. Mrs. Gorman did not know when this curiosity had begun but she had been embarrassed because Jennifer had asked several questions in the presence of the aunt and the older woman had not tried to conceal her horror concerning this behavior. Jennifer's mother was interested in the advice of the staff members at the center. She was assured that Jennifer's curiosity was natural and that the teachers would help Jennifer to know that her noticing sex differences was acceptable.

During the first few days at the center, Jennifer seemed curious about the way boys urinated. She would stand and watch from the doorway with a serious expression on her face. As she began to be accepted by the group, however, she became interested in the lively conversations about general activities and ideas that accompanied the toileting and washing routines. By the end of the second week, Jennifer was as disinterested in staring when the other children toileted as were any of the other children. It appeared that her curiosity had been satisfactorily appeased.

Sometimes adults ask how the change to separation of sexes is explained to children when they enter the primary school. This, like other kinds of learning, seems to be a developmental readiness that occurs naturally. Older preschool children are capable of understanding social expectations. In the process of growing, and as adult behavior is observed and imitated, children recognize that the functions of toileting usually are performed privately. A well-adjusted child easily assumes the customs of his culture almost without instruction.

Masturbation is a form of child behavior that can be especially embarrassing to parents. Studies indicate that masturbation is a common practice in both sexes at all stages of development and may be associated with sexual enjoyment in the adult. No doubt children vary in this habit just as they do in thumb sucking, nail biting, and other similar behavior patterns. The causes of masturbation are of primary importance. Sometimes, local irritations due to uncleanliness in the genital area, too highly acid urine, or clothing that is too tight in the crotch will prompt children to handle and rub their genitals.

When these causes are eliminated, we need to consider the emotional needs of the individual child. The feeling in the genitals is one of the pleasurable sensations of the child's body so he is likely to resort to the stimulation of this feeling when he is bored, unhappy, or overtired. Thus, for the preschool child, distraction, a variety of activities, and careful planning for his health and comfort are logical deterrents. Since children do masturbate, we should accept the behavior as natural. It is important to reassure the child by accepting him. Adults should refrain from criticizing or threatening children. It is not the habit of masturbation that is dangerous but the worry and tensions that may ensue. If children feel that they have not measured up to expectations, anxiety and guilt feelings may result and these, in turn, may promote further comfort-seeking in masturbation. If the habit is persistent and overt, parents of children older than preschool age should seek medical or psychological advice.

Sooner or later, all children will begin to wonder where babies come from. Sometimes their questions occur when a new baby is expected. But, even if the preschooler has no reason to be interested in the birth of a child, the egocentric nature of his personality indicates that he will be interested in his own beginnings. Too often, parents are not prepared for children's questions. This is not surprising since our feelings about sex are likely to be uniquely personal. Regardless of the nature of the questions asked by children, they should be answered accurately and satisfactorily. Children will not understand the implications of many of the answers, but the answering will provide a beginning for understanding and a good basis for further learning.

Occasionally, adults will consider it unnecessary to impart information since children's limited experiences indicate that there are few facts of the reproductive process that they really can understand. These adults are similar to those who would not talk to a baby because he cannot understand word meanings. The affection and emotional tone that truthful answers denote are good for adult-child relationships and little by little children will learn the facts they need to know. Like all forms of verbal guidance, answers should be brief and accurate. For example, the correct vocabulary is important. When questions are asked concerning the origin of babies, children could be told that before birth a baby grows from a small seed inside the mother's body in a place called the uterus. The exact manner of this telling will depend on the personality of the adult. It would be as ridiculous to adopt a specific form of recitation with which to answer these questions as to answer those of any other type.

If the parents were reared in homes in which body parts and reproductive functions were discussed furtively, it probably will be more difficult to give matter-of-fact answers to children. Both mothers and fathers should give careful consideration to their responsibilities for providing sex information. When children are young, it is not too difficult to anticipate questions and to be prepared to answer them. Some parents supplement this information by reading stories to their children about how babies are born. These stories can be valuable, but they cannot replace the day-to-day communications between parents and children.

Children do not stay at the preschool age and considerable thought by parents is necessary for future planning in sex education. We must consider the long-time goals of guidance. During late preschool years or shortly thereafter, the role of fathers in the reproductive process will need to be explained accurately. The child at this stage may be provided with the fact that a cell from the father's body meets a cell from the mother's body, the two cells meet inside the mother where a baby begins to grow. If the child then asks, "How does the father's cell get inside the mother?", the parent can explain that whereas the father has a penis, the mother has an opening in her body and the two fit together. Descriptive words for parts of the body such as breasts, nipples, vagina, vulva, uterus, foreskin, penis, and testicles should be ready for inclusion in casual conversations between parents and children when youngsters show a readiness for knowledge.

SUGGESTED ASSIGNMENT

Part I

Observe the children in the washroom. Select two children who appear to differ markedly in their behavior during the washing routine and answer the following questions about each child.

1. Does he usually start to wash when he first comes in or does he use the toilet before he washes?

2. Does he turn the water on and off without assistance?

3. Does he tend to play with the water, the faucets, or the soap? Describe this behavior.

4. Does he talk with other children while he is washing or is he intent on the mechanics of the activity?

5. Does he request adult help?

Part II

Write an anecdotal record of one of the children who is engaged in water play at the water table or on the palyground. Analyze your record on the basis of your readings.

Part III

Observe the children in the toilet room. Select two of these children who appear to differ markedly in their behavior during the toileting routine and answer the following questions about each child:

1. Does he go directly to the toilet when he comes into the room?

2. Does he need adult help? How much help? Physical or verbal help?

3. Does he flush the toilet?

4. How is he affected by the presence of other children or adults? Explain.

5. Did he display any curiosity about sex differences? If so, describe.

Part IV

Visit a library where books for young children are available and find two or three books that explain the birth process. Review and evaluate these books indicating when and how you would introduce them to the child.

SELECTED READINGS

1. Breckenridge, Marian E., and Margaret Nesbitt, *Growth and Development of the Young Child,* 8th ed., W. B. Saunders, Philadelphia, 1969.

The authors describe the effects of elimination and health habits on the healthy growth of young children. A description of cultural pressures as they relate to expectations of self-care is especially interesting.

2. Dittman, Laura L., *Your Child From One to Six,* Universal New York, 1968.

Toilet training is discussed on pp. 28 to 34 and questions and answers about sex on pp. 70 to 73. Most discussions about child care are divided into age levels for easy reference.

3. Hymes, James L., *How to Tell Your Child About Sex,* Public Affairs Pamphlet, No., 149, New York, 1971.

This twenty-eight page booklet offers much valuable information in an easily-read style that would be appropriate as a suggestion to parents and a worthwhile addition to the day care center lending library.

chapter 10

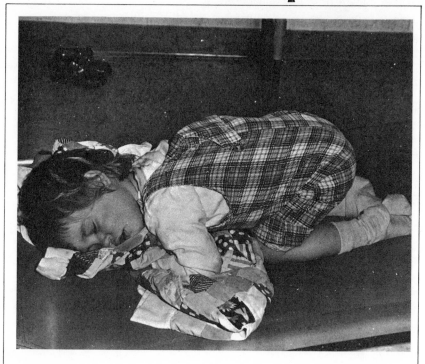

Sleep and Rest

An understanding of children's needs for sleep and rest is important in the study of child guidance for at least three reasons: (1) sleep is a physical need at all ages and, therefore, the child's sleeping habits are basic to his personal adjustment in all areas of living, (2) the alternation of vigorous and quiet activities that is so important to the optimal development of children indicates that adults in the child care center must be aware of how children can be encouraged to rest while in the invigorating group atmosphere, and (3) it is certain that a tired child is an irritable child, and misbehavior that is caused by weariness must be recognized as such if we really are to understand children.

PHYSICAL NEEDS FOR SLEEP AND REST

The newborn baby sleeps most of the time. In fact, his waking hours are only those during which he is being fed, bathed, and diapered. Sometimes, babies even drop off to sleep during these procedures. With increase in age, there is a definite and rapid decrease in the hours spent in sleep. These decreases, of course, are mainly a lessening of sleeping time during daylight hours. Sometimes, however, parents are troubled by the temporary tendency of babies to reverse this pattern—to sleep soundly during the daytime and to be restless when adults are attempting to sleep. Although this problem is likely to be an irritating one, like so many adjustments of infancy and childhood, it soon is replaced by a more acceptable routine if emotional tensions can be avoided. We repeatedly must recognize that the feelings of parents affect the behavior of children and that a relaxed parental attitude is beneficial to children at any age.

Very young infants sleep in a curled position and they usually move very little during their sleep. Before they can move their bodies from the positions in which they are placed, they appear to become tired and it is wise to vary the manner in which they are placed when they are put to bed. The very young baby does not seem to sleep soundly. Sometimes, there is little evidence that he really is asleep. He awakens abruptly when he is hungry, after he is fed he drops off to sleep again, and then he awakens to be fed. His sleep is disturbed by internal stimuli. He will awaken when he feels pain or hunger, but he usually seems impervious to his environment. Loud and sudden noises may bring some response of movement, but ordinary sounds appear to have little effect on his sleeping.

Older infants are slower in getting to sleep and they awaken less abruptly. When the child is capable of changing the position of his body, he usually assumes one that he prefers, and these positions for sleeping become habits. Possibly, people of all ages have unique positions that help to induce slumber. It would be interesting to know if these patterns might have begun in early childhood.

No doubt, the change toward less sleeping with increase in age is due partially to the child's increasing awareness of his environment. When children become interested in looking at their own hands and feet and at people who are nearby and when they become aware of sounds, they naturally spend more of their hours awake. If adults do not interfere nor attempt to set schedules, infants develop their own patterns of sleep. Of course, adult guidance of an indirect nature always exists. As children grow, their feeding, bathing, and sleeping habits become synchronized with the family pattern of living.

Logically, as a baby's stomach enlarges, he eats more at one time, becomes hungry less often, and his periods of sleep become longer. As feeding schedules change, sleeping habits naturally are altered. By the time the child is about one year old, he is sleeping through the night and napping in mid-morning and again in mid-afternoon. Later, the hours of sleep at night and those spent in the afternoon nap remain about the same, but the morning nap is usually discontinued. Obviously, the single naps are usually needed near the mid-point of the waking hours, in the early afternoon.

Individual children are unique in their patterns of sleep. Moreover, physical status, rate of growth, emotional tensions, and amount of motor activity are influential in establishing the needs for sleep and rest. The ill child, the fast-growing child, the child who is emotionally upset, and the physically active child need longer periods of quiet than do children who are not undergoing these stresses. Therefore, it is impossible to prescribe the amount of sleep that children in general should have. This is not surprising when we consider that adult needs for sleep and rest have similar variations from individual to individual and that we do not always know why this is true. Our best approach, then, is to provide opportunities for sleep and rest, to encourage children to set their own schedules, and to be alert for ways in which we can promote whatever pattern is best for each child. This does not mean that children should be allowed to choose their time for sleeping but rather that we can promote regularity in sleeping patterns by setting the general pattern of expectancy according to the needs of the individual child. As long as children are growing, we can assume that they need more sleep than do adults.

INDIVIDUAL VARIATIONS

Getting children to sleep and keeping them asleep seems to be a major problem to most parents, but it is no more possible to force a child to sleep than it is to force him to eat or to perform according to our demands in toilet training. Rather, the child needs to be guided toward a desire for rest or sleep in quantities and at times that are best for his specific pattern and stage of growing and living. It is evident, then, that parents and teachers must evaluate the needs of individual children. Children can be encouraged to rest by the way in which their daily schedules are planned.

Nap time is important in the schedules of preschool children. The majority of children are more willing to be left alone at nap time than at bedtime. Children vary in the napping time needed. Young children who attend school sometimes sleep as much as two to three hours in the afternoon. Many children awaken slowly and unless the nap is so late in the afternoon or so long that it may interfere with bedtime it is usually better to let the child awaken naturally. Some children seem to awaken easily, but others appear to feel miserable on awakening. These children may cry vigorously, and they usually will recover their composure more easily if adults pay little attention to them.

A quiet time in bed often is the only nap needed by the older preschool child and parents need not be alarmed if children do not actually sleep during these nap periods. Obviously, the very active child needs more rest than the less active one. It is not unusual to observe healthy children alternate periods of vigorous and quiet activity with no guidance from adults. Too often, probably, we find it difficult to permit children to do what is best for them.

David and Jerry were active four-year-olds at the preschool. They were never quiet during outdoor play. They rode the tricycles at a rapid pace around the yard, they climbed up and down the jungle gym several times during a ten-minute observation period, they played follow-the-leader on the slippery slides, and they frequently wrestled with each other as they rolled over and over on the playground.

When these children came indoors, they invariably chose listening to musical records as their favorite activity. Occasionally, students and visitors would remark that they thought these children should be encouraged to indulge in group activities indoors.

When winter came and outdoor play periods had to be shortened, however, David and Jerry of their own accord spent less time at the record player. They became more interested in block play, creative activities, and dramatic games indoors.

When these children were less weary, they no longer spent as much time in quiet activity. We should realize, however, that when children become too tired or overstimulated, it is usually extremely difficult for them to rest and they may need adult help. Environmental aids for these children are discussed later in this chapter.

When children rest or sleep at school, individual differences are evident. Sometimes, children who often resort to so-called misbehavior during free play are paragons of conformity during routine activities.

Fred had many characteristics that might be considered obstreperous. He had developed little emotional control, and firm support by the teacher was usually necessary at least once during each session.

During routine activities, there were no problems with Fred. He was capable of setting his own toileting schedule and he took special delight in his ability to wash and dry his hands in an adult manner. Sometimes, he resorted to water throwing or loud talking when other children were in the washroom, but he would return quickly to the routine when reminded by an adult or when other children left the room. Fred was adept with his clothing, and he moved quietly through the cloakroom. His eating patterns were exemplary and his ability to converse pleasantly at mealtime created a good situation for the other children at his table. His table manners met adult standards. He seemed to forget these manners only when other children interfered with his eating. At these times, he would show brief aggression and then revert to his quiet behavior. At rest time, Fred always was the best rester. Students who knew Fred but had not remained at school for lunch were amazed by his quiet demeanor during the rest period preceding the meal and during the mealtime.

Since human behavior is not caused by a single characteristic nor a single experience, Fred's attitudes and abilities in routine situations were no doubt based on several causes. As has been stated, children usually set their own best pattern and, since this child showed frequent emotional outbursts during play, he may have found needed security in the routines. In these activities, there is less variety from day to day, other children are not as likely to interfere with individual pursuits, and the skills necessary for good performance are always the same so that there is little need for problem solving.

Fred's advanced level of performance may have reflected adult pressures at home. There may have been an emphasis on learning adult manners and practices so that these behavior patterns had been mastered. In fact, rigid training of this kind might have explained his tendency to feel thwarted and frustrated when he was placed in a less structured situation and might explain his tendency for overt emotional expressions during free play. Whatever the reasons, it is evident that many responses of children depend on the situation and we cannot always predict the behavior pattern on the basis of observation in other activities. Occasionally, children who are conformists in group play become difficult to handle during rest periods.

Gary was a timid three-year-old. Most of his play was solitary. He would stand at the perimeter of the playground and watch the other children. Indoors, his favorite pastimes were working the jigsaw puzzles or listening to the record player. Sometimes, he would load one of the toy trucks with blocks or wooden animals and push it around the playroom floor, but he always was careful to avoid coming into contact with other children or their toys.

During the half hour rest period before lunch, it seemed impossible for Gary to be quiet. He would sit up on his cot and try to attract the attention of other children by waving his arms or making noises or he would lie on his cot and kick his legs so that the cot would slide noisily on the floor

Obviously Gary did not use enough energy during the morning activities to develop a need for rest. Also, it may be that this was one time when Gary found he was capable of attracting the attention of other children and adults.

Inducements for sleep should be chosen with careful consideration of the individual child. Most young preschoolers will be more likely to go to sleep if a quiet period precedes nap time or bedtime. Often, a story told or read is a good prelude. Usually, toileting and a drink of water will insure the child's physical comfort.

At home, a period of companionship with mother or father will often help to promote sleep. Of course, it is not always possible for a parent to devote much time to the child when older siblings and household chores need attention but the young child certainly needs reassurance that he is loved. Some children can be permitted to look at a favorite book or to play quietly in bed and then to turn out the light for themselves.

Children who are overtired or in poor health need more sleep than relaxed and healthy children but, frequently, it is difficult for these children to drop off to sleep even when we have provided comfortable surroundings. Occasionally, physical contact by an adult will help children relax.

Ellen Norris was small and agile. By nap time at the child care center, it was evident that she was very tired and that she needed to be quiet. Yet, Ellen wiggled and turned when she lay on her cot. Within a few seconds, she would be sitting on the edge of the cot, swinging her legs, or she would move to another child's cot and annoy him in some way.

Miss Rose recognized Ellen's need and tried to find some way to help her. In an effort to reduce Ellen's weariness, she asked one of the aides to suggest a story to Ellen as a break in the period of free play before lunch time. Ellen's ability to relax did not improve. Miss Rose then moved Ellen's cot apart from the other children, thinking that she would be less likely to be distracted. This, too, was ineffective.

Finally, the teacher moved her own chair close to Ellen's cot and, when Ellen seemed restless, she would place her hand affectionately on Ellen's head or shoulders. This gesture of physical contact seemed to help Ellen. Although she did not become a quiet rester, she usually was able to sleep for a part of the time set aside for naps.

Sometimes, centers should provide special opportunities for sleep to children.

Lucy was not a robust child and her home environment was not conducive to regularity of resting. There were four older siblings, two boys and a girl in junior high school and a boy in the fifth grade. Lucy's parents owned and operated a bakery and delicatessen in the front part of their dwelling and her mother and father baked the pastries during the very early morning.

Lucy always looked tired when she arrived at the center. She did not enter into play of any type and, sometimes, she would fall asleep during the story period. One day, when Lucy seemed to be especially weary, Miss Fisher asked if she would like to go in the teachers' lounge and rest for awhile.

Lucy fell asleep immediately and slept until time for outdoor play. On subsequent days, she expressed her desire to take a nap and she was permitted to do so. Sometimes, these naps would last only a few minutes. On other days, Lucy would sleep an hour or two each morning but she was always ready to relax again at nap time.

Although parents do not send their children to the preschool to sleep, this appeared to be this child's most urgent need. No doubt, small living quarters, the diverse sleeping schedules of the various age levels in the home, and the confusion and noise of the family business all served to rob this child of the sleep she needed. This case also indicated that sometimes children can be too weary to relax.

It is not uncommon to detect unusual signs of drowsiness at the preschool. When children seem to be unusually lethargic, it is wise to watch them closely with the possibility of incipient illness in mind. Sometimes, the child's actions will indicate that he should be isolated for a short period of rest and observation or even that his parents should be called and a report made to them.

Frequently, parents report that their child does not sleep soundly because he has bad dreams. Since young preschoolers are not skilled in telling us all about their experiences, it may be that they dream more often than we know.

Probably we can be certain that they do have dreams. By middle preschool years, children's imaginative thinking is apparent in their daytime activities, so it would seem logical that their dreams would have become more elaborate and varied.

That children's dreams often are frightening is demonstrated by the fact that some children occasionally awaken crying in the middle of the night. Sometimes, they will give us clues as to the nature of their dreams. It is not surprising that some of these dreams are frightening when we realize that, by this time, adults consider it necessary to caution children concerning the dangers in their environment. Probably, stimulating activity, a heavy meal, or television viewing may be contributing causes. Of course, it is wise to avoid anything near bedtime that may disturb the sleep of a preschooler. When children awaken crying, usually it is easy to reassure them and to help them get back to sleep. Sometimes, a small light in the room or in a nearby room will be comforting.

Many young children are afraid of the dark. This may be promoted by parents in their efforts to instill caution in the child. Other children, or even adults who have taken care of children during parents' absences, may have laid the foundation for these fears. Other causes may be guilt feelings, illness, overfatigue, overstimulation, the absence of parents, a strange room, or bad dreams.

Some children can be reassured quickly by parents who comfort them and who explain that their fears are normal but that they need not feel afraid. Other children may need prolonged reassurance of some kind. Occasionally, fear of the dark can be dispelled for the older preschooler if he can have a small flashlight to tuck under his pillow. Sometimes, children will attempt to gain special attention or to postpone bedtime by pretending to be afraid of the dark or of dreaming. Knowledge of the child is the best gauge for our judgment in these situations. The best way to help a child to sleep varies from child to child and from age to age and no particular way is certain to be successful.

Several techniques for promoting rest at the child care center are practical. Screens or other devices that separate one child from another may prove helpful. A well-ventilated room and a lightweight, warm cover of some type will promote the child's comfort. Sleep will be easier to attain if the room is darkened, and the arrangement of the room should be uniform from day to day.

Moreover, children will be more likely to sleep if the room is not one in which they are accustomed to playing. If the building is not large enough to provide a separate room, screens or curtains should be placed so that toys will not be visible. Thoughtful preparation is necessary. Children should be encouraged to use the toilet and to wash before they lie down, and shoes and tight clothing should be removed. Vigorous play just before nap time is stimulating, so planning a story hour or a period of listening to quiet music is a wise program choice.

The adults who supervise nap periods should be those with whom the children are well acquainted and comfortable. If these teachers or assistants know the child well, they will allow each child to set his own pace and to prepare for sleep in his own special way. Sometimes, a child will seem to need extra time to get settled. Adult patience is likely to be rewarding. Interestingly, the ability to relax sometimes seems somewhat contagious and it may be easier for children to relax in a group situation. The placement of individual children often is a good form of indirect guidance. The child who rests easily, if placed next to a child who has difficulty in relaxing, occasionally will have a good influence on the second child.

Adults who have infrequent assignments or who are new to the day care center usually will not be successful in supervising nap periods. If a student finds herself with this responsibility, she should not be surprised if the children do not relax in their customary manner. Quiet times provide opportunities for children to test the limits of behavior that are set for them, and only those adults who have good rapport with the group are likely to be successful in maintaining a semblance of order when children are unoccupied. Moreover, only an experienced teacher will be able to judge what techniques will promote rest in a specific group of children. Some teachers may choose to play quiet music on the record player or to sing quietly; others sometimes tell stories that are not stimulating.

Children who have regular and sufficient sleep at home usually are healthy and happy children. When groups of parents discuss their preschool children, it is not uncommon for them to mention the factor of noise as it affects their children's sleep. As stated previously, the very young infant does not seem to be aware of external auditory stimuli except for extremely loud or sudden noises but, as children become alert to their surroundings, they are more alert to the sounds around them. Probably it is unwise to try to eliminate ordinary noises after children have gone to bed since absolute quiet cannot always be maintained in any household without curtailing family activities. In fact, a quiet place for the child is impossible in most dwellings. Several decades ago, the majority of families lived in large houses and sleeping rooms were set apart from living areas in these dwellings. At present, the majority of families live in small houses, small apartments, or in mobile homes. These circumstances are not necessarily detrimental, however. If children become accustomed to a certain amount of noise when they are sleeping, they are likely to be able to sleep under diverse conditions later.

Just as adult attitudes are important in all areas of child guidance, children are more likely to go to sleep promptly and to sleep soundly if adults regard regualr sleeping hours as an accepted part of the daily schedule. The fact that early evening hours often are the only ones that parents spend with their children creates a problem. These parents would be wise to develop their talents in quiet story telling, lullaby singing, watching a television program suitable for children, and providing companionship for the child in so-doing, or scheduling a brief and leisurely walk outdoors with the child. Giving the youngster time for parental companionship is the important circumstance. Energetic play should be postponed for Saturday afternoons and Sundays.

Impatience and haste at bedtime probably are worse than vigorous physical activity. The late afternoon and early evening hours usually are hurried times in most homes. All family members tend to be tired and hungry. Probably, older children want to discuss the day's problems, perhaps the parents are expecting company or are planning to go somewhere. At the same time, the young child needs to be bathed, fed, and made comfortable for the night. Studied consideration of what things are most important is necessary.

Certainly, if parents and young children can be unhurried, the child's bedtime can be a time for close companionship, and the resultant feelings of trust and affection will be helpful in all parent-child relationships. For some reason, companionship and affection are especially satisfying at this time of day.

When there are older brothers and sisters, going to bed is particularly difficult for the young child. Older siblings are heroes and heroines to many preschoolers and they want to copy their behavior. Then, too, an early bedtime means separation from the family and, naturally, this is not pleasant. From the child's point of view, we are being unfair to him. Since young children need more sleep than older people, it is necessary that they go to bed earlier, but we can make it as pleasant for them as possible. Parents must be careful to let the child know that going to bed is not a punishment. They should take the child to bed, not send him to bed.

Here are some suggestions for a successful bedtime for the preschool child.

1. Set a regular bedtime for the child so he will know what to expect.

2. Avoid stimulating activity for the child near the bedtime hour.

3. Do not schedule a meal near the child's bedtime.

4. Avoid excessive intake of liquids after his evening meal.

5. Give the child a few minutes warning so he can become accustomed to the idea of going to bed.

6. Show consistency and firmness and indicate that you expect the child to go to bed and to sleep.

7. Be patient and unhurried so the child will be encouraged to relax.

8. Provide a cool, quiet, darkened room and a comfortable bed with lightweight covers.

9. Never send a child to bed as punishment for misbehavior. Use your influence toward his belief that bedtime is a pleasant time.

Sleep patterns of perschool children are not easy to study during a field experience because long-term observation of both naps and night-time sleeping is not possible. Moreover, these patterns are affected when visitors are present. Also, it is difficult to assess the soundness of sleep unless the adult is well-acquainted with the individual child. Students, however, can observe evidences of fatigue in children, children's attitudes toward rest, and their specific and unique abilities to relax.

SUGGESTED ASSIGNMENT

Part I

Observe a group of children for at least thirty minutes and answer the following questions.

1. What evidences of fatigue did you see? Tell why you think the behavior described resulted from fatigue and discuss your evidence.

2. Describe and comment on any subsequent behavior that you think was caused by fatigue.

Part II

Observe nap time at the preschool and answer the following questions.

1. What specific features of the room were conducive to good rest?

2. How did the teacher encourage the children to rest? Be specific.

3. What methods of guidance were employed for individual children? Were they successful? Describe.

Part III

Talk to at least one parent of a preschool child and record that family's procedural plan for the late afternoon and early evening hours.

SELECTED READINGS

1. Breckenridge, Marian E., and Margaret Nesbitt Murphy, *Growth and Development of the Young Child,* rev. ed., W. B. Saunders, Philadelphia, 1963.

These authors emphasize the need for a balance of activity and rest by the young child. Developmental patterns of sleep as reported from research studies are described in detail. Levels of sleep as they occur at various stages of development are discussed.

2. Jersild, Arthur T., *Child Psychology,* 5th ed., Prentice-Hall, Englewood Cliffs, N. J., 1960.

Jersild presents approximate amounts of sleep needed at various stages of development and discusses parental guidance that is likely to encourage pleasant family interaction at bedtime.

3. Landreth, Catherine, *Early Childhood: Behavior and Learning,* 2nd ed., Alfred A. Knopf, N. Y., 1969.

This author discusses recent research in classifying levels of activity as related to children's sleeping patterns. This description would be helpful to the student who is planning a major field of study in child development or child psychology.

4. Stone, L. J., and J. Church, *Childhood and Adolescence,* 2nd ed., Random House, 1968.

Patterns of rest and sleep at various stages of development from birth to adolescence are described in an interesting manner. This book would be a good choice for the student or parent who desires to gain knowledge about growth beyond the preschool level.

chapter 11

Food for Children

A child's eating habits are influenced by his nutritional needs, his level of development, his individual likes and dislikes, and the impact of the culture in which he lives. How hunger can be satisfied and how to plan the ingestion of necessary nutrients by the child are of primary importance to those who guide young children.

NUTRITIONAL NEEDS

Normal children are much alike in their nutritional requirements. During preschool years, they are gaining rapidly in weight and height. They need food that will make them grow, food that will build muscles, bones, blood, and sound teeth. They need food that will keep their bodies in good running order. They need food that gives them energy to play and work and learn.

There is concern at present about the effects of malnutrition not only on physical growth but also on mental development. This concern has been magnified by the extent of malnutrition among children in many parts of the world. Nutritional status during the time of development of the nervous system is considered to be especially important because of the probable formation of fewer brain cells in the malnourished child. Since brain size is almost complete by age two, we can assume that the prenatal period and infancy are critical times.

Experts have suggested that more research is needed to determine other periods of life when mental development may be influenced by nutritional patterns, what degree and duration of malnutrition may produce functional changes in the ability to think and reason, and whether such changes are permanent. Studies of malnourished children have shown slower intellectual development as measured by mental tests with especially low scores in visual-motor ability, pattern perception, and short-term memory. Certainly, it is reasonable to believe that lowered vitality and energy due to lack of adequate amounts or kinds of foods would have an effect on physical efficiency. Both physical and mental activity are dependent on the energy supply available within the individual.

Planning a balanced diet is easy. Nutritionists list foods in four basic groups: (1) protein foods consisting of meat, fish, eggs, fowl, lentils, dried peas, dried beans, nuts, or peanut butter; (2) milk foods that include milk, cottage cheese, cheddar-type cheese, and ice cream and ice milk; (3) cereal foods consisting of anything made of whole or enriched grains including bread, breakfast foods, spaghetti, rice, grits, cornmeal products and baked goods; and (4) vegetable and fruit foods that consist of oranges, grapefruit, tomatoes, dark green vegetables, and deep yellow fruits or vegetables. Some experts include potatoes in the cereal group.

A primary food at all ages is milk. Milk is especially valuable in the child's diet because of the kind and amount of protein, calcium, phosphorus, and vitamins it contains. During early preschool years, the child's meals should be planned with careful consideration of his intake of milk. Milk is excellent for bone, tooth, and muscle building. Usually, it is easy to get a child to take an adequate amount of milk. Since milk is the first food children consume and is supplemented gradually by other foods, a large majority of preschoolers consider milk an important part of the mealtime menu.

When foods are prepared for young children, it is wise to use large quantities of milk in cooking. It can be used in soups, sauces, casserole dishes, custards, and puddings. Milk used in food is just as good for the child as milk that he drinks. Milk intake also can be supplemented by mid-morning and mid-afternoon snacks composed of milk in combination with another food such as a cracker, a simple cookie, toast, or fruit.

If a child is not fond of milk or tends to drink only small amounts, usually it can be made more attractive by changing the pattern of service. Children may be tempted if it is served in decorative glasses or cups, with colored straws for sipping, or if a bit of sugar and vanilla extract, maple flavoring, or chocolate is added. Sometimes, milk is more appealing if it is served in a bowl with animal crackers or small pieces of toast floating on top.

Cheese can be used to supplement milk consumption. Cheddar cheese is the type most nearly like milk in calcium and phosphorus content. Cubes of cheddar cheese present an intersting change from the fruit juice or milk customarily served at mid-morning or mid-afternoon. Cottage cheese is a good source of protein also, but it does not contain as great an amount of minerals as an equal quantity of cheddar cheese.

When we plan to meet the nutritional needs of children, eggs are much more likely than some other kinds of foods to be provided in insufficient quantities. One egg a day is an accepted rule for nutritional needs at all age levels past infancy. Eggs are excellent for muscle building and since they are a protein they can be substituted for meat if provided in excess of the requirement just mentioned. Variety of service should be stressed and ingenuity can be exercised by including whole eggs in most pudding recipes and in many casserole dishes. Despite the recent controversy about the damaging effects of cholesterol, we can assume that the diets of young children should contain eggs unless an allergy exists.

Meat, too, is an important food for the young child and he should have at least one helping each day. For the preschooler it should be lean and tender and in an easy-to-eat form. If meat is too difficult to manage or to chew, young children may decide it is not worth the effort. It is not unusual for older children to dislike meat because of these original impressions, whereas if it is served in an acceptable form and the child learns to enjoy the particular flavor he will not be adverse later to making more effort to eat it. Occasionally, some adult will express a dislike for certain types of meat and it is interesting to speculate about the background reasons for such dislikes.

Meats can be served picnic style in small sandwiches, chopped and added to other well-liked foods, or cut in strips of a size for easy finger-eating. Careful preparation with the child's hand and chewing skills in mind probably is the key factor that will indicate his like or dislike of the meat. Peanut butter is a good source of protein and can be used as a meat substitute. Most preschool children like peanut butter. If the texture of this food seems too gummy for the child, peanut butter sandwiches can be varied by mixing it with soft butter or margarine or small quantities of jelly or mayonnaise.

Leafy green and yellow vegetables should be included in children's diets. Carrots, green beans, peas, green lima beans, spinach, sweet potatoes, asparagus, lettuce, celery, cabbage, onions, cauliflower, broccoli, turnips, and beets are all nutritious. Types of preparation of some of these may dictate acceptance or rejection by young children who are likely to refuse foods that are dry or stringy in texture. Frequently, cream sauces will make a vegetable more appetizing. Moreover, sauces can give enough consistency to make eating easier. We must remember that small children have not acquired sufficient manipulative skills to handle spoons and forks easily. They may become discouraged when they try to pick up peas, string beans, or diced carrots with the utensils provided. Sometimes, their refusal to eat these foods may be caused simply because it does not seem worth the effort. Occasionally, it is good to serve slippery foods in combination with strips of toast or raw vegetables that can serve as pushers for elusive morsels. Since children will eventually learn to conform to social practices, it usually is wise to allow a child to use his fingers for eating rather than create emotional tensions that prevent his eating the foods he needs. Table manners are usually learned through modeling rather than through admonition.

One leafy vegetable such as lettuce or spinach should be served each day. These often are more appealing if they are offered raw. Carrot or celery sticks, pieces of raw cauliflower or lettuce, usually are special favorites since they are attractive and easy to eat and add variety to the texture of the meal. Children who will not eat some vegetables when they are cooked often like them raw.

When children do not like vegetables, a good practice may be to let the child choose the vegetable he wants for a particular meal. Children, like adults, do not always want the same food day after day. Self-selection within limits dictated by nutritional needs is good. This practice is in accordance with wise methods of guidance and often promotes better eating habits. Sometimes, adults cause eating problems in children by insisting that they eat specific foods when substitutes are just as nutritious and may be more acceptable to the child.

Potatoes, macaroni, spaghetti, rice, and flour contain large amounts of carbohydrates. They are inexpensive, energy-giving foods. Potatoes definitely should be included in the diets of preschoolers. Macaroni, rice, spaghetti, and flour combinations can be used satisfactorily in planning well-balanced meals, and it is easy to prepare them in combination with milk so they can be especially nutritious. However, since they are cereal foods, they should not be used to supplant potatoes.

Cereals are essential in the diet of a small child. They are an economical source of elements necessary for energy and are also rich in B vitamins. For younger children, cooked cereals are preferable since they are more likely to contain the whole grain and to be less bulky and filling. If children are resistent to eating cereals, variety in methods of service will be helpful. A drop of food coloring may make the cereal more attractive or a piece of fruit, a piece of chocolate, or a marshmallow hidden in the bottom of the bowl may create interest in eating the cereal to reach the surprise. Cereals served with cinnamon-flavored milk or with honey instead of sugar often are more appealing to children. These practices are preferable to providing sugar coated cereals and other foods that are high in sugar content and, therefore, dull the appetite for other foods.

One slice of bread is considered equal to a serving of cereal, and as children grow older much of their daily need for cereal can be provided by serving sandwiches. Graham bread, whole wheat, and rye breads will furnish the extra nutritional values of the whole grain cereal foods.

Fruits should be included in menus for young children. Apples, plums, peaches, pears, cherries, pineapple, and well-ripened bananas are good for children. Sometimes, it is good to serve a variety of small pieces of colorful fruit since its appearance may make the meal more interesting. Dried fruits such as raisins, prunes, apples, apricots, and peaches in bite-size pieces are good for between-meal snacks. One citrus fruit such as oranges or grapefruit should be served each day unless tomatoes or tomato juice is consumed. Vitamin C is the essential element in these foods, and it is wise to remember that when tomatoes are substituted for citrus fruits, twice as much in quantity is necessary for the same intake of the vitamin. Most canned and frozen juices are comparatively high in vitamin content.

Butter and fortified margarine are important when we plan meals for young children. These foods supply energy and contain vitamin A. One or two tablespoons of fat are sufficient for preschoolers, however, and greater amounts are likely to reduce appetites for other necessary foods. Butter and margarine can be used to best advantage on toast strips or as flavoring for vegetables.

Sufficient quantities of fluids usually present no problem with preschool children. The five to six cups necessary in the daily diet are often exceeded through the intake of milk and fruit juice. It is sensible, however, to offer water to very young children between meals and to make it possible for older children to help themselves to water when they are thirsty.

Many wholly acceptable foods have not been included in this discussion. Some of these are: plain cookies and cakes, bland salad dressings, gelatin puddings, jellies, preserves, and jams. Although these should never supplant the essential nutrients, they are sources of energy and are helpful in adding variety to menus.

Desserts often present problems for parents. Young children should not have rich desserts because they are difficult to digest and an abundance of sweet foods tends to lessen appetites for foods that children really need. Sweets are energy foods, however, and should be provided regularly as a part of the meal. Appropriate desserts for children are: custard, junket, stewed or raw fruits, fruit whips, sherbet, ice cream, or jello. These should be served casually at the end of the meal and never offered as bribes either for eating or for other behavior. Using desserts or candy as bribes is likely to enhance their value and to create a greater desire for them by the child.

Soft drinks often are considered a treat but they should be provided sparingly because they have no food value except for calories. By providing a variety in milk drinks and in kinds of fruit juice served, we can satisfy most preschool appetites. If a child has an excessive craving for sweet foods, it may be that he is not receiving enough energy-producing foods and his diet should be reviewed for evidences of deprivation. Conversely, he may have developed poor habits previously. For example, there may have been too much sugar content in his formula. In this event, perseverance in breaking the habit may be the best resource.

Highly seasoned foods are not good for young children. Interestingly, many accepted rules for the care of preschool children have sound reasons when we know how children grow. In this instance, physiological structure indicates that condiments should be supplied for children's diets in only limited amounts. Children's taste buds are not only on the surface of the tongue as they are in adulthood, but they also line the insides of the cheeks. This is evident when we see children roll their food around in their mouths in order to test the flavor. Moreover, much of our sense of taste is enhanced by the way foods smell and, since children do not possess the hairy covering that lines the nasal cavities, we can be assured that taste differentiation is more clearly defined for them.

Food jags are not unusual for preschool children. Sometimes, we must remember that it is not the specific intake for a particular day that is important but rather the fact that, over a period of several days or even a week, the child's dietary requirements are met. It is wise to remember that adults, also, crave certain foods at some times. Some leniency in letting the child choose his own foods within specific limits is our best policy.

Many factors should be considered when children have poor appetites. If we are assured that they are healthy, it is well to consider what the reasons might be. Perhaps children drink water or milk thirstily before they approach solid food. In this case, it is wise to suggest a drink of water several minutes before mealtime and, perhaps, to be a little slow in providing the milk that will accompany the meal. We should remember that milk leaves the stomach more slowly than most other foods and, therefore, influences the appetite for a longer time after ingestion. Frequently, children are too tired to be hungry. Quiet activities or a few minutes of rest before mealtime are good practices. Sometimes, too, children may be too hungry. If we suspect this to be true, we should increase amounts served at mid-morning or mid-afternoon.

Our cultural familiarity with eating three meals a day has led us to believe that this is a nutritionally sound pattern and often parents consider it undesirable for their children to eat extensively between meals because it might spoil the appetite at mealtime and thereby interfere with good nutrition. However, research has proved that a specified intake of nutrients taken in small amounts at relatively frequent intervals may be more desirable than eating the same quantity of food in larger meals. Eating between meals is good for young children if nutritious and sensible foods are provided and if servings are not large enough to jeopardize normal appetites at mealtime. The stomach capacity of the young child is not large and it is logical that he probably needs to eat more often than adults do. Between-meal snacks should be provided at regualr times. If food is given to a child whenever he asks for it, however, he probably will increase the number of his requests and detrimental eating habits will be formed because, ultimately, this practice will interfere with his enjoyment of regular meals.

Children acquire their food habits in their homes. Cultural and home factors in dietary choice are important in planning meals for child care centers. It is not uncommon for the child who is new in the center to eat sparingly because the food is dissimilar to the menus of his family. Many preschools include food check-lists as a part of enrollment procedures. These should be comprehensive. They should include lists of meats, casseroles, vegetables, breads, cereals, fruits and desserts. Under each of these categories, the parent can then check: (1) "likes," (2) "dislikes," or (3) "has never tasted." Giving the parent an opportunity to present a simple recipe that the family enjoys may provide the cook in the preschool a new menu idea that will enable the child to feel more at home during his introduction to the group.

EMOTIONAL ASPECTS OF FOOD

Infants really discover the world through their experiences with food. The need for food probably brings their first feelings of discomfort and their being fed brings their first physical satisfactions and their first feelings of emotional security because of the affectionate ministrations of the adult who cares for them. The importance of eating habits is apparent in our culture. Even in adulthood, our most pleasant social experiences are likely to be closely associated with eating in the company of other people.

During the first few months of life, all eating consists only of sucking and swallowing, and it is important that children are provided with adequate amounts of milk whether they are breast fed or bottle fed. The processes of eating should be emotionally satisfying to them, also. Each infant appears to have his own rhythm of eating just as he has his unique rhythm of sleeping. Mothers soon become aware of the quantities their children desire as well as the approximate feeding schedule that seems to satisfy the child. During the early months of life, babies grow rapidly and healthy babies usually have excellent appetites. If the breast milk or the formula is readily digested, feeding problems are almost nonexistent.

When children begin to eat solid foods, servings should be small. An accepted rule is one level tablespoonful of a basic food for each year of age during the preschool years. Like all rules, this standard should not be considered definite. Children vary as to the amounts of food they need for proper growth and health, and individual appetites vary from one time to another. The important fact is that we should consider food from the child's point of view. Large servings can be discouraging and it is far better to insure a feeling of a pleasant mealtime experience by serving small quantities and providing second servings according to the child's requests.

The rate of growth in height and weight decelerates during the second year of life and we cannot expect children to be as hungry as they were when they were younger. When adults are accustomed to hearty eating by children, it is easy to become alarmed when appetites lag. Thus, there may be a tendency to coax the child and, by this coaxing, to create an eating problem. Children soon learn that refusals to eat are likely to result in increased attention from grownups. In fact, this behavior probably is the child's most successful method for controlling the adults with whom he lives. Many examples are evident when we study children who attend preschools.

Scott was four-year-old. His parents often worried about their methods in his guidance. They requested frequent interviews with staff members. His mother, Mrs. York, was aware of her lack of consistency in setting limits for Scott's behavior. She was apprehensive about his tendency to treat other children aggressively and his many refusals to conform to acceptable behavior patterns. During parent-staff interviews, she often reiterated her determination to display anger toward Scott less often and to be more patient with him. She stated that she had not encountered these problems with his older brother who was six years his senior, but that she had always had a tendency to indulge Scott one minute and to berate him the next.

Scott was not considered a problem child at the center. Sometimes it was necessary to take measures to avoid his impending aggression but he appeared to welcome this support from adults. He displayed more than average affection for his group teacher.

One morning in the middle of a school week, Mrs. York telephoned and excitedly asked if Scott were eating normally at school. No differences in his food habits had been noted by the teachers. He had eaten as heartily as usual at snack time and at lunch time the day before. Mrs. York stated that Scott had refused to eat anything for supper the night before and that it had required coaxing to get him to taste his cereal at breakfast. He had eaten only a teaspoonful of the one food. She had taken his temperature, but it was normal and he did not appear to be ill.

That morning, Scott seemed unusually hungry at snack time. He ate three of the finger-size rye bread and butter sandwiches and drank three small glasses of orange juice, the maximum amounts available for each child. At lunch time, Scott ate heartily as usual and he seemed satisfied with second servings of only the foods that he liked especially well. His light afternoon snack seemed to have unusual appeal.

On the following morning, Mrs. York called and reported that Scott had refused both supper and breakfast at home. She seemed puzzled by the report of his natural behavior at school and said that if it were not for her confidence in the teachers she certainly would have called a doctor and made other arrangements for Scott that day. The director assured Scott's mother that he was eating well at school, that she believed he would resume his usual eating patterns when he was really hungry, and she advised Mrs. York to try to ignore his refusals of food at home for a day or two at least.

Soon after Scott came indoors on the third morning, he went to the kitchen door and spoke to the cook who was well-liked by the children, "I'm hungry. Can I have something to eat?" The cook explained to Scott that the food for snack time had not been prepared but that it would not be long until time for the children to eat.

At snack time, Scott seemed ravenously hungry and he whined and refused to leave the table when the student teacher told him there was no more food.

His appetite did not seem quite as good as usual when lunch time came, however. The long week-end vacation followed and, subsequently, Mrs. York reported that Scott gradually had resumed eating although not as heartily as usual.

We can only speculate that some emotional tension may have been responsible for Scott's behavior and that the attention that his refusal of food brought to him at home must have been satisfying in some way. Seldom do we have the opportunity to observe such an obvious example of a child's attempts to cause anxiety in his parents. From the child's point of view, we must recognize that there was some good reason for his behavior, but we certainly feel sympathy for the mother in her efforts to accept his unusual actions. This example also demonstrated that excessive hunger can be detrimental to a good appetite. This was shown by Scott's decreased appetite on the third day at school.

It is surprising how quickly children learn the power that they can wield by their refusals to eat. Ironically, the most conscientious parents often are the ones who have eating problems with their children and who find it especially difficult to accept this behavior calmly.

Bobby was a three-year-old who was slight in build. Both of his parents were professional people and he was an only child. The last words his mother spoke when she left him at the school in the morning always concerned her hope that he would eat a "big lunch" and when she called for him at the end of the session, she always said something like, "Did you enjoy your lunch today?" Frequently, she would call to one of the teachers and say, "I noticed there wasn't a thing on the menu today that Bobby likes. Are you sure he really ate at lunch time?"

Bobby was not growing rapidly and he did not eat as heartily as some of the other children. He was considered "a good eater" at school, however, since he seemed to enjoy all foods and often requested second servings when he liked a food especially well.

Some of these experiences reaffirm one of the advantages of preschools. Occasionally, children seem to be more relaxed when they are in the care of someone who does not have the sole responsibility for their well-being. Then, too, when other children are eating and apparently enjoying their food, it is much easier to do likewise. This, of course, is not limited to the preschool age.

In Bobby's case, it is probable that many of the eating problems at home would have been lessened if his mother had not been so worried about the quantities he ate. It is interesting to note that his mother was likely to discuss what she considered a food problem in Bobby's presence. Obviously, this conversation with a teacher might have provided a form of attention that was pleasing to Bobby or it might have created guilt feelings because of his failure to meet parental expectations. Neither reaction would have been helpful to Bobby. The importance of not discussing children's behavior in their hearing cannot be overemphasized. A telephone call or a note slipped to the teacher would have been preferable.

Sometimes, emotional tensions in both children and their parents result from interference by other adults. It is not unusual for outsiders to be critical concerning the manner in which children are trained in the routines of toilet training, sleeping, and eating. Derogatory comments often are heard when these training procedures are observed.

A pediatrician recommended that Karen Thompson's mother take her to a nearby town so that she could be hospitalized for a tonsillectomy. Karen was five years old.

Karen remained in the hospital overnight and spent the following night with her mother in a hotel. The next morning they had breakfast there. Cinnamon toast was a special favorite with Karen. Her mother suggested that she should eat a cooked cereal instead, but finally acquiesced and asked the waitress to make the toast very soft. When the toast was placed on the table, Karen's mother tore the crusts off as Karen ate the soft centers of the slices of bread.

When they had almost finished eating, a dignified older woman whom they did not know left a nearby table, stopped by Karen's chair, and said to Mrs. Thompson, "I'd think you'd be ashamed of yourself, letting that child get by with not eating the crusts of her toast."

Some mothers would be amused by this incident and some would be angry, but often such an experience is not pleasant for either parent or child.

Preschool children are great imitators and adults should refrain from discussing or displaying their own dislikes for certain foods. Children definitely acquire their food likes and dislikes in the home. These depend not only on ethnic patterns but also on family preferences because parents usually serve the foods that family members like the most. Sometimes, the variety is surprisingly limited and we can conclude that children have had opportunities to explore food interests in only a narrow range. This is regrettable since, during these years, children are intent on learning about their surroundings, indicating that it is the best time for them to learn to know and to enjoy a variety of foods.

From the child's point of view, eating can be an interesting procedure apart from the pleasure of satisfying hunger. When new foods are offered, it is wise to observe the way in which children react. Children are likely to be interested enough to taste the food, but if they do not it is best to ignore the refusal and to try the food again at another time. A new food always should be introduced in very small servings. It should be offered several times, but if the child demonstrates a specific dislike it is best to delete that food for the present time and to substitute another with similar nutritional qualities. If this is done, the child will be much more likely to approach the food later in an accepting manner. As with other experiences, grownups often have a tendency to try to force their attitudes on the children whom they guide.

It is better to combine one less popular food with several well-liked ones in a meal. This is a good plan for any age. Since young children naturally like to test and taste and try new things, it is probable that the combination may be pleasing to them. Combining foods of varying textures is also a good practice. Sometimes, we tend to think that the appearance of children's meals makes little difference, but when we consider that they are extremely alert to trivial things in their environment, we know that their sensitivity indicates that food should be attractive, varied in texture and in taste.

A good rule to consider is to plan a meal that includes a crisp food, a soft food, and a food that requires chewing. Although children's foods should not be highly seasoned, the meal will be more appealing if it contains foods with contrasting flavors. Color is important, also, and colorful meals are not difficult to plan when we consider the kinds of foods recommended for young children.

The following menus exemplify these rules:

Meat loaf	Baked eggs	Beef stew
Sweet potatoes	Beet slices	Letuce wedges
Buttered raisin	Creamed cauliflower	Whole wheat toast
bread	Toast strips	Whipped cherry
Celery sticks	Pineapple rice	gelatin
Fruit cocktail	pudding	Milk
Milk	Milk	
Macaroni and	Chopped liver	Scrambled eggs and
cheese	Green lima beans	bacon
Fresh tomatoes	Raw apple wedges	Green beans
Spinach	Bread and butter	Carrot strips
Toast strips	Baked custard	Bran muffins
Fruit cup	Animal Crackers	Chocolate pudding
Milk	Milk	Milk
Salmon loaf	Spaghetti and meat	Fluffy omelet
Peas	balls	Stewed tomatoes
Raw cauliflower	Buttered carrots	Cottage cheese and
Toast strips	Cellery sticks	pineapple
Peaches	Toast strips	Raisin bread and
Milk	Applebrown betty	butter
	Milk	Pears
		Milk
Creamed dried	Tuna soufflé	Baked potatoes with
beef	Asparagus	cheese
Boiled potatoes	Carrot strips	Breaded tomatoes
Spinach	Celery strips	Apple wedges
Tomato wedges	Bread and butter	Peanut butter
Toast strips	Fruit cup	sandwiches
Orange sherbet	Milk	Banana pudding
Milk		Milk

Overstimulation or fatigue will create emotional tensions conducive to poor eating habits. Frequently, children's appetites are affected by the lively conversations of older siblings at the table. Moreover, it is not uncommon for adults to expect more expert behavior in the eating situation than in other activities. Adult admonitions and instructions are frequent and these are more numerous as the number of adults at the table is increased. Examples are: "Sit up in your chair," "Don't spill your milk," "Use your fork," "Chew your food thoroughly," and "Don't talk when you're chewing." It is small wonder that these young children may lose their appetites. Such conversations will not make the meal pleasant for older people, either.

This indicates the importance of each family choosing its own best plan for food service. Mealtimes should be restful, happy, and unhurried times and this kind of an atmosphere may be difficult to provide when there are older children. Often, children who show little interest in food when the entire family is present at dinner will eat heartily at lunch when only their mother is with them. Usually there is very little conversation when very young children eat at school. We must remember that these children are not experienced enough to concentrate on talking and eating at the same time. When manipulative skills have improved, pleasant conversation will serve to increase food consumption.

There are other reasons that sometimes necessitate children's eating away from the family table. Since fatigue and excessive hunger tend to lessen appetites, it is not always possible to postpone mealtime for young children until the entire family can be at home for dinner. In this event, it is better to feed children at an earlier hour. This does not mean, however, that children should be expected to eat when isolated from companionship. A high chair or a small table and chair in the kitchen will enable a mother to proceed with her work and at the same time to lend assistance and attention to the young child.

As stated earlier, parents' attitudes toward their children's eating habits are extremely important. It is impossible to make a child like all foods. Our best procedure is to insure his health so his appetite will be good, to provide opportunities for fresh air and exercise, to make his meals attractive and palatable, to make mealtime a pleasant time, and to set a good example by our attitudes.

Teachers are sometimes questioned as to how table manners are taught at the preschool level and when this teaching should occur. As in other kinds of etiquette, the best method of training in good manners is to be patient with the child and to set a good example for him. When we recognize how much children must learn before the mechanics of eating can be mastered, we will be more lenient of their awkwardness and will understand that refinement of behavior can be expected only after they are comfortable and capable in mealtime procedures. When we review the sequence of manipulative skills, we are aware that feeding oneself requires good eye-hand coordination. Again, it is wise to consider eating from a child's point of view and with his experience and growth in mind.

The young child who can grasp only with his whole hand is capable of picking up a piece of toast and clumsily getting it to his mouth, but very young children often seem to get more food on their faces than in their mouths. At this stage, of course, the child is probably still drinking from a bottle at least part of the time and is being fed semisolid foods by his parents at regular times.

Later, the task of eating may be tiresome for children. They may begin to eat energetically until their hunger has been partially appeased, and then they may find the mechanics of eating too enervating. When children begin to dawdle and we suspect they are tired, it may be wise to assist them. Assistance may consist of scraping the food into a form that can be placed on a spoon by the child, of filling the spoon for him, or even of spooning the food into his mouth. Our knowledge of the individual child must dictate the kind and amount of help we give. Here again, the form of service may be the deciding factor. For example, preschool children may have difficulty in eating soups with spoons but will be quite successful if thin soups are served in cups.

Sometimes grownups can feel repulsed as they watch some children's messy eating behavior. When we are aware of the wide variation in motor skills among children in other activities, it is not surprising that some of them can assume adult mannerisms far earlier than others. Doubtless, children are aware of how adults feel about their abilities. At home, parents can be accepting of children's awkward efforts. At school, it is best to give careful consideration to child and adult placement at mealtime. Time after time, it is demonstrated that the pleasure of mealtime for the child is affected by the adult near whom he sits.

Obviously, children will be expected to conform to cultural patterns in time and as soon as their growth makes the handling of knives, forks, and spoons possible, parents are justified in expecting them to conform to family practices in table manners. We should remember, however, that the purpose of good manners is to make the child more acceptable to other people. Etiquette should not be considered as an end in itself. Children can be told, "We eat potatoes with our forks," "It bothers other people when we sing at the table," or "We swallow food before we talk." Children want to conform and kindly firmness by adults is reassuring. Mealtime is more pleasant for children who know what is expected of them but these expectancies should depend on their ability to perform.

ENVIRONMENTAL AIDS TO GOOD APPETITES

Since children need to develop pleasant attitudes toward foods and eating, it is logical that we should help them to do so. Many of the factors that were discussed as being helpful in encouraging children to rest are equally influential in helping them to eat: (1) children are likely to have better appetites when they eat in familiar surroundings, (2) rooms should be light, cheerful, well ventilated, and comfortably warm, and (3) toys should be removed from sight and noise and confusion in nearby rooms discouraged.

When children are capable of grasping with thumb and forefinger, foods that can be handled in this manner are good. By this time, children will have become adept at placing food in their mouths without smearing it on their faces. Many foods that they need, however, cannot be eaten by hand and they need to begin to use spoons and forks. The so-called baby spoons with curved handles have lost favor since the majority of adults believe that children should learn to use the utensils that they will soon be expected to employ. Light-weight teaspoons or salad forks probably will be most easily handled by young children. They need a lot of practice with these utensils before they can use them as adults do.

Small tables and chairs are among the most useful pieces of equipment available for small children. These can be used for several purposes and over long periods of time, but they are especially important for mealtime. The table should be sturdy and strong. Among those available, the tables that can be adjusted in height are preferable since they can be raised as the child's height changes. Most table tops are hard-surfaced and attractive so that table covers are usually unnecessary. Chairs should be comfortable and should conform to the child's size so he can sit with his feet flat on the floor. A variety of higher chairs suitable for children who eat at the family table can be purchased. A choice of these will depend on the money and storage space available, but the child's comfort should be the criterion.

Children are usually pleased if their dishes are bright in color. Certain types of plastic dinnerware are good since children frequently have accidents and both children and adults will be happier if breakage can be avoided. Dishes should be light in weight and shaped so they can be grasped easily, of course, if children are to be allowed the fun of helping serve themselves. Glasses are more easily handled than cups. They should be small both in height and in circumference. The child's size is of special importance in the choice of glasses. Obviously, adult-size portions of liquid can seem overpowering to a small child and, moreover, his hands will not be large enough to grasp a large glass securely. Since children enjoy helping themselves to second servings, small pitchers for refilling glasses will prove useful.

Most young children below the age of three will accept bibs or aprons as a part of the mealtime plan. Coverall aprons or bibs that can be easily slipped on by the child himself are especially good. An elastic band at the neck instead of tapes to tie will enable children to be more independent.

All these factors contribute to the child's feelings of comfort and security. As has already been mentioned, nothing is as influential to these feelings, however, as the atmosphere of the home or school. Television viewing is a mealtime accompaniment in many homes and probably is a main deterrent to relaxed and unhurried eating habits.

Mealtime had never been a pleasant time in the Harper household. Mr. Harper was a finicky eater. Mrs. Harper was not particularly interested in cooking, and three-year-old Lana seemed to care little for food. When meals were discussed, Mrs. Harper often shrugged her shoulders and said, "What food tastes like really doesn't matter. We never eat a meal without the television turned on."

When Lana entered the child care center, mealtime seemed to be completely uninteresting to her. The fact that she was unwilling to sit still at the table for more than two or three minutes at a time might have been a reflection of the eating pattern at home when her parents' interests were centered in television programs.

When child guidance is considered, three facts are evident: (1) instead of Lana's experiencing the pleasure of eating, she was forming a habit of indifference toward food, (2) one of the best opportunities for family fun and interaction was lost, and (3) the mealtime procedure constituted poor training in social grace which, in our culture, is likely to combine mealtime and companionship.

SUGGESTED ASSIGNMENT

Part I

Observe a group of preschool children at lunch and answer the following questions.

1. What factors in the school environment appeared to encourage good eating habits? Be specific.

2. How did the teacher contribute to making lunch time an acceptable social experience for the children? Give examples.

3. How did the children contribute to the procedures of serving?

4. Of what value do you consider child participation in lunch procedures? Be specific.

Part II

Choose one of the children at the lunch table and answer these questions.

1. How was the child helped to be ready for mealtime?

2. Estimate the quantity of food actually eaten by the child. Do you think these amounts were sufficient? Why or why not?

3. In what ways was the child helped during the meal?

4. What, if any, comments did the child make about the meal?

Part III

If food preference charts are available, answer the following questions.

1. According to the child's food preference lists, which items on the menu does he like, which does he dislike, and which has he never tasted at home?

2. Comment on discrepancies between food actually eaten and the preferences on the child's food list.

Part IV

Observe a preschool child in his home or at a restaurant. Describe his eating behavior in relation to his developmental status and the apparent attitudes of his parents.

Part V

Plan meals and snacks for three days for the child care center. Furnish recipes or descriptions when necessary. Estimate daily costs per child.

SELECTED READINGS

1. Beal, Virginia A., "Nutrition during Infancy and Early Childhood," *Nutrition News,* Vol. 33, No. 4, December, 1970, National Dairy Council, Chicago.

This article stresses individual differences in requirements and reports on actual intake as measured in research studies. Developmental variations are described clearly.

2. Birch, H. G., and J. D. Gusson, *Disadvantaged Children, Health, Nutrition and School Failure,* Harcourt-Brace, N. Y., 1970.

Students who plan to work with disadvantaged children or in school lunch programs will find this book valuable.

3. Callahan, D. C., "You Can't Teach a Hungry Child." *School Lunch Journal,* p. 26, March, 1971.

This article describes present concerns about the relation of malnutrition to mental functioning. It should appeal to those who are interested in the findings of recent research but do not desire to read the actual research studies.

4. Committee on Nutrition, "Factors Affecting Food Intake," *Pediatrics,* Vol. 33, No. 1, January, 1964, American Academy of Pediatrics, Evanston, Ill.

The authors of this article discuss emotional, cultural, and educational factors of human development as they are influenced by nutrition. Environmental situations and individual differences are described. The article is well-documented and would be a good source of information for the person who plans a professional career in dietetics, psychology, or anthropology.

5. Dayton, Delbert H., "Early Malnutrition and Human Development," *Children,* Vol. 16, No. 6. Nov.-Dec., 1969, The Children's Bureau, Washington, D. C.

The author has reviewed research studies now in progress and suggests the need for more long-term studies. Malnutrition among children in the United States and several other countries is discussed.

6. McEnery, E. T., and Margaret Jane Suydam, *Feeding Little Folks,* National Dairy Council, Chicago, 1966.

This attractive, twenty-one page booklet includes recommended practices for menu planning for young children. Suggestions for preparation and service of food for children are helpful.

7. National Dairy Council, *Food Before Six,* Chicago, 1969.

This leaflet, in semioutline form, describes foods that fulfill dietary needs of young children, lists sizes of recommended portions, and presents environmental guidelines. It would be a good hand-out to parents in the day care center.

8. U. S. Department of Agriculture, *Food for Fitness,* leaflet No. 424, Washington, D. C., 1967.

This is another inexpensive leaflet that would be valuable for the child care center library. Food groups and vitamin content of specific foods are listed.

9. Wetzel, Norman C., *Instruction Manual in the Use of the Grid for Evaluating Physical Fitness,* NEA Services, Cleveland, Ohio, 1941.

In this booklet, Dr. Wetzel has provided simple and concise information. Growth, body build, nutritional grade, physical status, maturation, basal metabolism, and caloric needs are presented as qualities that can and should be measured to assess the individual's level of physical fitness at sequential stages of development. Students who plan to do graduate study in foods, nutrition, or child/development will be interested in the grid technique described.

chapter 12

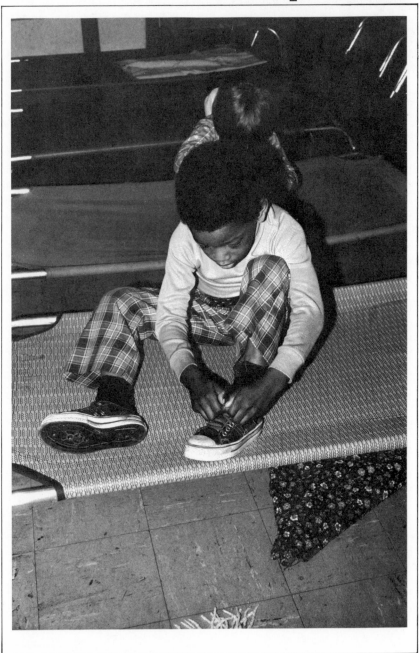

Clothing the Preschooler

Modern guidance principles indicate that we should consider clothing as the child sees it, feels it, and as it affects his actions. Just as the child's skeletal structure and physical characteristics dictate his feelings about himself, the manner in which he responds to other people and their reactions to him, so the covering that encases his body can enhance or detract from his feelings about himself and his ability to be physically active or constricted in movement as he develops social relationships with his playmates. Furthermore, children learn through the development of sensory perceptions and their clothing represents an important facet of their tactile and visual experiences.

THE EMOTIONAL ASPECTS OF CLOTHING

Very early in life infants seem to receive satisfaction and comfort from soft fabrics. This is demonstrated when babies rub their groping fingers over the soft surface of their blankets and gowns. Later, babies derive security by fondling soft toy animals, tiny blankets or even soft pieces of cotton or yarn.

Mr. and Mrs. Levenson adopted Rebecca when she was five months old. For two months they had visited the nursery in a nearby city regularly and when the day on which they were to take Becky home was scheduled, they drove to the city early and purchased sufficient clothing for the immediate future. Among these purchases was a soft blanket with matching hood, both bound in soft satin.

During the three hour drive home Becky snuggled comfortably in Mrs. Levenson's arms. Two or three times her new mother remarked that the infant seemed to like the feel of the satin that she had grasped tightly between her fingers and rubbed incessantly. By the time they reached home, the threads in the satin were broken as a result of Becky's evident enjoyment of this tactile experience.

Throughout childhood some children appear to insist on clothing that is soft and often they will choose to wear much laundered apparel in preference to new garments that retain the initial stiffness. The many washings requested before jeans are ready for wear may not be based entirely on peer standards but also on the comfort of increased pliability of the fabric.

As children grow older it seems that their needs for self-acceptance are at least partially met through their clothing.

Carl Massey, four years old, was small for his age. He was quiet but he usually was included by other children in their play at the preschool. Carl's father was a jet pilot and recently had been stationed several hundred miles from their home. Carl's mother maintained the home for her children: Carl, his six-year-old brother, and a younger brother and sister. Mrs. Massey reported that Carl was enthusiastic about the school and he always seemed happy to be there although his facial expression usually was very serious.

Carl always wore a large, felt, sombrero-type hat to school and the hat was never removed from his head. At the beginning of his attendance, his mother was embarrassed by this behavior but, when she would insist that she should take the hat with her, Carl would burst into tears. Interestingly, the children did not comment about Carl's hat. It almost seemed as if they accepted it as a part of him. The teachers could only surmise that this garb afforded some sense of security for Carl.

Whether wearing such apparel is indicative of role playing and this hat was chosen because of the specific style or whether it was symbolic of some kind of protection is not obvious. During the following term another quiet child whose pattern of family living had been disturbed wore a knitted cap, day after day.

As children grow older, wearing specific items of head gear, dress, or shoes may become status symbols that identify the child with his group. Adults should recognize that the emotional implications of such conformity are important.

During the preschool staff meeting, Mrs. Ryan who was a volunteer described an incident she had observed from her kitchen window on several occasions. The Ryan home was located less than a block from a private kindergarten. On several successive mornings, a five-year-old boy paused on the opposite side of the street on his way to school, removed his low rubber shoe coverings, crammed them into his jacket pocket and then proceeded through water puddles toward the school building.

Mrs. Ryan surmised that possibly this youngster had been teased by his peers because he did not have boots such as the other children wore. She expressed sympathy because of his probable feelings of guilt because he was trapped between the dictation of his parents and the expectations of his society.

Style and fashion usually are not important to the preschool child. True, he will appear to be proud because he is wearing a jacket similar to those worn by the teenage crowd, but his pride probably is the result of comments by adults and because he enjoys their admiration, not because he feels a need to conform to the latest clothing fashions. Many grownups find it difficult to converse with young children and clothing seems to run close competition to physical growth as a favorite topic. Stereotyped comments are: "What a big boy you are!" or "That's surely a good looking sweater you're wearing."

Children's clothing often is bought to satisfy adult standards of style. It can become a factor of parental projection. Many parents buy garments for their children in order to fulfill their own unsatisfied desires to be dressed in the height of fashion. Clothing advertisements tend to appeal to this characteristic in parents. Children are eager to please adults and they often are pleased with a garment just because the parents admire it. Moreover, it probably is a strong-willed and secure parent who can feel self-assured in the company of a disheveled child when confronted by another parent and child who are impeccably dressed in the latest styles. Children's feelings can be hurt, too, when adults vocally admire the dress of other children and leave the impression that style reflects negatively on the child who does not wear it.

THE IMPORTANCE OF COLOR CHOICE

We all have heard the statement that the woman who is depressed can bolster her spirits by purchasing a colorful dress, or scarf, or shoes. However, surprisingly little has been written about the effects of color on children despite our recognition that even young infants seem aware of color and interested in brightly hued mobiles or plastic toys. As in other experiential learnings, adults can foster the interest of young children by conversing with them as they play.

Mrs. Morse's nine-month-old grandson, Jason, spent much time at her house while his parents attended college classes. She usually spent the time with him in her guest bedroom in which the bed was covered with a multi-colored patchwork quilt.

Jason was intently interested in looking at the blocks in the quilt and Mrs. Morse would name the colors as he would point to them. Within a few months, as their game continued, Jason learned to point to a block of a specific color in response to his grandmother's pronouncing the name of that color.

Interior decorators frequently attempt to set the mood for the intended use of a specific room by choosing a bold or a soothing color combination that is appropriate to that use. Industrial employers are experimenting with color schemes as a means of increasing production or sales, and school planners are convinced that colors will influence the achievement of pupils and teachers. People of all ages appear to respond in certain ways to color. Indeed, recent research is concerned with the effects of color on the intellectual responses of children.

Could it be that many adults are not aware of how children feel about colors? When youngsters are given an opportunity to choose colors for crayon, paint, or paper activities, individual preferences and differences are apparent. It would seem, therefore, that some colors are more pleasing to the individual child than others. Parents sometimes dress their children almost exclusively in colors that they find unbecoming to themselves or which they consider especially becoming to the child. It is possible that a long-time dislike of these colors by the child may result or, conversely, that these colors may become permanent favorites, It is interesting to speculate that color patterns worn by adults may be the result of parental shopping for young children, that as adults we may enjoy or dislike colors that our parents chose for us.

Certain color combinations are displeasing from an adult point of view, but these values probably are the result of our cultural training. When children are allowed to choose clothing colors, combinations often resemble the bold blends of other cultures. The amount of freedom of choice that can be allowed the preschool child probably depends on the parents' dispositions. As in many other areas of child guidance, it probably is best for the parent to be firm about a minor decision if it allows that person to be a more relaxed and accepting person with whom to live. The introspective adult will realize that clothing colors often set the mood, that bright colors in dress for recreational activities are likely to enhance feelings of freedom and enjoyment.

CLOTHING SIZE AND CONSTRUCTION

Obviously, ill fitting and uncomfortable clothing will affect the emotional outlook of a young child. We too seldom recognize the misery that displeasing or ill-fitting clothing may cause the child nor to what extent the clothing he wears affects his behavior. We should be alert to clothing construction that permits freedom of movement and unhampered feelings.

Many preschool toileting accidents could be prevented if little boys' pants were comfortably loose and did not press on their genitals.

A serious emotional uspet resulted from daily toileting accidents by Jerry, a four-year-old. Jerry always wore extremely tight pants and his toileting accidents always occurred during vigorous play. He appeared to be embarrassed and his social response to the group was affected. His tendency toward withdrawal was accompanied by a facial tic. This was slowly overcome only after his parents bought a different style of clothing, better suited to his needs, as suggested by his teacher.

Fads appear in children's clothing just as often as they do in fashions for adults. Manufacturers are alert to clothing types worn by movie and television actors, and similar garments are worn surprisingly soon by the preschool crowd. These garments not only affect the behavior of the child who wears them, in that he probably will try to enact the role that they represent to him, but they often hamper normal activity.

Sometimes, little girls are permitted to wear soft-soled ballerina slippers to school. Small pebbles, the rungs of climbing apparatus, or even simple jumping games will be painful through these soles. Moreover, such shoes are harmful because they do not give adequate arch support and children who wear them probably will become onlookers to vigorous play.

The effects of wearing clogs and platform soles can be equally detrimental. In the first instance because clogs are difficult to keep on the feet and in the second instance because body balance is altered.

Susan, age three, was permitted to buy clogs because she wanted shoes like those of her older sister. These shoes slipped off her feet easily and many of her school activities were interrupted while she groped for her missing shoes. Other children, in turn, were affected by Susan's inattentive behavior to their play. Thus, ill-fitting shoes can create problems in group guidance.

Probably parents should remain adamant in assuming full responsibility for buying children's shoes and permit selection by the young child only in the purchase of less important items of apparel.

CHOOSING CHILDREN'S CLOTHING

Choosing clothing is so much a part of our everyday living that clothing for preschoolers is likely to be chosen quite casually. We devote time and effort only when we shop for a special gift, for attire for a special occasion, or when we strive to satisfy our own pleasure by visualizing the child in something "sweet", "cute," or "stylish." When groups of parents discuss children's clothing, their conversations tend to be completely adult-centered. They seldom mention how the child feels about his clothes. Usually, the high cost of garments is mentioned or the comparative ease of laundering is stressed.

The economic aspects of clothing the preschooler are important indeed.

Children grow rapidly and clothing often is outgrown and must be discarded when it shows little sign of wear despite the fact that clothing for the small child is almost as expensive as that for the adult. As a result, there is a likelihood that parents may purchase snowsuits, coats, and shoes that are too large for the child at the present time and that he will continue to wear them until his movements are hampered because they are too small. We should try to imagine at least two-thirds of our time spent in ill-fitting clothing.

When there are several children in a family, some items of clothing can be passed on to younger siblings but others, such as shoes, become shaped to individual contours and may affect posture and growth. Adults usually can relate their own experiences with "hand-me-downs." Children seem to vary in their attitudes toward wearing older siblings' clothing. Some children will gain self-esteem and will consider the wearing of the clothing of an older child a boost in status. Others may feel abused and even unloved if they must wear cast-off clothing. Probably a great deal depends on the parents' attitudes in such situations. Children imitate adults not only in behavior patterns but also in attitude formation. If parents are pleased with what their children wear and how they look, these feelings are reflected in the child.

Children's movements should be unhampered and their vigorous actions should be encouraged. Therefore, in order that bulkiness can be reduced, it is wise to choose lightweight, warm fabrics that are very closely woven. A complete snowsuit made of these materials, however, may become a veritable steam cabinet for an active child. Consequently, it is probably best if these fabrics are used only for jackets that can be put on or taken off in accordance with the weather and the type of activity in which the child is engaged.

Clothing chosen for children by adults influences how the child feels about himself and his abilities. Clothing that encourages self-help, such as garments with large buttons and buttonholes or easily manipulated zippers down the front or garments that can be readily pulled on over the head, will enhance the child's feelings of independence and self-confidence.

DRESSING AND UNDRESSING

Helping children gain independence in dressing and undressing is a responsibility of the adults who guide them. However, it is obvious that many garments are not constructed to encourage self-confidence in the child. These items can be frustrating to both children and adults. The assistant in the day care center who is left struggling with these clothing contrivances when everyone else has moved to the playground for midmorning play is in an uncomfortable situation. Many jokes are told about the problems teachers of young children meet during cold weather. Sometimes, preschool teachers are called "snowsuit stuffers." Indeed, the teachers of very young children spend a large proportion of their time during inclement weather trying to meet the challenges of "rubber legs" and "those booby traps" called snowsuits. Patience, understanding, and a well-developed sense of humor are necessary.

We may be more patient if, as in other routine activities, we attempt to view the situation through the eyes of the child. Adults are so accustomed to the tasks of dressing and undressing that many of the procedures are done almost unconsciously through habit. Putting on and taking off clothing can be a fascinating pastime for the young child to whom it is a novel experience, and the process offers an excellent opportunity for adults and preschoolers to converse and to get better acquainted.

Dressing and undressing provide wonderful opportunities for practice in manipulative skills. An advanced level of eye-hand coordination is required to master the intricacies of buttons and buttonholes, hooks and eyes, snaps and zippers. These all are remarkable items when considered from the child's point of view.

Of course, children can take off their clothes more easily than they can put them on. In fact, some parents are embarrassed because their toddler insists on removing his clothing at inappropriate times. We should remember that modesty is a cultural learning and that, from the child's viewpoint, unhampered nakedness is a pleasant feeling. There may be personal satisfaction, also, in the ability to get out of one's clothes. Another possibility, of course, is that such actions may serve as means for getting the attention of adults.

Assistants in the preschool often ask how much help to give a child in dressing and undressing. With the wide age range and the rapidly changing skills of preschool children, this is a difficult question to answer. Here, as in other kinds of guidance, our understanding of the individual child must set the rules.

1. Is his eye-hand coordination well developed so that he can manipulate his clothing easily?

2. Does his gross motor coordination permit a good sense of balance?

3. How much help does he receive from the adults at home?

4. Is he slow and deliberate so that long periods of time spent in dressing and undressing will prevent his moving on with the group and thereby make him feel inferior?

5. Does he have feelings of insecurity that might be eradicated by individual adult attention?

6. Is he testing the limits to see how much special help he can demand?

Possibly, we should give a little less help than the child demands. We must be alert, however, for the nonverbal child who, because of temperament or lack of language skills, cannot request help from the adults who are caring for him.

Children who have a tendency to procrastinate while dressing can be irritating to grownups. At about two years of age, most children enjoy routine and repetition in all their activities. Children at this stage are likely to be exasperating because of their insistence that dressing and undressing should be accomplished in a specific order of events, that shoes must be put on before hair is combed or that shirts must be buttoned before any other garment is considered. These children seem to be fascinated by repetitive details that are unimportant and even boring to adults. We should remember that children must experiment and that, by deliberate practice, they learn how to do things. It is encouraging that children soon outgrow this phase of ritualism.

Children sometimes procrastinate as a means of teasing adults or of testing the limits of adult patience but we must remember, also, that individual differences matter, that some children are slow in body movements and will probably continue in that pattern as they mature. An impetuous adult may find it especially difficult to care for such a child. We must rely on our knowledge of developmental patterns in order to recognize this child as different from the child who is slow in perfecting his motor skills.

Adults often lose patience with the child who stops in the process of dressing or undressing himself. His attention may be attracted by something entirely apart from the task at hand. For example, the four-year-old may have succeeded in putting on both socks and one shoe when his attention was diverted to his toy cars or his building blocks. It is necessary that we know that the child's concept of time is entirely unlike that of the adult. Present interests are more important to him than what he plans to do after his dressing is completed. After all, from his point of view why shouldn't he take time off to play with his toys for awhile? Although we cannot always permit him to interrupt the dressing procedure, we certainly can understand his desire to do so.

SUGGESTED ASSIGNMENT

Part I

Choose two children in the child care center who appear to be very different in personality and motor skills. Observe these children as they put on and take off their garments. Answer the following questions about each of them.

1. Can he take off his coat, jacket, cap, mittens, boots, and put them away? Does he need assistance? How much? Describe.

2. To what extent do you think his ability to put on and to remove his garments is related to the style or construction of his apparel?

3. Does he know when it is time to put on his things or to take them off? Does he do it at once or does he tend to dawdle or play? Describe.

4. How much is the child influenced by the activities of other children in the locker room?

Part II

Write an accurate anecdotal record of incidents during the school day in which you believe clothing affected the behavior of children.

Part III

Visit a store and select a full set of clothing for a four-year-old. Keep accurate records and answer the following questions.

1. Were you pleased with the selection of garments available? Explain.

2. Evaluate each garment you chose on the basis of the following points.

    a. Relative cost.

    b. Ease of laundering.

    c. Possibility for alteration as the child grows.

    d. Ease with which you think the child could cope with putting on or taking off the garment.

    e. Probable appeal to a specific four-year-old with whom you are acquainted.

SELECTED READINGS

1. Bobula, Katherine Ann. *Mediated Responses to Color and Form of Preschool Children In Two Socio-Economic Groups,* The Ohio State University, Columbus, Ohio, 1969.

This master's thesis was concerned as to whether children from different socioeconomic levels developed mediating responses at the same stage in their chronological development. The methodology employed will be of interest to advanced students in child development.

2. Hurlock, Elizabeth B., *Child Development,* 5th ed., McGraw-Hill, New York, 1972.

Hurlock's book, first published in 1942, can be considered a classic in child development. Reference to children's attitudes toward clothing and the effects of their clothing on their feelings and behavior has been retained in the present edition in abbreviated form.

3. LaToush, Elizabeth J. Rumney, *Influence of Clothing Upon Preschool Children,* University of Nebraska, 1969.

For this master's thesis, eighty preschool children were interviewed to determine the influence of clothing on children's first impressions as to whether or not an adult was happy or unhappy. Variables chosen were age, sex, and socioeconomic level. Advanced students in child guidance will find this study interesting.

chapter 13

The Meaning and Value of Play

Activity is a human need and through play children and adults are active, physically, mentally, and socially. Play activities vary according to age; type and availability of equipment; rural, urban, or suburban location; space and types of other people present. Moreover, individual traits, abilities and interests influence how one plays. Through play, the individual can develop skills, leadership, value systems, and he can have fun. Interest in play continues into adulthood in the form of recreation and leisure-time activity. For children and adults, the process of socialization is inextricably woven into play activities. People on the golf course mix play, skill development and social interaction with the same intensity that children work at these skills in the sandbox. Play is an ongoing activity that takes a variety of forms as people mature. It is an essential part of growing up.

THE EDUCATIVE ASPECTS OF PLAY

Many of the skills discussed in previous chapters are acquired through play.

Activity and general development are closely related. The child's level of maturation determines his interests, and his activities, in turn, stimulate his growth. Children learn through their play and their play indicates what they have learned, how much they know. At any age an individual's knowledge can be judged by how he acts. The infant who attempts to grasp a rattle hanging above his bed gains from the experience as he becomes able to focus his eyes, to control his muscles, and to coordinate these two processes. The play of infants and young children is spontaneous and casual, but it results in knowledge and it denotes knowledge.

When stimulation and motivation are present, play is the method a child uses to develop sensory-motor functions. When play materials, such as rattles or crib-attached toys, are present an infant will tend to reach toward these objects and to repeat the reaching persistently. At first this will occur only as long as these items remain in view. Later, the infant will attempt to retrieve objects that have disappeared.

Infants often watch their own hands and then reach out with one hand to catch the other. Or they may try to grasp at a pattern as sunlight is affected by a waving curtain or a flickering venetian blind. Concepts of spatial relationship develop more easily when an adult plays with the infant and offers objects that interest him. Tactile experiences influence sensory-motor development as the young child learns through play that his rattle makes a noise when he shakes it but that his blanket does not.

Sensory-motor intelligence depends on physical manipulation, social interaction, biogenetic maturation and the opportunities a child has to play with objects in various settings. The toy industry and learning theorists are equally interested in appropriate toys that may help parents and caretakers plan constructive play with and for young children.

As a child develops mobility, his opportunities for play increase. He tends to play with the many things he comes into contact with during his day. It is at this time that socially imposed limits influence play and learning. The child is likely to learn that it is all right to play with the pots in the cupboard, but it is not all right to play with the candy dish on the table. Social intelligence is demonstrated when a very young child walks up to another child, pushes him, and then steps back, obviously alert to what the reaction of the other child may be.

Manipulative skills are developed through play. The young child at the woodworking table expends much thought and energy to coordinate the hammer and the nail. He is content to display his piece of wood with one nail in place. Later he will play with a hammer and nails as he hammers many objects onto his piece of wood. The prekindergarten age child often will have developed enough manipulative dexterity and problem solving skill to create a representational object such as a truck or boat when he uses carpenters' tools.

Problem solving behavior is developed through play. The very young child who is pulling a toy across the room often is confronted by the problem of its being overturned or entangled. He may simply abandon the toy, he may cry out for help and be guided by an adult to extricate the toy, or he may be maturationally alert and attempt to solve the problem by manipulating the toy so he can resume his play. Learning through play occurs when a child uses past experience and his current skills to solve problems related to the material or social behavior involved.

The normal young child spends most of his waking hours in play. These activities are so commonplace that it is often difficult for some adults to recognize their educative value. It is not uncommon to hear an irritated person say, "Oh, go on and play." To the child this may mean, "Leave me alone." Under such circumstances, play can denote a negative value for the child who, we must remember, needs acceptance and approval.

Adults often interrupt a child's play without warning and express annoyance when the youngster remonstrates. Frequently, all that the youngster has created must be destroyed immediately without time to reflect on the pleasure of the activity. Television is a cleaner pastime than play and some parents wrongfully suggest that the child watch television because cleaning up is not necessary. Play areas usually are cluttered as young children sort through toys to select their choices of the moment. This is part of the learning process of selection and decision making and is an important aspect of growth. The current enjoyment of an activity will lengthen as the child matures and usually the variety of material needed for his play will decrease. With proper guidance, clean up time can be a pleasant learning experience, particularly when a youngster has a specific place to arrange his play materials and is helped to classify them as he puts them in their places.

Many early play patterns evolve as imitative reproduction of games adults play with a child such as waving "bye-bye" or "peek-a-boo" activities that are encouraged and praised. Parents, as the child's models, have a great responsibility to encourage play and to provide proper materials for developmental play. Occasionally, nurturers are shocked to see and hear aspects of their own behavior mirrored in a small child. Children learn nonverbal behavior much more quickly than they absorb verbal clues. Therefore, they are guided by what they see rather than by what they are told.

Mr. Lewin was attempting to teach Iris, age two years and three months, to treat the new puppy gently by patting and hugging it. He became upset one afternoon when the puppy found a sock and was chewing it, and he spanked the puppy with a newspaper. A few days later, he was horrified to see Iris slamming the puppy with a toy because the animal had taken one of the pretzels the child had placed on the floor for a moment.

Simple imitation is evident in the activities of the two-year-old group at the child care center.

Four two-year old children were busily engaged in playing in the housekeeping corner of the playroom. Kay was clumsily attempting to fasten a doll blanket to a clothesline by means of toy clothes pins, David was sitting in a chair rocking a rag doll that was slung across his knees, and Sheila stood by the doll bed placing a blanket over a rubber doll. She would place the blanket over the doll, snatch it up, cover the doll again, walk to the foot of the bed, uncover and cover the doll, and then repeat the procedure from the other side of the bed. Meanwhile, Carol sat at the table with the receiver of the toy telephone at her ear. Her facial expression was extremely animated.

Of course, interest span is short at the two-year-old level and not all of these activities continued for as long as the time required to read about them, but they are indicative of the imitative play patterns of young children. By acting out these situations, sometimes time after time, these children were learning to interpret behavior as it related to their experience.

The meaning of these activities for young children may be overlooked by adults for three reasons: (1) they are transitory in nature, (2) they are solitary pursuits, and (3) these children lack the language skills that emphasize the more complex dramatic play of older children. Adults guide development and intellectual growth as they present materials appropriate to the maturational level of the child and offer him secure environments for exploration, indoors and outdoors. Caretakers who offer a child a sense of self-confidence, appropriate materials and, eventually, a playmate can have the opportunity to watch the child's emerging understanding of the world around him.

DRAMATIC PLAY

Imitation accompanied by imagination is characteristic of preschool play. Children imitate the models around them but each child adapts the actions according to his maturational level and his own individuality. He creates, in his play, the things that have meaning and interest for him. Obviously, the ability to dramatize depends on the acquisition of locomotor and manipulative skills and the power to use ideas and language. Consequently, dramatic play increases with age during the preschool period.

Playing grown-up roles gives the child an opportunity to assume power over the situation and to enact· the adult role that may have been difficult for him to accept from his parents or teachers. Certainly, we can learn more about individual children than they are capable of telling us in words, and this release of feelings appears to make the child happy and relaxed. Often, when children play adult roles, they assume dictatorial mannerisms that probably reflect their ideas concerning adult authority. The child who is imitating adult behavior is learning how it feels to be an adult, and the way in which he enacts the role usually demonstrates his interpretation of the activities of his own sex.

Three-and-one-half year old Mary, in the role of mother, spent much of her time scolding her dolls for some kind of misbehavior, undressing them, putting them to bed, and getting them up and dressed only to repeat the sequence of activity, time after time.

Four-year-old Susan, whose mother was a popular organist, spent the majority of her play periods enlisting the aid of other children in acting out wedding processions. Her knowledge of the way in which these should be organized and conducted was surprising to adults.

Frequently, students are amused, and occasionally much too literal, as they interpret home living patterns that are reflected in dramatic play.

Clara, age three-and-one-half, was especially interested in playing with the housekeeping equipment. During free play periods, she would always suggest a play situation in which she would be the "mother," one of the boys would be the "daddy," and other children would enact roles as their "babies."

One day "daddy had arrived home from work" and the family started to pretend to eat from the toy dishes. Suddenly, Clara stood up and started to clear the table hurriedly. She carried the dishes to the toy stove and, as she opened the oven door, she stated, "Quick, let's put the dirty dishes in the oven. I hear company knocking at the door."

It is interesting that young preschool boys and girls usually confine their dramatic play to kitchen chores and the care of babies while older preschool children assume roles of community workers, television characters, animals and astronauts. Children move from playing roles they are familiar with toward sociodramatic play that explores and reassigns relationships based on the child's interpretation of himself in his environment.

Jamie's mother had died during childbirth and his father had abandoned him. He lived with his elderly grandmother and he was placed in a day care center at three years of age by a social service agency in order to relieve his grandmother of the task of total day care.

For many months his dramatic play consisted of play in the kitchen and frequent fussing with a "baby" to keep it neat, clean, and fed. Jamie was almost four when he began to assume the role of father, a concept he often had seen other children act out in the playhouse area. He then explored many avenues of fatherhood as he tried to find an image for the male figure he had not been exposed to.

The serious manner in which children assume imaginative roles attests to their feelings concerning these characterizations. Usually, as children grow older, situations become more complex and more diverse equipment is used in their play, but it is not important that these properties should always be realistic. For example, a tire pump attached to a hose in the area near the tricycles can provide opportunities for a variety of situations. In pretense, the pump can be used for its original purpose, it can become a gasoline pump, a part of an oil truck, or a watering device. Sometimes, only one small item can stimulate a complete situation of role-playing.

Gary and Jeffry were especially interested in transportation facilities. They enjoyed wearing striped caps that belonged to the school and frequently they had chairs arranged in a row and pretended that they were engineers aboard a train. One day, when they came in from the playground, Jeffry reached for one of the caps and, in a serious manner, said to Gary, "Let's put on our engineers' heads."

During classroom discussion, students commented that Jeffry's statement was indicative of his feeling, that the cap transformed him, that his head became an engineer's head when he donned the cap. Dress-up clothes stimulate social activity and dramatic play. When providing these materials, it is important to remember that boys enjoy dressing up as much as girls do and to include masculine attire as well as feminine. A chest of dress-up clothes is an important asset in a preschool.

The adults in the child care center are not trained as therapists and they should make no effort to interpret the actions of children whom they suspect of being seriously disturbed. These children should be referred for psychological help. Sometimes, however, it is evident that the needs of normal children for self-esteem are met at least partially through their imaginative thinking.

David, age three-and-one half, appeared to be a timid child. His mother was particularly apprehensive about this trait. In fact, Mrs. Martin seemed to worry about much of David's behavior. When she called for him after school, she always wanted to know every detail of his activities.

David frequently stated to students, "I am Batman." One day, Billy's mother was the first parent to arrive at the playground. David was standing nearby and Mrs. Clark said to him, "I don't believe I've met you. What is your name?" His very serious reply was, "I'm Batman." Mrs. Clark made no further effort to converse with him.

A few days later, a heated quarrel took place at the snack table when a child who was new to the school commented, "You're David." Immediately, David jumped to his feet, saying, "I'm not David. I am Batman."

Undoubtedly, television programs influence the choice of subjects in dramatic play and it seems that children sometimes are portraying these characters when we are not aware of their thinking. When children portray television characters, the classroom atmosphere can be influenced by the physical violence and super powers of those characters. Just as the cowboy and Indian and the cops and robber movies offered role playing opportunities full of stereotyped misconceptions for children during the thirties and forties, indiscriminate television viewing can influence the actions of preschoolers today. Batman on the climber may make a younster feel daring and more aggressive than being three and a half years old and a child may actually feel that he can conquer his peers, as someone else.

Tina was a five-year-old who was a television cartoon expert. Each day, she portrayed a series of cartoon characters as she recreated the daily morning shows when she came to the afternoon session at school. One afternoon, in her eagerness to portray a scene with accuracy, she pushed the "bad cat" off the climber and hurt her playmate.

The decision to permit role playing of television characters is governed by the director of the school or, in some cases, by an advisory board of parents. A good variety of dramatic play materials such as costumes, accessories, and uniforms of various kinds can offset the television syndrome and direct children toward more innovative encounters in the classroom and outdoors.

Children frequently enjoy dramatizing a favorite story or nursery rhyme, and adults who guide young children toward participation in creative drama as a story telling technique offer youngsters (1) an opportunity for group effort in a shared language experience, (2) an opportunity to discriminate between real and fantasy situations, and (3) creative experiences that permit identity with familiar storybook friends, both animals and people.

Miss Culbertson, the teacher of a three-year-old group, usually chose stories for her group that were realistic and concerned everyday situations. One day, however, she decided to read "Goldilocks and the Three Bears" and then to suggest that the children dramatize the story. The following results occurred: (1) Denny, who seldom entered into group play but often commented about the stories that were read, was eager to be a participant; (2) Miss Culbertson had an opportunity to comment, "Of course, bears don't really talk but in stories it's often fun to pretend they do"; and (3) Kay, who had a frightened expression on her face when she listened to the account of Goldilocks' experiences, was a relaxed and happy heroine in view of the fact that the three bears were her friends, Don, Pat, and Dorothy.

Dramatic activities can be stimulated by recreating a favorite story using puppets, flannel board figures, or other materials. These accessories sometimes can help children gain confidence in the child care center. A totally unstructured dialogue may occur.

Melissa, a reserved four-year-old, entered school at mid-year. She seemed lonely and avoided play situations with other children. Miss Kahn, her teacher, brought out a large, boxlike puppet stage with puppets. Mellisa went behind the stage, took a puppet, and began to converse with it. Jane wandered in, took a puppet and began to answer Melissa. The puppet conversation between the two girls was overheard by Miss Kahn who suggested that they put on a show for Sue and John who had just come in from outdoors. Melissa apparently enjoyed this idea and, soon, others joined the audience or were talking to the puppets. After the performance ended, the girls were busy planning a program for the next day.

The example indicates the importance of a flexible program so that the children have time to play out the situations they choose. Even when long periods of time are allowed, groups of four- and five-year-olds will often resume the same roles and the same kinds of situations on many successive days. Of course, dramatic play needs supervision, but adult intervention should be kept at a minimum if children are to derive full value from their experiences. The quarreling that so often occurs in children's play is usually due to the immaturity of the participants. When two children have a pleasant experience playing together, we can be assured that social learning has taken place. By trial and error, the nature of reciprocal relationships is learned and this learning accompanies dramatic play.

Little evidence of imaginary playmates will be seen at school, but some mention of this type of companion is warranted since these "friends" are common with young children. These imaginary children or adults seem to be lifelike to children and to fill a need in their social lives. Children who do not have siblings or companions near their own ages are more likely to create these playmates.

Make-believe friends usually are similar to the child in age and are of either sex. They have names that may be ordinary ones or may be of an unusual form that has been originated by the child. Children talk to these playmates as if they were real. Sometimes, they appear to accompany children wherever they go. At other times, they appear only in certain situations when children are lonely. It is not unusual for young children to request toys that can be shared with these "people." Of course, whatever the situation may be, there probably is personal satisfaction since the real child is the leader in all planning and the imaginary person always is cooperative.

Girls are somewhat more likely to create make-believe friends and the high point in their incidence is when children are around three and one-half years old. From the standpoint of child guidance, the important facts are: (1) since so many children of preschool age have imaginary companions, the practice should be considered completely normal, (2) by the time children reach elementary school age, they usually discard their imaginary friends although sometimes they may reappear when children are lonely, and (3) children who seem to be perfectly well-adjusted are just as likely to have these make-believe playmates as timid, shy, or withdrawn children.

THE WISE CHOICE OF TOYS

Careful consideration of the tools for play is extremely important. Public concern about the importance of early education combined with the abundance of television commercials relating to the sale of toys have made toy selection an emotionally charged activity. Toys designated as learning devices by manufacturers often are designed to make the purchaser believe that these items will foster early intellectual development. Toys are packaged and designed for instant eye appeal, but many do not offer children safe and vigorous manipulative and creative play opportunities. Toy purchasers for the home or school should guide their toy selection by the age and interest levels of the children rather than by their own wish-fulfilling fantasies. Toys that require close adult supervision or intervention because of complicated structure, electrical mechanisms, or fragility serve only to frustrate children and to foster dependency during situations when independence and skill development should be occurring.

Adults often buy toys without thinking seriously of the individual child who will play with them. It is not uncommon to hear remarks like: "I simply had to buy that toy. I could play with it all day myself," or "It's just exactly the kind of toy I'd have liked when I was a child."

When we consider the recipient of the gift, there seems to be little humor in the situation when the father buys an electric train for a Christmas gift for his preschool son and the adults spend Christmas Day playing with it. A simple, wooden train that could be pushed or pulled around the room regardless of tracks would be much more fun for a young child. The three-year-old girl who receives the beautiful doll dressed in nylon and lace is to be pitied, also. A cuddly rag doll with easily manipulated clothing would be much more beloved by children. Moreover, toys that are above the age levels of children are likely to cause emotional tensions because it is difficult for the adult to refrain from cautioning the child to "take good care of the beautiful doll" or to "never run the train unless Daddy is at home."

Sometimes, toys can be extremely dangerous. As a result, in 1966 Congress passed the Child Protection and Safety Act giving the Food and Drug Administration the right to ban any toy that might prove hazardous to children. As an outgrowth of that Act, in 1972 the presidentially appointed Consumer Product Safety Commission was established. In a list compiled by that commission late in 1973, forty-six pages of toys were itemized as being dangerous either to all children or to very young children who might misuse them. The sale of such toys is illegal and companies that make or sell them are subject to fine and imprisonment but it is obvious that it will continue to be difficult for the retailer and the purchaser to be alert to the nature of new toys that will appear on the market.

When choosing toys for children, we should keep the levels of social development described in a previous chapter in mind. The infant and toddler need toys that encourage exploration and sensory-motor development. Groups of young children should have access to toys that are appropriate for solitary play, duplicates of some types of toys should be available for children who need to play near other children with similar interests and abilities, and toys that stimulate cooperative play are very important.

Young babies play with their ears, hair, toes, and fingers, but very soon they need to include toys in their explorations. Since they explore by means of sight, taste, touch and hearing, it is apparent that their toys should be brightly colored, lightweight, and of varied textures, that they should be washable, too big to swallow, and free of rough edges. By the age of three or four months, most babies will enjoy a rattle or a plastic object that can be grasped easily. Colorful mobiles, safe crib gyms, and soft stuffed animals also are appropriate toys for these children.

After children begin to walk, push toys and pull toys that encourage exercise are helpful to developing muscles. It is probable that between two and six years of age, children are influenced more by play materials than at any other time. During this period, they are growing at a rapid rate in all areas: physical, mental, social, and emotional. At each preschool level, children are perfecting abilities preparatory to the learning of new and difficult skills that they will acquire somewhat later.

Trucks and cars that are sufficiently sturdy and large enough to straddle are good early in this period and wagons, wheelbarrows, doll carriages, and other wheel toys are special favorites. Stuffed animals of all kinds are satisfying toys for many young preschoolers. Dolls, doll accessories, and housekeeping equipment are interesting during the preschool years. Sand toys for digging, pouring, and molding are always popular. Blocks of all sizes and shapes will encourage various kinds of play both indoors and outdoors. Toys for this period should be simple and it is wise to remember that fine muscle coordination is not possible.

That one should keep the individual child in mind when buying toys does not mean that each child in the home or at school must have his own special set of toys. Some toys at home, of course, such as tricycles or a favorite ball or doll are usually individually owned and these toys can be used by the same child for several years. As the child grows, he will use the toy in different ways. For example, the very young child will spend many hours riding his tricycle. At that age, he is not capable of combining the skill of riding with other ideas for play. He is intent on the mechanics of pushing the pedals and guiding the toy. By late preschool years, his tricycle becomes a tool for dramatic play and he rides it so competently that it is no longer necessary for him to concentrate on the techniques of riding. His mind and energy are free to create situations for cooperative play.

A ball in the hands of the very young child is of interest to him as an object to be handled and sometimes rolled across the floor. Later, he will become aware of its resilient qualities or of the possibilities of rolling it or tossing it to another person. The doll of a two-year-old child will be cuddled or carried around by a leg, an arm, or the hair. As the child matures, ideas for dramatic play will include the doll as a baby to be cared for, fed, bathed, and pushed in the doll carriage. As the child's manipulative skills increase, there will be more emphasis on careful dressing and undressing and other activities demanding more precision skills.

The point here is also that one can choose materials that can be used in different ways by different children at various age levels. Examples of these universal types of toys are blocks that will be discussed in detail in a later chapter. A wagon is another good example of a long-lasting toy that is appropriate for all children. The two-year-old likes being pulled and, if the wagon is small, he may like pulling it just for the pleasure of exercise and self-confidence. By about three years of age, his social life with his age mates has begun to develop and he may sometimes pull a friend or get a friend to pull him. By the time he is four to four-and-one-half years old, the wagon probably can become any of a number of things that will be used in his play. It may be a part of a train, it may be a passenger automobile, a fire engine, or any other vehicle desired.

For vigorous outdoor play, opportunities for the exercise of locomotor skills are afforded by many kinds of apparatus: walking boards, barrel tunnels, swings, seesaws, slides, and climbing bars. In warm weather, the sandbox and appropriate tools provide enjoyable activities. Housekeeping equipment is welcomed by both boys and girls. It gives wonderful opportunities for dramatic play. Usually, toys should be of good quality. Toys that break easily can cause frustration and develop destructive qualities in the children who play with them.

Certainly, the number of toys is an important factor in the guidance of children's play. If too many toys are available, children sometimes become confused as to what toy is of most interest and may move from one to another and enjoy none of them. Conversely, if too few toys are provided, children are not encouraged to perform according to their increasing abilities. In evaluating available toys, the following check list will be of value:

1. Are there toys that stimulate healthful physical activity? (pedal toys, wagons, wheelbarrows, balls, tricycles, things on which to climb)

2. Are there toys that satisfy the desire to manipulate, take apart, and fit together? (nested blocks, peg toys, large beads, easy puzzles)

3. Are there materials that can be used for construction? (blocks, boards, hammers, nails)

4. Are there materials that stimulate the dramatization of adult activities in which children are interested? (dolls, housekeeping toys, transportation toys, toy animals, garden tools, work costumes, male and female apparel)

5. Are there creative, dramatic play materials that accurately provide for ethnic and racial diversity?

6. Are the materials free of sharp corners, rough edges, splinters? Is there ample space to store them and space to use them without possible danger to the other children?

SPACE REQUIREMENTS

As mentioned in an earlier chapter, one of the best ways in which schools can supplement homes is in providing plenty of space for children to play. A lack of adequate space creates unhappiness in children who need vigorous exercise for their development. Crowded conditions are likely to cause outbursts of anger in groups of children since their activities are restrained and, therefore, frustrating. Many states require certain allotments of outdoor and indoor space for play before licenses will be granted for the care of preschool children outside their homes.

The arrangement of equipment in the space available is also of importance. Interest can be stimulated if materials are easily visible and accessible. Group play can be encouraged if there is space for more than one child near appropriate accessories for play. For example, ample space in the doll corner will encourage more than one child to play there. Sometimes, students are assigned the responsibility of rearranging equipment indoors or outdoors and it is interesting to observe the differences in the play activities that result. Often, playrooms will appear more spacious and will be more usable if rearrangements are considered carefully.

In some preschool centers, new and challenging space arrangements for indoors and outdoors offer the young child carefully designed facilities to assure ample opportunities for creative and dramatic play experiences. Inside space may be arranged with structures of varying shapes and sizes as designated areas for various play interests and curriculum centers. Spatial arrangements vary according to the developmental level of the children in the group. For example, five-year-olds who build roads and cities with blocks need different block space and block storage space than two and three-year-olds who usually prefer to build towers or single lane highways around the room.

SUGGESTED ASSIGNMENT

Part I

1. Write an anecdotal record giving an example of simple imitative play. Record the time that was spent in this activity.

2. Write an anecdotal record giving an example of dramatic imitation in a play situation.

3. Give an example of how a teacher encouraged dramatic play.

Part II

1. List toys or equipment that you think promote the following types of play:

    a. Active-physical

    b. Manipulative

    c. Imitative-dramatic

    d. Solitary

    e. Social

2. List five toys for children of the following ages and explain why you would select them for a children's toy library to be set up by a group of preschool parents:

    a. Infants
    b. Toddlers
    c. Two-year-olds
    d. Three-year-olds
    e. Four-year-olds
    f. Five-year-olds

Part III

Visit a preschool to which you have not been assigned and observe and record how the spatial environment influences how the children interact with each other. Be specific.

SELECTED READINGS

1. Herron, R. E., and Brian Sutton-Smith, *Child's Play*, John Wiley, New York, 1971.

This is an historical compilation of significant research concerning play. The sociological and psychological descriptions presented may help the reader define the value of play to the preschool child. Various kinds of play are described in the context of the developmental process.

2. McVickar, P., *Imagination: Key to Human Potential*, National Association for the Education of Young Children, Washington, D. C., 1972.

The author has written an interesting, small book about the need for imaginative teachers who can, through their own experiences and with the effective use of time, space, and materials, create a climate for insight and imaginative learning in all curriculum areas. Creative learning and environmental techniques are emphasized.

3. Millar, Susanna, *The Psychology of Play*, Penguin Books, Baltimore, 1968.

In Chapter 4, Millar discusses the initial responses of infants and describes how, through exploration and movement, the onset of play evolves. This discussion should be of interest to students and parents.

4. Montessori, Maria, *The Montessori Method*, Schocken Books, New York, 1912.

Chapter 8 of this classic book presents a concept of discipline based on respect for children and a belief that a child must be active and curious. The theory expounded should be helpful to the student who is seeking a personal theory of children's attitudes in play.

5. Parten, Mildred, and S. M. Newhall, "Social Behavior of Preschool Children," in *Child Behavior and Development*, Barker, Kounin, and Wright, eds., McGraw-Hill, New York, 1943.

This book contains brief and easily-read reports of research concerning infants and young children that have become bases for much that is being written today. Parten and Newhall have outlined the developmental stages of social behavior. These concepts provide information by which types of play can be evaluated.

6. Smilansky, Sara, *The Effects of Sociodramatic Play on Disadvantaged Pre-school Children*, John Wiley, New York, 1968.

Chapter 2 describes and informs the reader about research concerning dramatic play and play as a developmental process. Chapter 4 offers a view of the literature relating to dramatic play and accounts for the variations in levels of achievement in dramatic play for diverse groups of young children.

chapter 14

The Use of Creative Media

The effective use of creative media serves many purposes when (1) it provides each child with opportunities to express himself uniquely with a variety of materials, (2) there are opportunities to experiment with texture, color, form, and consistency, (3) children can develop skills with materials and tools used for creative experiences, and (4) there is time to build and refine language as a child learns to describe what he is experiencing. These criteria should guide the adult toward assuring preschoolers ample chance to work with media as a meaningful, creative, learning experience. Young children should feel satisfaction and joy when they are involved in a creative encounter and they can work through their ideas, interests, and feelings as they develop their abilities.

Creativity can be expressed in every area of living and every child has the potential for it. Certainly, children are creative in many of their behavior patterns. A child who finds it difficult to express himself in other forms of play or through language, often will be able to employ certain materials as a means of communicating his feelings. These media are also beneficial because children of different ages may adapt them to their current interests and abilities. Most adults probably wish they could experience childlike freedom in creative pursuits.

THE SEQUENCE OF INTERESTS AND SKILLS

When the very young child is given a pencil and paper, his actions are exploratory and his first concern is the tools confronting him. His thought seems to be: "What is this pencil and what do I do with it?" Similar curiosity is evident when children first become acquainted with crayons or easel paints. Testing these materials usually includes general sensory exploration; they like to see and taste and smell the materials that they manipulate. For this reason, special care as to the contents of the tools for creative work should be taken. Many of these materials can be made at home or at school from palatable and safe ingredients. If they are purchased, the nature of the ingredients should be investigated to make certain they are safe for children.

As children continue to wonder about the medium, they appear to think, "What is this sheet of paper and what does it have to do with the pencil or crayon or brush?" A wonderful discovery is made when, through bodily motion, children make lines appear on the paper.

Only brief mention of pencil work for preschoolers seems necessary for students. Most children will have been introduced to pencils and crayons at home and will have learned that manipulating them is enjoyable. These tools, however, are more appropriate for use by older children who are no longer so interested solely in the technique and have developed an interest in the products to be made. Thick crayons should be used in the preschool so that they can be grasped easily by young children. Some teachers think it is good to remove the paper wrappings and to break the crayons in assorted shapes in order that small children can grasp them more easily. This practice, also, may lessen quarreling over the newest crayons and unhappiness if a long one snaps into pieces.

The very young child is a scribbler. In pencil or crayon work, scribbling will begin, of course, at the time when children are provided with the materials and have developed a readiness to try their use. This may be as early as eighteen months of age or it may be considerably later. Children learn by doing and their early experiences with graphic materials promote this learning as they recognize the coordination between their movements and the effects of those movements. The child becomes aware of the relationship between his arm movements and the marks that appear on the paper. Thus, the activity becomes interesting to him.

Early scribbling forms are unique to individual children and children's methods of approach to the materials are as different as their social or locomotor activities. These differences, which probably persist to a marked degree in their later graphic work, are interesting to observe during the preschool years. Some children scribble in wide, sweeping motions, others tend to scribble in short, jerking movements and may use only a small area of the paper.

We can recognize rhythm in many activities of preschool children: in their motor activities as they run and jump and pound, in their language as they repeat syllables and phrases. Rhythm is always characteristic of young children's scribblings as well. The preschool child with pencil or crayon will establish a rhythm and a timing that seem to be particularly satisfying to him. A similar rhythm is apparent as children make marks on paper with paintbrushes.

Painting seems to have special interest for children. That it is more fun for the child than the use of crayons or pencils is not surprising when we consider the greater possibilities for freedom of movement, the texture of the medium with its diversity of uses, and the opportunities for color blending. Painting is first of all a motor activity, but it is not illogical that, as such, it is a good agent for expression of children's feelings since, as has been stated previously, one of the characteristics of young children is the overt quality of their responses to life. Painting by preschoolers should not be considred as an achievement but as a means toward healthy growth.

After the child has been assured of his ability to use the brush on paper, he is likely to test the materials further. For awhile, his interest may be confined to dipping the brush in the paint and dribbling one color into another in a separate container. In the school environment, such messiness should be permissible. If the child is wearing a coverall apron and the floor is covered with oilcloth or linoleum, adults can be relaxed enough to appreciate this experience from the child's point of view. The mechanics of handling a dripping paintbrush can be a fascinating procedure for the child.

The next step is likely to be an exploration of the paper with the paint-filled brush. The very young child at the easel will often paint around the border of the paper and will test the results of smearing the paint on the easel and on himself instead of on the paper. It is interesting that, as in other kinds of behavior, there seems to be tendency to test the limits of action before expected behavior is adopted. In the same way that children often experiment in social behavior by pinching or hitting other children and watching the responses, they seem to test the materials that they handle before they learn correct procedures.

After children learn to confine their efforts within the edges of the paper, they continue to work for the sheer joy of performance. The satisfaction that is demonstrated as the child designates his completion of the activity or asks for another sheet of paper is definite evidence of the emotional release that has been afforded.

By the time children are three to three-and-one-half years of age, their paintings assume more definite form. Crossed lines and curves appear in their drawings. These products are not often realistic by adult standards, but it is not unusual for children to name their paintings on completion.

Luella had been dabbing with the paintbrush, first with one color and then

with another. The dabs of paint were in orderly rows and the symmetry of her painting was attractive. Suddenly, as the page was almost filled with dots, she stood back and surveyed her work. A happy smile appeared on her face and she seemed especially interested as she returned to her activity. As she worked, she commented, "I'm making cookies and they're almost ready to go in the oven."

Sometimes, we are surprised at the knowledge children display when they name or talk about their pictures.

Judith had been painting rhythmic, blue, horizontal lines across the paper. She changed to black paint and painted a figure just above the lines. As she looked at her work, she said, "That's a whale." The realism of the drawing was striking and the teachers were surprised that she should know how a whale is shaped. A later conference with her mother, during which the episode was described as interesting, presented no information as to where or when her knowledge had been acquired.

The freedom with which children employ their symbols is demonstrated when the child, by the addition of a few lines, will decide that his painting is something very different from the initially announced subject. For example, putting a trunklike appendage on a dog will make it an elephant in spite of the fact that it may be small in comparison to the stick-figure man by whom it stands. In other words, a single differentiating characteristic rather than general appearance will identify an object or creature.

Adults who have not thought much about children's paintings are likely to think that the absence of correct proportions is due to the child's poorly developed manipulative skills or carelessness, but this lack of realism is often the result of his level of comprehension. Since his painting portrays his interpretation of his world, he gives precedence to those things with the most meaning for him. When the drawing of human figures begins, they usually have large circles for heads with only a straight line representing the body. Probably this signifies the importance of the head to the child. After all, the head is the area that denotes pleasant or unpleasant facial expressions and the origin of language and of laughter or crying.

Sometimes, the body will be deleted completely and the figure will consist merely of a head to which arms and legs are attached. Although we might conclude that this is because the head, arms, and legs are the features that express action, sometimes, no doubt, we may be mistaken in our suppositions.

Larry and Dan were four years old. Dan studied the painting that Larry had just completed and Larry said, "That's me." Dan commented, "But you don't have any body." Larry replied, "Of course not. I don't have any clothes on."

Depicting important items as of greatest magnitude is often characteristic. When the child draws "a house—and Daddy is going to work," "Daddy" is likely to be as tall or taller than the house. The father is the central theme as the child thinks of the situation. Usually, children appear to have no need to provide a setting—objects or people are drawn without a background and need not be placed on a base line in the picture.

Children's drawings gradually become more realistic as they learn to perceive more realistically. The process of growth can be observed as the details with which people and objects are symbolized become more numerous, as proportions become more true-to-life, as more objects or people appear in their pictures, and as fewer unidentifiable parts are included. Few children of preschool age will have reached the stage at which they will purposely set out to draw a specific item or situation. When they do, it is probable that older siblings, parents, or teachers have influenced them toward a striving for the product, and some of the pleasure in unstructured creativity has been lost. Of the three stages that have been described (1) exploratory, (2) symbolic, and (3) realistic, all are recognizable in children's behavior in the use of all types of creative media; however, the third stage is not characteristic of young children.

The young child should be provided with clear, harmonious colors since these provide a variety of experiences for him.

Fred, age three, was the son of a professor in the art department of the college in which the laboratory nursery school was located. Fred's father stated that he had made no effort to teach Fred anything about art and that Fred had not had access to any materials not usually provided for children of his age. However, Fred appeared to have an intense interest in combining colors to make other colors. Since he was a talkative child who liked to explain all his activities to other children, free playtime often resembled a demonstration period during which Fred and his friends spent long periods of time at the easels painting splotches of color, covering these spots with other colors, blending them, and discussing the results.

During each school term, there is likely to be some child or children who express delight when two colors are blended and the formula for a third color is discovered. It is thrilling to watch children's pleasure as they learn through their activities.

Research has shown that the persistent use of certain colors or color combinations is indicative of certain personality characteristics. Such factors of analysis are not appropriate to child guidance classes but rather are in the area of psychiatry or clinical psychology. Nevertheless, we cannot help being aware that children, like adults, do have favorite colors. A record of colors chosen by children over a period of time will show some striking consistencies in color choice. We must remember that color choices sometimes may reflect current interests, however. They may be influenced by the time of year, a current holiday observance, or the nature of what the child is thinking about at a particular time. For example, we would presume that red and green would be favorite colors before the Christmas holidays. Occasionally, we may be surprised when we learn the reasons for certain color choices.

During the last week in April, Douglas had chosen brown easel paint on several occasions. The subject matter of his paintings on these days was not recognizable to adults. Sometimes, he would cover the entire sheet with the brown paint. At other times, he would paint the lower one-half of the sheet with brown. On the third day, when he asked the teacher to replace his painting with a clean piece of paper, he remarked, "This is my garden. The seeds haven't come up yet."

It is interesting, also, that from a child's point of view it is not always necessary that colors are realistic any more than that proportions are authentic.

At a parents' meeting in December at the nursery school, Mrs. Murray, the mother of Jennie, age four, and John, age seven, reported that she was irritated by the quarreling that occurred when the children used crayons and paper. As an example, she said the children had been drawing Christmas trees and Jennie usually made her trees purple. John was terribly upset each time this happened. He would insist that Jennie make green trees and, when Jennie continued with the same color, he would scream at his mother to make Jennie conform to realism.

It should be easy for adults to allow children like Jennie to create according to their desires and we would hope that Mrs. Murray could convince her son of the unimportance of his sister's behavior. Some children appear to set high standards of realism for themselves and others in their work with creative media. These children are probably the ones who need our help in guiding them toward enjoyment and satisfaction in the processes of working with some of these materials. The standards that these children set for themselves can often eradicate the fun of creativity.

THE CHOICE OF MATERIALS

Although easel painting is enjoyed by a large majority of young children, our recognition of individual differences indicates that it may not be as satisfying to some children as to others. If they are tense and do not derive pleasure in their painting, it is probable that the use of another medium should be encouraged.

A material that offers one of the most desirable outlets for self-expression is finger paint. In using this material, the child who feels a necessity to conform to arbitrary standards is not hampered since pictorial images are not as likely to be expected by the child himself nor by other people. The principal satisfaction in finger painting is the "feel" of the finger paints, and the procedure does not include the mechanical difficulty of manipulating a brush, crayon, or pencil. Therefore, even very young children can enjoy finger painting.

It is an accepted opinion that children enjoy a certain amount of messiness, that the texture of messy materials is a needed factor in their preschool learning. Since most homes are not planned to allow for the freedom of such activities, the pressure to keep clean brings on tensions for most children. Finger paint provides an acceptable outlet for sensory and emotional experience that children are likely to be seeking. Since preschools are planned specifically for children, these activities are acceptable and offer a good way to supplement the child's home experiences.

Personality differences, inherent and learned, are striking when finger paint is first introduced to young children. We soon learn the extent of control that has developed within the child. Some children respond to this medium with great interest and freedom, others seem loathe to participate wholeheartedly until careful exploration has been experienced. Often, a timid child will place the tip of one finger in the paint hesitantly, and his painting may continue to be confined to his fingertips during several sessions. Or, he may use the base of the palm of his hand with his fingers held above the surface on which he is painting. The versatility of these paints is demonstrated when one child will approach the material as if fearful of getting his hands dirty, another child will pat and slap and scoop the paint much as if he were working with a form of semiliquid mud, and a third child will use his entire hands and lower arms in smearing the paint. The early handling of finger paint usually resembles the child's characteristic attitudes toward life.

If timid children are encouraged in finger painting activities and their interest is stimulated, the differences of techniques among individuals in time become less noticeable than with other creative media. After they have had finger painting experiences, the quietest children in the school often plunge in with both arms in a manner similar to that employed by more vigorous children. Frequently, we are surprised by the freedom and spontaneity with which usually quiet children use finger paints. These expressions seem indicative of their needs for the release of tensions.

A cumulative intensity of expression seems evident when children are permitted to use finger paints without limits of surface or time. Since the end product is not the important factor in children's creative work, finger painting is a particularly wise choice of activity. When easel painting is done, there is a product and only wise parents and teachers can give sufficient praise so as to encourage further painting and yet not enough so that he feels he is expected to produce an admired picture. Finger painting can be done on glossy, dampened paper that can be preserved or it can be done on oilcloth surfaces that are wiped clean when the child has lost interest in the activity. In other words, the fun of the process can be made the sole result.

Sometimes, ingenuity is required to engender a beginning interest in creative work. Children often get as much pleasure from cleaning up as from the actual procedures.

Dick was almost three-years-old. He never had been interested in any of the

creative media at the nursery school. By indirect means, Miss Blaine, the group teacher, had tried to encourage all children to participate. Two or three kinds of materials were always placed on the tables and, when the children came into the playroom, screens had been placed in front of the toy shelves so the children would not be distracted by toys.

When, after several sessions, Dick continued to show no interest in these materials and wandered around the room as if he were bored, Miss Blaine tried a more direct approach. She would suggest to him that he would enjoy joining the other children at the tables. Dick was completely unresponsive. He would try to engage the college students in conversation or he would sit on a small chair in another part of the room and watch the proceedings with a disinterested expression on his face.

As the children began to lose interest in the activity and to move toward the toys, Miss Blaine would move the screens so other types of play could begin. One day, when the other children had gone on to play with the housekeeping equipment, the puzzles, and the blocks, Miss Blaine asked Dick if he would like to help a student clean the finger paint table. He seemed delighted and he scrubbed the table vigorously with a sponge.

On the second and third days, as the children left the tables, Dick would walk to that part of the room and ask for the sponge. On the third day, Jerry and Diane joined him and they laughed and talked as they scrubbed the tables and the floor around them. On the fourth day, Dick watched as two of the children began to finger paint; he then reached for an apron, slipped his arms into it, and stood at the table waiting for a jar of paint to be provided for him. It seemed that the scrubbing activities had demonstrated that the painting would be fun after all.

Finger painting is likely to promote a more sociable experience than easel painting since several children usually work at a table facing each other and their work is more easily observed by other children. Rhythmic imitation often occurs as they correlate their hand and arm movements in tempo with the strokes of other children.

To a somewhat lesser degree than in easel painting, the sequence of expression may be observed in finger painting. Surely, all children will test and try the texture and use of the medium when first introduced to them. Since a greater variety of movements and effects of those movements are possible in this kind of painting, the exploratory stage is logically of longer duration. It is not uncommon, however, for older preschool children to give a name to or to tell a story about a finger painting picture and school age children often plan the finished product during the initial stages of their specific paintings.

Another material that has kinesthetic value is water-based clay. This clay has the texture and pliability that provide children with many opportunities to push, pull, squeeze, pound, and manipulate. It can be rolled, pinched, pounded, and made into an infinite variety of forms. Children learn that water makes it soft and that air dries it out. Clay work is a table activity that provides a time for solitary experiences or intense group interaction. If the product is to be saved, twigs, pipe cleaners, buttons, or any number of other materials can be stuck into the clay. Creative limits are bound only by a child's imagination. Homemade play dough can be used as a clay medium and it can be made with flour, salt, water, and vegetable dye. This dough, however, serves a different purpose because it is less likely to hold form and, therefore, is a more tactile medium than a creative one. Clay based on grease offers some opportunity for manipulation but it lacks the pliability of water-based clay.

Working with clay can offer opportunities for the active child to encourage his more passive peer, since clay can be pounded vigorously without harmful results and it can be manipulated gently with great satisfaction. Once routines are established for using clay, it does not require direct supervision but is enhanced by adult comments. Moreover, it provides an excellent time for staff to listen and observe the conversations and attitudes of children.

The sequential stages of play that are characteristic of all creativity are especially evident when children play with clay. They first appear to wonder, "What is this?" and "What do I do with it?" Poking, punching, rolling, pulling, pinching, and pounding usually are practiced as children become acquainted with clay. In the second stage, children continue to manipulate with no preconceived notions concerning specific products, but an accidental form often appears that impresses the child and is named by him. Here, as with other creative media, a simple change of feature will allow the child, according to his level of perception, to rename the object. For example, a tug on the neck of a dog may create a giraffe regardless of the differences in realistic sizes of the two animals. At the third level of creation, manipulation will become a purposeful activity. Because of the dimensional form and the simplicity possible in the products, the stage of realism is likely to appear when children are younger than the ages at which realism appears in their graphic work. The age limits characterizing each stage are extremely varied and it is impossible to predict at which ages certain kinds of manipulation will occur, but it is likely that all three stages can be observed when we watch one child in a play session at the clay table. This is probably another factor that makes clay activities especially worthwhile from an adult point of view. It seems natural that many adults become more interested in watching children when their creative work assumes realistic form.

Effective artistic experiences for young children evolve when there are a variety of objects and many ideas to draw on as a child explores how color, line, and form can create patterns and meaningful thoughts graphically. A child needs many opportunities to explore the properties of glue with a variety of collage materials before he is ready to move from an exploratory experience to a preplanned creative endeavor. Very young children glue objects from nature such as pine cones, twigs, leaves, and weeds onto surfaces and create random designs. Older preschoolers use these same materials and carefully place them in patterned forms. Some mature, sophisticated preschoolers implement preconceived forms as they carefully plan before they use the glue.

Boxes of collage materials that contain everything from pieces of colored paper to styrofoam egg carton sections can be glued to anything from newspapers or wall-hanging materials to scrap wooden plaques. Children can be guided to use the adhesive nontoxic glues for designing one, two, or three dimensional creations that satisfy a natural desire to think, feel, and create.

Art materials can serve many purposes. Property and texture can be explored as children work with macaroni, salt, beans, and pebbles. Shape and form can be discussed as leaves, buttons, or fruit seeds are arranged on paper, in a box, or on a piece of wood. Color and color changes can be observed as dry sand is mixed with water or as red paint is spread over a piece of yellow cloth. Young children usually work individually. Occasionally, large mural-type collages can be put together by small groups of children when they have a common goal.

A group of four-year-old children had just completed a "junk" collage of objects they had found on a series of walks around the urban neighborhood of their school. They had glued the objects onto a long sheet of vinyl wall-hanging material that their teacher, Mr. Herman, had set on the floor. When Mr. Herman hung the collage on the wall after it had dried, Esther stepped back in order to view the panorama and called out, "That junk looked plenty messy in the street but it sure looks pretty when you put it in a picture."

Block painting that recreates forms, such as those made by sponges or vegetable sections, is another art form that children enjoy. This medium can be set up easily and repeated with a variety of materials, thus offering children a variety of materials while they develop skill with a particular technique.

Blunt scissors are important tools for art experiences. Young children can master cutting skills as they are encouraged to fringe paper. Older preschoolers enjoy cutting pictures from old greeting cards or magazines to paste on paper or on supermarket pressed paper package trays. It is important that left-handed scissors be available for those children who need them.

Wide crayons and chalk provide opportunities for young children to experiment with line and color. As children move from random scribbles to nonrepresentational shapes, they gain mastery over tools they will later use to create designs and representational forms. Developmental levels are clearly observable through crayon pictures as random color choice and picture form gives way to selected colors and perceived forms and shapes. Young children often describe their scattered markings and identify their drawings before the discerning adult can notice readily identifiable objects. The adult who observes a child's art work must remember that a comment concerning color and space can encourage a conversation but that an attempt to identify an object can dampen the creative spirit of a young child who cannot create as he perceives or who has been so busy exploring the medium that the final product is not his primary concern.

Wood and woodworking tools are an exciting and sought-after preschool activity. Scraps of soft wood gathered from lumber yards, furniture factories, or do-it-yourself family projects can be used as an art form for gluing wood sculptures and as a craft project at a workbench. Supervision is necessary as a child learns to use a hammer and saw. Three-year-olds often display amazing dexterity as they persevere to hammer a nail through a soda cap into a block of wood while a four-year-old will use great amounts of energy to saw his wood and be content to take both pieces home as a sign of his strength and dexterity. As the youngster approaches five, he often begins to nail blocks of wood together and to saw appropriate sized pieces to use as he builds a model of transportation or a piece of minisized furniture. Finished products are rough in design but very satisfying to the creator. Some children enjoy painting their woodwork in order to complete a preconceived idea. The stages of activity: exploratory, symbolic, and realistic will occur in this area as well as in others.

A variety of sturdy, splinterless blocks of varying shapes and sizes will provide experiences in block play with many opportunities for creative experiences. Children work with form, design, and structure as they move through exploratory, sumbolic, and realistic levels of development. It is not unusual to see four three-year-olds each trying to balance his own tower or building his own road on which to push a car. Sometimes, they will strive to construct a framed enclosure around themselves or around wooden animals. As children approach their fifth year, block building often becomes a group activity for four or five children as they construct superhighways, bridges, tunnels, and towns and create their own environment for dramatic play. Block play can be a solitary or group experience depending on the age or mood of a youngster.

Block play is particularly satisfying for the child who may be timid or fearful about handling the messier media and yet who desires to create. When the block area is spacious, several children can be engaged in this gross motor activity on the floor without the danger of spilled paint or paste. Children can alter their creations without concern for a finished product, and group experiences can occur in an area that does not depend on close teacher-supervision. A teacher, however, should observe behavior in the block area and enhance language skills as she encourages children to discuss the shape and form of blocks that are necessary to build a sturdy structure. It is sometimes helpful when an adult writes a sentence in the child's own words about a product on which he has worked. This enables a parent to understand the shcool program when a child comes home and says, "I played blocks today." It is especially important that girls be encouraged to work with blocks and woodworking. These activities often are offered to boys without effort to involve girls in these forms of creative activity.

TECHNIQUES OF GUIDANCE

Many of the adults who guide young children through art experiences have not had the opportunity to grow up practicing and creating with art materials. Frequently, the student experiences art along with the children and finds it difficult to free herself from the craft concept of a finished product or a realistic form. It is helpful when adults (1) realize that creative expression has been part of a man's heritage, (2) recognize the diversity of forms for aesthetic appreciation, (3) understand that art is a form of creative expression along with music, dance, and drama, and (4) communicate an appreciation of color, form, and line as part of an aesthetic concept of artistic creations.

Adults have the responsibility for providing materials, space, and encouragement for preschool experiences with creative media. Skillful adults guide children toward initiating ideas appropriate to their own developmental level. Models created for children to imitate violate the concept of expressive individualism. They (1) inhibit and intimidate the child who may feel inadequate with the materials, (2) deprive him of the opportunity to think things through in an original way, and (3) stress and end product rather than a creative encounter. Adults who present models show a lack of trust in the child's ability to use materials effectively and are presenting adult concepts instead of allowing for a child's unique perceptions.

If children ask how to draw or paint specific items or objects, we should stimulate their thinking by talking with them about what they want to portray. For example, if a child asks, "How do I draw a tree?" the teacher or parent might ask, "What does the trunk of a tree look like?" "How tall is a tree?" or "Do trees have branches and leaves?" When we stimulate pictorial images in the child's thinking, he can be encouraged to depict what an object looks like to him, not to us. When children have learned to enjoy the medium and have developed skill in working with it, they will choose their own models if they wish to imitate.

Children cannot be free in expressing their ideas and their feelings if we attempt to "teach" them how to paint or model. Encouragement and guidance are the best forms of adult supervision. Teahcing the child how to paint will destroy his initiative. Creative activities become "busy work" and individuality is squelched when all the children in a group are trained to make similar products. Moreover, frustration may develop if children are unsuccessful in producing according to the standards set by the teacher. This will often cause the child to lose interest as a participant.

Asking the child what he is making is one of the most common blunders made by adults who supervise the creative activities of young children. Such questions are harmful for several reasons:

1. The child may not be making anything. He may be merely experimenting with the materials and his enjoyment will be lessened if we make him feel he must always be making something.

2. The child may not have decided what his product will be, in which case he may feel he is inferior or incapable since we have implied that his activity should be definitely purposeful.

3. The child may not care to tell us what he is making. Children have little privacy and they deserve some activities which they can enjoy without our questioning.

4. The child may lack the verbal skill by which to explain his drawing and, from his point of view, this will make him lose self-confidence.

5. The child may believe that his picture or model is quite realistic and, by asking, we have signified that he is incompetent.

6. The child may lose confidence in our judgment when we let him know that we are not intelligent enough to recognize what is perfectly clear to him.

Color books should not be provided for children because freedom of movement, which is one of the pleasures of creative expression, is hampered. Young children have not reached a level of eye-hand coordination that makes it possible for them to stay within the lines, and the inability to do so may be frustrating to some children. Moreover, dependence on the lines may become a set pattern and the ability to create independently may be lessened or even lost. If these reasons were not enough to discourage the use of color books, a survey of the books available demonstrates that the majority of them contain pictures of objects and situations with which preschool children are completely unfamiliar and which, therefore, have no meaning for them.

One of the most baffling problems is how much or how little praise we should extend to children when they work with creative materials. Praise by adults is good because it serves as motivation for children. Yet, praise of a specific picture or model may result in a tendency by the child to repeat the theme or technique in subsequent products and thereby to stereotype his work. No definite rules for good verbal guidance are possible, but the following comments will provide encouragement and self-confidence in children: "The colors you've used are certainly pretty," "You've had fun painting today, haven't you?" "You worked for a long time on this picture," or "You and Carol chose the same kinds of brushes for your painting today." When we review the rules for good verbal guidance, it is evident that these remarks are reassuring to the child.

Sometimes, models of clay, drawings, paintings, and other creative products are displayed temporarily at the school. When this is done, care should be taken that, over a period of time, all children will have had their work exhibited and that adults do not comment effusively about any one item. In the home situation, a similar practice is wise.

Frequently, children and their parents will be pleased if some of their graphic and plastic art work can be preserved and taken home. Pressure toward this practice often results because older siblings of school age bring completed work home from school. Specific schools handle this problem in various ways. Sometimes, in order to eradicate the possibility of undue attention, favorable or unfavorable, to any one piece of work, a good practice is to place the date and the child's name on his work each day and to allow him to take an accumulation home at certain intervals. In this way, when children ask to take something home to their parents, we can assure them that the item will be saved and that they can take it home in a few days or on a certain day.

Frequently, it is necessary for teachers to interpret children's creative work to their parents. Parents who have been trained in stereotyped art work are likely to place undue emphasis on their children's products. It is not unusual for a mother to express her concern about the messiness and unrealism of her children's paintings or drawings. Also, comparisons are often made with the work of other children or even of older siblings.

Teachers should offer suggestions about how to comment on a child's creative work to assure that stress is placed on line, color, and arrangement rather than on the completed project. A meeting for parents held early in the school year can provide opportunities for the parents to work with the media and will serve as a learning experience as to how to comment effectively about a child's work. Adults should help preschool children explore, manipulate, and symbolize as they gain dexterity, aesthetic appreciation, and perception through the use of creative media.

SUGGESTED ASSIGNMENT

Part I

Observe a child working with crayons, chalk, easel paint, or finger paint, and answer the following questions:

1. How many colors were available? How many of these did he choose to use?

2. Did the child comment during his work? What were his comments?

3. Do you think the child was interested in the materials, the colors, his movements, or the finished product? Explain your answer.

Part II

Observe a child working with sand, clay, or water, and answer the following questions:

1. How did the child use the material?

2. Was this activity principally solitary or social?

3. What were his comments during his work?

4. Do you think this activity served as an outlet for the child's feelings or do you think he participated just for enjoyment?

Part III

Observe a child working with blocks and answer the following questions:

1. What did he do with the blocks?

2. Was this activity principally solitary or social?

3. What were his comments during his work?

4. Did the child use his product after it was completed? Describe.

Part IV

Observe a group of children working with collage materials and answer the following questions:

1. How was their dialogue related to their work?

2. Select two children of different age levels and explain how their performance differed in reference to

a. length of time spent at the task

b. preplanning of placement of materials

c. concern for and interest in the finished product

Part V

Select five creative media at the preschool and work with them for a period of one week. Describe your experiences.

SELECTED READINGS

1. Alschuler, Rose H., and La Berta Weiss Hartwick *Panting and Personality*, University of Chicago Press, 1969.

This book will be especially informative for those adults who seek to understand the art products of two, three, and four-year-old children. Illustrations throughout the text are reproductions of actual paintings by children.

2. Bland, James, *Art of the Young Child*, published by Museum of Modern Art, distributed by Simon & Schuster, New York, 1957.

This is a graphically illustrated book showing ages and stages of children's art. The last few pages recommend simple materials and tools that are important for a good preschool art experience.

3. Cherry, Clare, *Creative Art for the Developing Child*. Lear Siegler, Inc./-Fearon Publishers, Belmont, California 1972.

This is an excellent source for information about appropriate creative art experiences in all media, for young children. Precise information is presented about materials, methods and levels of expectation. The author's stess on the creative process is supported by direct suggestions for implementation. Photographs clarify the concepts that are presented.

4. Hurlock, Elizabeth B., *Child Development*, 5th ed., McGraw-Hill, New York, 1972.

Chapter 13, "Creativity," offers interesting ideas concerning correlative facets of several kinds of activities for young children. Those who are interested in a good curriculum for the preschool will gain understanding from reading this explanation of how the child can be encouraged toward creativity.

5. Jameson, Kenneth, *Art and the Young Child*, Viking Press, New York, 1968.

This is an illustrative book on art as a process and as a means of expression. Developmental stages of art expression are described. The author also makes excellent suggestions to help teachers and parents guide children toward creative, meaningful art expression.

6. Lowenfeld, Viktor, *Your Child and His Art*, The Macmillan Company, New York, 1955.

This book would be a good choice for all parents. Adult attitudes toward children's art are recommended specifically. Most chapter headings and subheadings consist of questions and problems that occur to all people who observe children's work with creative media. Illustrative materials make the text attractive and easily understood.

7. Taylor, Barbara J., *A Child Goes Forth*, Brigham Young University Press, Provo, Utah, 1973.

Chapter 2, "Creative Expression," presents practical information as to how to present various media to children. The entire book would be helpful to a person who is planning a program for a preschool or a day care center.

chapter 15

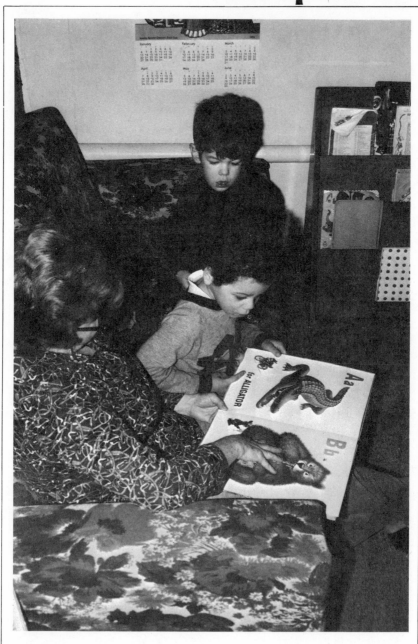

Stories, Poems, and Television

Children have always liked stories. Traditional conceptions of the adult-child relationship entail communication by means of story telling or story reading. Indeed, story telling is part of man's heritage. Adults, as well as children, are entertained and informed by books. Books are important in the lives of children and, in order to choose books for them, adults must be acquainted with children's books and with the children for whom the books are chosen. Although not every book will be of interest to every child, with the tremendous number of children's books available many interesting ones can be found that are suitable for each child. Through pictures and stories, children learn about their world, seek humor, enjoy fantasy and gain understanding about relationships.

A good preschool will have a variety of carefully selected books, film strips, films, tape recordings, and records that (1) span many interest areas, (2) clarify a child's concept of his world, (3) expand the child's perceptions about people, animal life, and other places, (4) enhance vocabulary and offer various rhythms of speech, (5) contain warmth, humor, and feelings, and (6) have attractive aesthetic formats of design and language. Children should be permitted to handle books of many shapes and sizes and to learn how to care for them. Even young children can also become involved with using audio visual materials correctly and can enjoy listening to a story of their choice on a tape recorder or phonograph.

CRITERIA FOR GOOD BOOKS

Among books that appeal to a young child some usually reflect an aspect of his world that he can identify with through the stories and pictures. Children respond eagerly to stories that present familiar scenes. Many good books for children are published that describe the variety of life styles of families that form our American culture. If a preschool library is to be meaningful, it will contain books with stories and poems that offer children an understanding of their own culture and glimpses into the culutres of other young people.

When the adult chooses a book to which the child can relate she provides opportunities for him to talk about familiar things and thereby may increase his feelings of security and self-confidence.

Jason Hays was an intense and uncomfortable appearing four-year-old child in Mrs. Kahn's day care center. He had joined the group in November when his family moved to the suburbs from a large city.

Jason usually played by himself and seemed unable to join in conversation with the children. Mrs. Kahn, in seeking some way to help Jason, decided to check with the local librarian to see if there were some books that stressed the urban environment with which Jason was familiar. The librarian suggested one particular book because it was the story of a black child who lived in a high-rise apartment house and another that contained a collection of simple poems about city life.

Mrs. Kahn read the story to Jason and his group the next day and he smiled in a relaxed manner as she read. After the story, Jason began to talk about how small the people looked when he had looked out of his window in the city, of his elevator experiences, and of supermarket shopping without a car. Mrs. Kahn encouraged Jason to talk about his city experiences and a few days later she was pleased to observe Jason busy at work with several children who were building a high-rise house in the block corner.

Humor is an important quality in children's literature, particularly when there is an element of surprise or of gross exaggeration that the young child can understand. Stories about animals or people who are silly looking, out of place or mischievous delight children, particularly if the language is concise and the pictures are graphic and colorful. Children laugh raucously at slapstick, pie-in-the-face humor that occurs in a story or during a television program.

Fantasy can be fanciful or frightening for children depending on the nature of the story, the age and background of the children, and the ability of the reader or story teller to present the proper perspective according to the understanding of the children. Fantasy and reality often are interchangeable in the mind of a preschooler who is still unsure of the limits of the real world. Therefore, traditional fairy tales may have frightening, fearful elements that can cause confusion and concern in the minds of very young children.

Before Mrs. Hubert registered her four-and-a-half year old daughter, Paula, at the nursery school she made a special request that the story of the three pigs should not be read to her. The family had been living in a brick house in another city until they moved into a cedar shingle house in their present home town. Paula had been acquainted with the story about the three pigs in the past without apparent effect but was now fearful about going to sleep because she was afraid that her new house would be blown down.

This twilight zone between fantasy and reality causes confusion for preschool children and fantasies that cause misconceptions can be sources of conflict for them.

David, age three-and-one-half, refused to put the blocks away. A volunteer at the preschool was trying to persuade him to do so and decided to try an imaginative way to convince David to follow her direction. She said, "Those blocks are tired. They want to go back to their house. They will be very angry with you if you leave them on the floor and they will not play with you again."

David looked from the volunteer to the blocks and ran to the teacher in tears. He related what he had been told and cried, "She's making fun, isn't she? The blocks are my friends. She is making believe, isn't she?" It took several minutes to reassure David that the volunteer had pretended and that people get angry, objects do not.

Children enjoy stories and poems about feelings and emotions that they can understand. For example, it is easy for a child to identify with someone in a story who cannot go out to play because he is sick or to share the joy of a person in a story who obtains a new pet.

Unfortunately, most children's literature makes it easier for boys than for girls to identify with success and high achievement. Female characters in many children's stories have only minor roles. They usually are far less adventurous and much more passive than male characters. Recently there appears to be an increasing awareness of this problem and, just as there have been many fine books about minority cultures published in recent years, new books with more adventurous female characters are now available. Children learn about relationships between people through stories and it is important that they learn that boys and girls have equal opportunities to be adventurous, heroic, humorous and gentle.

Perennial favorites of young children are not all realistic, however. The Mother Goose rhymes have remained popular throughout the years in spite of features that would appear to be contrary to some of our knowledge about the wise choice of children's stories. Their rhythm and rhyme are probably largely responsible for their popularity. Poems have special interest for children due to their liking for rhythm and sound. Moreover, this story form is especially appropriate for preschoolers because of their level of language learning. At this age, when children's vocabularies are expanding more rapidly than at any other time, the use of words represents adventurous experience for them and specific words appear to derive more attention in poems than in prose. Many classics for children are poetic in form, which indicates the universality of their appeal.

Certainly, the language of the story, the style of writing and the length of the story affect the book's appeal for children. Young children prefer succinct stories that can be completed in one session. They enjoy repetition within a story theme and often join in when the text has repetitive elements. The words of the story should be appropriate in language, rhythm and style to the tale it tells.

Books contributing to our understanding of ourselves and other people are popular at all age levels and especially so with young children. This is not surprising when we consider their egocentricity and their eagerness to find their places in their world. Stories that relate to children who have mothers and daddies, brothers and sisters, playmates and pets, and the everyday behavior of these people are favored by children. Tales descriptive of community services such as the activities of the baker, the grocer, the postman, and the filling station operator are usually favorites. Transportation is as interesting in story form as in dramatic play situations. Also, many good books for children enhance the pleasures of the physical world. For example, books that describe the sounds of rain, the changing colors of the sunset, the beauty of snowflakes, and the falling of the leaves in autumn are chosen often by all preschoolers.

Above all, stories should be interesting and entertaining. The information that children gain from literature is important, but preschool children will learn only if they enjoy what they hear. Sometimes, adults are so intent on teaching children that they forget that learning can be a pleasant experience, that our main purpose is to encourage a liking for literature. With the flexible schedule at the preschool, children are usually not pressed to listen to stories unless they like to do so.

The criterion of interest indicates that stories should have good plots, good characterizations, and appropriate actions. Doubtless, children today, through conditioning by their experiences in diverse activities such as busy family life and television viewing, will demand these three elements more than children of a generation ago. Too often, adults try to force their own tastes in literature on children. It is disappointing to parents and teachers when children do not enjoy a book that brought special pleasure to them when they were young. Not only are children unique in personality and interests but their experiences are different from those of children of a few years ago. With the tremendous amount of available literature, it is possible to find many stories that both adults and children will enjoy. Sharing pleasure in books creates a close feeling between grownups and the children with whom they associate.

Illustrations in children's books are indicative of their worth. Obviously, these should be appropriate to the subject matter and should be placed on the same pages as the part of the story that they illustrate. Factual material should be accompanied by accurate drawings or photographs, whereas imaginative illustrations can be more varied. Younger children will be more attracted by simple, mass drawings than photographs since the latter are likely to include distracting details. Illustrations for young children should be simple and uncluttered. This is obvious when we consider what we know about children's impressions as shown in their own creative products. For the same reason, only a few colors are necessary. These colors usually should be of rather intense hue and should be free of the shadings that are attractive to adults. The sepia-colored pictures that were popular several decades ago probably will not have appeal for children today, but a few relatively recent books in which illustrations have been composed of only one or two colors seem to be pleasing to preschoolers.

The format of a book usually indicates the cost of the book. Although it is not necessary that every book should last indefinitely, it is disconcerting to children if their favorite books fall apart. Obviously, books chosen for preschools should be sturdily constructed with good paper and strong bindings. The general appearance of books is important to children. Frequently, this factor is the reason for the child's original interest in looking at the book or requesting that it be read to him. Since young children cannot read, it is good if some picture on the outside of the book indicates the subject matter of the story.

The dimensions of children's books seem to be relatively unimportant as criteria of popularity. When a large number of books are placed on an open rack at the school, there appears to be no tendency by children to choose books because they are small or large.

TECHNIQUES OF PRESENTATION

Parents sometimes ask, "When should we start reading to our child?:" In view of what we know about babies' responses and learnings when they listen to adult voices, very young infants enjoy the monologues of those who care for them. The one-sided conversations that parents carry on with their babies represent the beginnings of story telling to children.

By about eighteen months of age, the majority of children will enjoy being read to. Although not all words may have meaning to them, the rhythm and inflection of adult voices may be enjoyable and they will begin to relate these pleasures to books. With the advent of the understanding of words, children show their first personal interests in books and pictures and they delight in hearing adults name objects or people as they designate the appropriate drawings or pictures. The first books possessed by children usually have cloth pages and are composed simply of pictures that sometimes are labeled by name. Story hour at home presents a time when adults and children should have an uninterrupted time together. Thus, the child's early experiences with stories is accompanied by social and emotional satisfactions.

Preschools should provide a variety of books that are available to children at all times. When an open book rack is placed near a low table, the stage is set for interest and experience in handling and looking at books. It is wise to have enough books so that children can choose from several and yet not so many that their choices are difficult to make. When too many books are on display, some children are likely to spend only a minute or two with one book and then to choose another only to discard it for a third one. Certainly, books should be placed so that they can be seen and reached easily. A pile of books placed haphazardly on a table will not promote interest in exploring this pastime.

Obviously, the youngest children at school cannot sit still and listen for more than a few minutes at a time. Therefore, their stories should be simple and brief and it is good to alternate singing, action games, or finger plays with story telling or reading. In some schools, children sit on small chairs in a circle at story time. This plan probably will insure enjoyment by older preschoolers, but younger children may feel closer to the teacher and be more willing to listen if rugs are placed on the floor and the teacher sits on the child's level during the story period. Often, it is wise to divide children into small groups who are in similar stages of development or have similar interests.

Preschool teachers become adept at reading a story and at the same time holding the book so that each child in the group can see the appropriate pictures as the pages are turned. Illustrations tend to increase and prolong interest in a story and, therefore, provide a good means for holding the attention of a group of children. There is a possibility, however, that children may become dependent on visual perception at story time and that pleasure in the style of writing or even the meanings of the words may be curtailed. Occasionally, children become so accustomed to pictures as a part of stories that they fail to concentrate when stories are told or when it is impossible for them to see the illustrations.

At rest time, Miss Harrington sometimes told a simple, unexciting story to the children. It seemed as if the sound of her soft voice and the children's concentration on the story helped them to relax.

When Richard entered school, apparently he had never heard a story told. That he was accustomed only to illustrated stories was demonstrated at rest time when he sat up on his cot and said, "But where are the pictures?" Miss Harrington explained that there were no pictures, that she simply was telling this story, but Richard continued to ask for "the pictures." It was apparent that the story alone was not very meaningful to him.

When we consider how much of children's experiences with literature is visual through comics, movies, and television, it seems important that we provide opportunities for informal story telling as a means of offering them more varied experiences. Adults, as well as children, become dependent on the pages of a book. They are likely to feel incompetent and self-conscious when they relinquish this support. A wise student, teacher, or parent will evaluate her self-confidence in this area and will attempt to learn techniques of good story telling. Story telling has at least three advantages over story reading: (1) there is more opportunity for freedom of expression and adults and children become better acquainted, (2) appropriate gestures are possible when one is not hampered by handling a book, and (3) deletions or additions can be improvised in accordance with the child's interests and mood.

Certainly, preparing for a child's experiences with literature should be painstaking. Our discussion has indicated that the adult must choose stories carefully so that they are interesting to the children. Moreover, in order to read and at the same time to display illustrations to the group, the teacher must be familiar with the details of the story. At school as well as at home, children will almost completely memorize a beloved story and their displeasure is evident when portions are omitted or read incorrectly. If students are to be expected to assume responsibilities for story reading or story telling, the importance of careful preparation should be emphasized. Participating students should spend ample time in becoming acquainted with books for planned periods and also with those that children may request be read during free periods. Beginning students are seldom expected to read or tell stories to groups of children, but sometimes they are privileged in being permitted to share stories with one or two children. This practice is helpful since there is no better way of gaining rapport with and becoming well acquainted with children.

When we are aware of the wide range of individual abilities and interests of children, we know that we cannot expect them all to be equally attentive at story time. The advantages of the laboratory school are strikingly apparent in meeting the needs of individuals in this situation. Since the ratio of adults to children is large in a laboratory school, the teacher need not sacrifice the enjoyment of the group when one or two children are unable or unwilling to be attentive. Usually, one adult other than the teacher will be free to supervise at story time. As stated when techniques helpful in promoting relaxation were discussed, physical contact will often enable a child to sit quietly and happily. In a group of two- to three-year-olds, it is not uncommon to see a restless child crawl on an adult's lap and cuddle there at story time. When children are older, by moving near a child and placing a hand or arm on his shoulder, an adult sometimes can give just enough support to make him comfortable for a period of quiet listening.

Children enjoy participating in storytelling in various ways. The simple dramatization of a story or poem provides a new dimension for language growth, sequence development and story sharing. Children enjoy seeing and using puppets, also, as a part of a story telling situation.

Books made at school or at home concerning a particular situation are a fine source for listening and viewing. Simple books can evolve from a story a child dictates such as a sentence about a school trip. He and other children will enjoy choosing illustrations from a catalog or magazine. A story book with photographs about the school may provide satisfaction and pleasure. Children enjoy these materials because the content is egocentric in concept and directly related to their lives.

Occasionally, a very young child will refuse to sit and listen to a story. If the room arrangement permits, it is probably wise to allow him to play elsewhere if he can do so without distracting other children. Later, as he becomes more interested in other children and what they are doing, he will likely join them in the story circle. Sometimes, older children flaunt adult authority by misbehaving at story time. Since this is likely to prevent interested children from concentrating on the story, it may be wise for another adult to remove that child and perhaps another child with similar interests to another part of the playroom and to read to them alone. Such a procedure may (1) provide the special attention that the child desires and probably needs, (2) promote his ability to concentrate because he is nearer to the adult and less distracted by the presence of other children, and (3) help him to know that story periods are a definite and regular part of the school routine. On the next day, or within a few days at the longest, a desire for social acceptance and reciprocity usually will prompt this child to join the story group and to adopt desirable behavior.

As in other activities, sometimes children are so fatigued or emotionally upset that it is difficult for them to conform to group behavior at story time. When children consistently seem unable to remain in a story group, we may suspect physical illness, mental retardation, or perhaps a hearing deficiency. Of course, none of these maladies should be determined on the basis of this behavior alone. Careful consideration of the child's over-all behavior by professionally trained teachers should be planned and appropriate referrals made if deficiencies of any kind seem probable.

One of the main purposes of stories is to promote children's learning. Permitting children to ask questions and to make comments during the reading or telling of a story is a good technique at school just as it is at home. A good teacher not only will allow questions concerning the story but will encourage them. Answering one child's inquiries and, at the same time, maintaining the interest of other children sometimes is difficult. Methods of accomplishing this feat will depend on the teacher's personality, the nature of the story, and the children involved. Usually, if the children are four to five years of age, most of them will be interested in the conversation. If they are not interested, a teacher sometimes suggests that the two of them talk about it after the story is finished and she sees to it that they do so. When children are younger, it is probably best to reply to questions very briefly. Continuing with the story usually will distract the questioner toward thinking of new developments in the plot.

Obviously, the developmental level of the children is the best criterion for choosing good methods of presentation. A child in a group of two-year-olds listens to the story as if he were the only person present. He is seldom interested in the reactions of other children unless they deviate greatly. Older children display interest for far longer periods of time but, with their increased sociality, they are interested not only in the story but also in the behavior and responses of other children.

All preschool children enjoy stories that relate to themselves, and the way in which stories are presented will often emphasize this pleasure. Interest can be encouraged when children are permitted to describe their own experiences or possessions that are similar to those mentioned in the story. Often, a child who is usually timid and reticent gains group recognition by his participation at these times.

Story time should be a leisurely, relaxed period of the day and it is wise to make it a flexible part of the daily schedule. The amount of time that is to be spent with stories should never be definitely planned. Children's needs for relaxation are closely related to the length of time that they will spend sitting quietly in a story group. These needs depend on such factors as the weather, their physical status, their routine habit patterns, the amounts and kinds of play that have preceded the story period, their interests in the material presented, and the ability of the adult to present these materials in an appealing manner.

SOURCES FOR CHILDREN'S BOOKS

Inexpensive books for preschool children are available at most supermarkets and drug stores. They are found in medical and dental offices where a child may need something to amuse him. Many of these books are of poor quality, design and story theme. Yet, this literature does provide opportunities for identification and some of it refers to popular television programs that children view. The contents are as varied as those of other books and they have the added attraction of being easy to handle and inexpensive. Guidance toward discriminating choices is the best method of adult supervision.

A liking for these books need not eliminate interest in good literature. In fact, a desire for stories of other kinds may be stimulated. It is wise to recognize that, during the preschool years, adults wield their greatest influence in giving direction to the choices children make. If parents guide children toward a wise choice of books and inform themselves concerning these books so children recognize their interest and sanction, possibly this is the best kind of training toward wise self-selection of literature in later years.

The local library is a source for good literature for children and the librarian usually has information concerning appropriate materials for specific age groups. Moreover, several resource books are available to help in the selection of children's literature. Books can be ordered, then, through a local book store.

TELEVISION AND FILMS

Television is the most influential story media today and, undoubtedly, its influence is seen in all preschool classrooms. Some programs are viewed in preschools and day care centers but most television viewing occurs at home.

Children interpret what they see not only on the basis of their levels of comprehension but also according to their unique dispositions. Thus, the degree of tolerance for vicarious experiences of excitement, anxiety or fear possible in many television programs and movies will depend on the developmental level of the child and also on his unique patterns of feeling and response.

Children's television programs often present false values, stereotyped people, and sick humor and, therefore, are poor sources for guiding personality development. Until the creators of these programs produce themes that respect the rights of children and show awareness of the developmental differences among children, television will remain an uncertain learning tool. According to a government report on violence in 1969, most children watch television without adult supervision and spend hours absorbed in fantasy and violence-oriented situations. This media has influenced the behavior patterns of some children who confuse television with real life situations. The graphic reinforcement of absurdity, insult and violence can distort a young child's concept of the world around him.

Adults and young children can enjoy certain educational and entertaining programs together but adults should monitor what a child views and determine to exclude programs that offer unrestrained violence and hostility, that distort perceptions about other people and insult the intelligence of the viewer. Television can be an effective teaching tool but it cannot offer an exchange of language, a tactile experience or an opportunity to explore. It can only show and tell. It cannot feel or discuss or move about. Therefore, it is not a substitute for the human relationships that are the true guiding forces for learning behavior.

Carefully chosen educational programs can be used appropriately for young children, particularly if they relate to the interests of a particular child or group of children. However, the use of television as a babysitting device is of no positive value and can have harmful side effects.

Carl, age three-and-one-half sat passively on a chair in the playhouse, sucking his thumb and staring into space while the children around him were busy playing. Mrs. Laurel, his teacher, approached the playhouse and quietly asked Carl if he needed help. "No," he replied, still gazing into space, "I'm the baby and I'm being quiet and watching TV until dinnertime."

Sometimes the effects of television are felt in the preschool even more directly.

Carol, age five, needed several stitches in her head because Peter and Jill pushed her into a spaceship in the climber on the school playground. They did this because they were determined to save her from a TV monster who, they were sure, would blow them up if they did not find a shelter immediately.

Some children can tolerate television fantasy more readily than others and are not inclined to be intimidated nor fearful of most programs. Parents should guide children's choices, however, and be constantly alert to the programs seen by their children. Children enjoy sharing a discussion about what they are viewing or have viewed and adults who work with children can benefit from these discussions.

Older preschoolers enjoy appropriate films and film strips of favorite stories, animals and people. These strips can be used as effective supplements to learning, particularly when first-hand experiences are not available. A child will be pleased in seeing himself on film, particularly when he can view a shared trip or the highlights of a day at school or at home. Children can be guided toward a better self-image in seeing themselves in this way. There are many ways that audio-visual equipment can be used effectively with preschool children and the interested adult can provide helpful opportunities for personal and intellectual growth in children who are growing up in this audio-visual era.

SUGGESTED ASSIGNMENTS

Part I

Write anecdotal records describing the following kinds of experiences with stories or poetry at the day care center.

1. Listening.
2. Retelling or adding to a story or poem.
3. Creating a story or poem.
4. Telling personal experiences.
5. Dramatic interpretation.

Part II

Record specific incidents in which the story period helped a child

1. to learn new words.
2. to secure information.

Part III

Select a book that seems to appeal to young children. Write a synopsis of the story and a critical analysis of its content, illustrations, construction, and worth.

Part IV

Monitor an educational television program for preschoolers and a cartoon program for that age level and answer the following questions about each program:

1. Were the commercials directed toward pressuring children to buy a product?
2. Was there unwarranted violence?

3. Did the program set out to teach something? If so, do you think it was successful?

SELECTED READINGS

1. Arbuthnot, May Hill, and Zena Sutherland, *Children and Books*, 4th ed., Scott, Foresman and Company, Glenview, Ill., 1972.

This book is a valuable resource for those interested in understanding the relationship between children and books. Chapters 9 and 10 discuss the value of poetry for and with children and describe the range of poetry that is available for literary, linguistic, and emotional learnings for the young child.

2. Feminists on Children's Media, eds., *Little Miss Muffet Fights Back*, Box 4315, Grand Central Station, New York, 1971.

This is an annotated bibliography of children's books that stress girls and women as successful characters in children's stories.

3. Griffin, Louise, *Books In Preschool*, ERIC—National Association for the Education of Young Children, Washington, D. C., 1970.

This pamphlet describes the use of books in preschool education. It contains suggestions for selecting, reading, and making books as well as presenting sources of books for nonenglish speaking children. This would be a valuable source for preschool teachers and parents.

4. Moore, Vardine, *Preschool Story Hour*, Scarecrow Press, New York, 1966.

The author presents good suggestions about how to read to young children. These include ways to react to children during story time and information about when to involve children during the reading.

5. Mukerji, Rose, *Television Guidelines for Early Childhood Education*, National Instructional Television, Bloomington, Indiana, 1969.

This book has several purposes: (1) to help people plan for effective programming for children, (2) to help teachers make better use of television as an educational tool, and (3) to help parents select effective programs for children's viewing.

6. White House Conference on Children, *Child Development and Mass Media*, Washington, D. C., 1970.

This selection tersely describes the influence of the mass media on children and proposes a list of guidelines for changes in programming.

chapter 16

Music and Movement

Because adults' minds are crowded with other things, they seldom listen to the rhythms of sound in everyday living. Music is such a commonplace part of our lives that we hardly are aware of it. Grownups often do not hear the chirping of birds, the sound of wind in the trees, or the distant whistling of the engines switching in the railroad yards. Yet, sounds are everywhere and children learn about the world through the sounds they hear. It is not unusual for a child to say, "What is that?" when his parent or teacher does not realize there was a sound. This presents an interesting challenge to the adult. We can share the pleasures of listening with children and we can grow through sharing their appreciation of sounds. An interesting experience awaits the adult who closes his eyes and listens to the noises that are in progress at all times. This is "listening to the world as children hear it."

Children naturally move rhythmically to sounds they hear and imitate the movement of people and nature. Adults owe children the opportunity to listen and to recreate their musical heritage. Music and movement are natural to man and provide pleasure as well as a valuable means of expression and communication. Music may be a solitary experience or a social encounter and children grow and create through their encounters with sound and movement.

Three-year-old Jennifer was watching the duck in the small pond in the corner of the day care center playyard. Suddenly, her body seemed to take on a new dimension as she squatted down, raised her elbows to her sides and waddled along, singing, "Swish, swish, quack, quack, splash, swish, swish, quack, quack, splash."

ORIGINS OF INTEREST

Children first experience music through their interests in sounds and rhythm. This begins when they listen to the voices of the adults who care for them during infancy. Speech is very similar to music since it has changing pitch, tempo, rhythm, accent, and varying volume. The rhythm of adult voices seems to impart comfort and pleasure to babies long before words have meaning for them. The traditional popularity of lullabies attests to the social and emotional values that music has for children as well as for adults. These songs comprise one of the first forms of communication between the child and his environment. The universality of this form of communication between the child and his parent is evident when parents who would not think of carrying on one-sided conversations with young infants will sing to them. Thus, emotional needs for companionship are met and the beginnings of social experience originate through music.

Children display an enjoyment of rhythm in many of their behavior patterns. They explore and experiment with sound just as they do with things they feel, taste, and smell. They learn to talk by experimenting and listening to themselves. Babies discover their ability to babble and their babbling becomes a pattern of repetition and rhythm of certain syllables. All preschool children enjoy rhymes and repetition and it is not unusual for their physical actions to signify that these verbal forms are the representation of a kind of music to which they respond. Music is enjoyed not only through the ear, the mind, and the emotions but also through the entire body. Children as young as six months bounce or wave their arms in time to music that has definite rhythmic patterns. Many mothers of children less than one year of age report that their children seem to enjoy polka music or folk-song rhythms. These experiences seem to be meaningful to children.

In accordance with other kinds of early responses, babies respond to rhythm with their whole bodies. Later, these preschoolers will clap their hands or tap their heels in definite rhythm. These activities prepare them for enjoying a variety of rhythmic experiences. Preschool children repeat nonsense syllables as they swing or play on the seesaw. The motor play of children is frequently accompanied by chanting that resembles the rhythm of primitive music. These accompaniments appear whether children are indulging in vigorous physical play or manipulative play with crayons, brushes, finger paints, or hammers and saws. Music appears to be a natural phenomenon of childhood. In planning guidance for children, adults often neglect considering what music is from a child's point of view.

In our culture, children are even more likely to be repressed in their freedom of expression in music than in their work with graphic and plastic materials. Sometimes, there seems to be a greater lack of freedom and spontaneity in music experiences at school than in any other activity. Probably this is a reflection of the self-consciousness that many teachers feel when they themselves participate either vocally or in dancing. Certainly, children's experiences are affected by the adults who guide them. Unfortunately, it would seem that this hesitancy to take part in musical activities and to enjoy them is being perpetuated in our children.

Adults often think of music as a performing art only. They set standards that are rigid and inconsistent with the wholesome approach of child guidance that offers encouragement as children strengthen their perceptions of their environment through music as a creative force. When only the gifted child is nurtured, two things happen: his spontaneity is lost and other children become self-conscious and concerned about their failure. The preschool environment should be designed to strengthen self-images and to promote the ability to respond to the environment. It is not a center for polished performances. Children can learn to appreciate their own expressions and the expressiveness of others when there is a well-defined policy to incorporate many kinds of musical experiences ranging from fingerplays to listening activities.

Obviously, other areas of ability and interest will affect children's responses to music. Since both body rhythms and singing depend on motor coordination as well as on audio-perception, it is logical that children differ greatly in their ability to participate. Certainly, forcing them to take part in these activities and comparing one child to another constitute poor guidance practices. It is not uncommon for a discerning adult to realize that the child who plays a spectator role may be enjoying the activity as much as the children who are performing. Frequently, children's facial expressions will indicate their pleasure in merely listening to music and watching.

LEVELS OF PARTICIPATION

If they are not inhibited by timidity and self-consciousness, the youngest children at school appear to listen to music with their entire bodies. Sometimes, we must watch minor movements in order to understand children's levels of interest. Children nod their heads, tap their feet, or sway in a tempo appropriate to the tunes that they hear. Between two and three years of age, most children are capable of changing rhythmic movements. Therefore, music that is markedly rhythmic is especially pleasing to them, and adults can use music with success to insure quiet or vigorous action. Although these children will not march or run in unison, they will enjoy these activities with record players or pianos in accompaniment. During a music period, rhythm sticks or bells provide special fun for these young children and they will like attempting to imitate the adult's manipulation of these instruments.

Around three years of age, children have better muscular control than formerly and most of them can reproduce sound patterns. Simple musical instruments become very interesting. Instruments that sound when they are waved, hit, or hammered on are appropriate to their interests and abilities. Bells, cymbals, rhythm sticks, rattles, and all kinds of drums are excellent choices. Individual differences in conceptions of tempo are more marked than with younger children. Usually one or two children in a group will continue to be more intent on the manipulation of the instrument than on the sound that it makes.

Most of the children in Harry's group semed to enjoy activities with percussion instruments. They would listen quietly as Miss Gidden suggested that they shake or beat the instruments simultaneously and they would march around the room watching and listening intently and demonstrating great pride in the sounds that they made.

Harry, however, seemed to indulge in these rhythm experiences for the sheer joy of physical action. He would start slowly and with appropriate timing, but he seemed to be carried away with the noises and activity and he would ring the bells or beat the sticks or drums with increasing vigor and speed until the noises he made set him on a pattern of his own.

Sometimes it is wise to provide more opportunities for children like Harry to pound on the drums or to make noise with other instruments with the hope that his desire for this kind of activity will be satisfied. On this occasion, the group began to resent Harry's individual perception of sound and rhythm in their band. With the teacher's encouragement, he was offered the position of leader in hopes that he would use his baton without interfering with the common group sound. This opportunity helped him to learn to guide his rhythm and to prepare for patterning his beat more precisely.

Young children need space as they improvise movement to music or poetry. As they move about in an uncluttered area, they enjoy responding to the mood of the lyric as it describes flowers swaying in the sun or pumpkins rolling about at Hallowe'en. Musical stories that describe sliding snakes or drifting snowflakes provide the basis for creative learning through music. Supplementary materials add a new dimension to movement. Getting under a bridge table or slaloming around stacks of blocks may induce physical reactions to movement and encourage creativity. Scarves, hats, and other accessories influence the perception and expression of sound and movement.

As children become more agile, they gain control over their bodies and often enjoy responding with specific repetitive body movements such as galloping, hopping, bouncing or skipping as they move rhythmically to the patterned sound of a drum or other instrument. As children approach kindergarten age, they enjoy singing games and very simple folk dancing movements that lend meaning to the song text. Songs with repetitive phrases help children coordinate their movements to verbal cues.

The adult who guides children through musical experiences should enjoy music and movement and should feel free enough to join with children on occasion. Successful experiences occur when the adult knows the children and can maintain a sense of control without demanding conformity.

Record players are especially good for very young children, although adult manipulation of these instruments is necessary until eye-hand coordination is developed to a stage wherein skill in placing the needle carefully on the record is possible. If a record player is used, it should be placed on a low table so that children can watch its mechanical functions.

Of course, records should be chosen carefully but, after a discriminating choice has been made by the adult, usually it is wise to let individual children choose those they want to hear at a specific time. Their choices often will provide clues to their feelings. For example, children who have been playing vigorously and who want to rest are more likely to choose records that are entertaining but do not encourage vigorous physical movements. Moreover, sometimes it appears that children derive feelings of security at preschool from certain records.

Jack usually appeared to be fairly happy at school, but he was not likely to remain with another child when something displeased him. At these times, he would retire to a small chair by the record player. He always asked a teacher or student to play a specific nursery rhyme record that he had said was like one he had at home.

In classroom discussion, the students speculated that, when things went wrong for Jack, he might have become homesick and this record was comforting because it made him feel at home. However, requests for the same record to be repeated do not always indicate unhappiness. Like familiar books or toys, familiar tunes are usually the most popular. Frequently, adults in the school will become bored with the repetition of the same record over and over and over again. When we consider the over-all behavior patterns of children of this age, however, their interest in repetition is not surprising. These children appear to gain self-confidence in this manner. During song time, it is common for younger children to request the same song, time after time. As in other activities, it is usually reassuring for children to know what is coming next, to be familiar with procedures of all kinds.

Occasionally, it seems wise to discourage children from seeking to escape group activities by dependence on listening to records. Of course, how much time should be spent in this manner depends on the individual child.

Henry, age two-and-one-half, was a quiet and timid child as evidenced by his attitudes at school. Although he seemed contented, he seldom took part in any vigorous play nor in play with the other children. During outdoor periods, Henry stood on the periphery of the playground and watched other children. Sometimes, he would dig for awhile in the sandpile.

Indoors, Henry spent all his time sitting by the record player and requesting that the staff members play certain records for him. Miss Hewitt, the group teacher, permitted this behavior for several weeks at the beginning of the semester. Occasionally, another child or two would wander to the record player but none of the group except Henry seemed to enjoy it particularly.

In keeping with a practice of alternating toys, it was not inappropriate to remove the record player from the playroom before the beginning of each period. In this way, Henry was encouraged to explore the playroom and he began to develop some interest in handling the blocks in the block corner, playing in the indoor sandpile, and manipulating the color towers. If he made a verbal request for the record player, Miss Hewitt sometimes made an effort to distract his attention and to encourage his further interest in other activities. At other times, she brought the record player from the closet. As an experienced teacher, she appeared to be aware of the extent of Henry's need.

Later in the semester, two boys in the older group spent almost all their time indoors at the record player. Play periods outside had been lengthened due to warm weather and these boys were extremely active on the playground. Every day, after snack time, they would take small chairs to the table on which the record player was placed and often they would remain there until the teacher suggested that it was time to go back outdoors.

A student who had observed Miss Hewitt's guidance of Henry asked why the group teacher did not remove the record player and thereby encourage the older boys to engage in other types of play. This question certainly was warranted in a discussion of how to choose good methods of indirect guidance for general behavior. However, classroom discussion demonstrated that, unlike Henry, the older boys did not need experience in vigorous or social play. Obviously, their greatest need during indoor play was some quiet activity and, as long as extensive periods were spent outdoors, this kind of rest was important for them. These periods of relaxation as promoted by music emphasize one of its important values. Adults are often surprised at the ability of children to schedule their own activities according to their physical, mental, and emotional needs.

Available records should include a variety of kinds: classical, semi-classical, folk songs, sea chanteys, and story records. They should all be good for their kind. Music by a variety of instruments and combinations of instruments should be included. In most schools, children are free to listen to records at any time, but group listening is also planned often. Enjoyment is usually increased when several children listen at one time. Moreover, the teacher and children have an opportunity to talk about the records being played. The social and educational aspects of music appreciation are important to children at school or at home.

Singing is a natural activity of young children. When children are happy, they will sing and it is not necessary that adults plan a specific time for music experiences in order to help children in this learning. Just as teachers can encourage children in increasing their speaking vocabularies, so they can provide stimulation for vocal expression in music. Even very young children sometimes accompany their play with songs concerning their activities and their pleasure can be increased when adults join them and enrich these experiences.

Miss Charles frequently began to sing when the children were playing on the playground. She stated that her family always had been a "singing family" and had enjoyed creating songs for every occasion.

As Miss Charles pushed a child in the swing, she was likely to sing a simple song something like, "Up so high, toward the sky, it's fun to swing as I sing and sing." Some of the children usually joined her in song. Often, as a child walked past her in the playroom, she would softly sing, "Where are you going, little lady? Where are you going today?" The children all were delighted with these fragments of song, pitched to their levels of ability and with only a hint of a melody. Many of them would answer in a similar manner and would show their pleasure by smiling widely.

Children are fortunate if their parents and teachers can develop a relaxed pleasure in casual singing during everyday situations. Often, such singing seems to appeal to children so much that is valuable in guiding their other activites. An impromptu song will make a boring task more enjoyable. It is not uncommon for a clever teacher to improvise a song about putting blocks away in the cupboard or hanging wraps in the locker room. Children often respond and work energetically as they sing.

Mrs. Beam reported at a parents' meeting that she had experienced difficulty in getting her preschool children awake from their afternoon naps. She believed they should not sleep more than a certain length of time or they would not be sleepy at bedtime. Yet, if she awakened them, they were likely to be cross and irritable the remainder of the day.

One day, she had stepped to their door and sung, "Lazy Nina, will you get up? Nap time is over," and then repeated the song with Larry's name. The children had responded pleasantly and a custom was inaugurated in their daily living pattern.

The high voices that often are considered an attribute of childhood are not realistic. Children of preschool age have an average range of vocal tones from about middle C to C or D above and songs that are composed of only three to five tones are more easily learned than those with a wider range. Some children's singing voices seem to have a monotony of inflection just as their speaking voices do. Although some children never will become talented singers, this need not imply that they must be classified as "monotones." Logically, every experience that promotes their ability to differentiate in tonal quality may be helpful in their enjoyment of music. It is interesting that, in their spontaneous play, children are likely to pitch their voices somewhat higher than when they are consciously intent on singing. Of course, they should be provided with listening experiences comprised of songs with much more variation in tone than they are capable of producing. As indicated in an earlier chapter, children's understanding vocabularies far exceed their speaking vocabularies and the same is true when we consider their music experiences.

Songs for very young children are little more than simple sentences sung on only three or four notes on a descending scale. Frequently, the teacher composes these and they describe something in which the children are currently interested. Since these children like to be near adults and the songs are simple, one or two teachers often sit with a group of children and there seldom is any instrumental accompaniment. Singing games are especially interesting and often children who will not enter into the singing will make appropriate gestures in imitation of the teacher or other children.

By late preschool years, songs with imitative noises such as animal sounds and train whistles are interesting to children. With their longer spans of attention, songs with several verses can be chosen and they like songs that tell a story. Some divided responsibility of participation may be good. The five-year-old child will wait with pleasure for his cue to perform.

ADULT INFLUENCES

The best way to introduce songs to preschool children is for the adult to sing the song several times. Usually, one or two children will sing a word or two on the second or third repetition. The same procedure is repeated on the following day and, at that time, the children who participated on the first day probably will learn the entire song. These children will like the same, simple songs day after day. It is important that we should not urge children to participate. Most of them will enter in when they feel comfortable and capable.

Sometimes, one or two children will continue to be nonparticipants, but this should not be discouraging to teachers or students. Almost always, the parents of these children report that they sing these songs frequently at home. Sometimes, these children become angry at their parents due to their lack of knowledge concerning the words or tunes of these school songs. This presents good reason for parents to visit schools and to become familiar with what children are doing. Occasionally, school administrators ask that teachers or students make copies of songs for distribution to parents.

Of course, as children grow, the songs they enjoy are more varied. A greater number of notes and words are included and piano accompaniment will be helpful. Most schools are equipped with a number of song books appropriate for children. The subject matter of favorite songs is usually something with which children are familiar. Sometimes, nonsense syllables will create special appeal. Some song books include attractive illustrations that encourage interest. Everyday activities such as dressing, eating, going to the park, or crossing the street are favorite themes. Children's songs often describe the weather, seasonal changes, or are appropriate to certain holidays. Thus, music becomes a usual part of the child's perception of his world.

Music periods are sometimes completely planned and controlled by the teacher and sometimes by the children. Each of these kinds of experiences will be helpful to some children. The former types may discourage participation by some children and the latter may not be effective for children who are timid or inhibited. Therefore, both kinds of experiences and modifications of these types should be provided.

A skillful teacher gives enough support for children who need direction and encourages rather than urges all children to participate. Rhythm instruments of various kinds, records, and record players are usually available all during the preschool session and spontaneous singing is encouraged so that music assumes its proper perspective as a normal concommitant of free activity.

Although children should be allowed to choose according to their own tastes and to express their unique feelings through music, adults' likes are important, too. Musical expression and interpretation are personal attributes and, whether at home or at school, the way music is presented to children will depend on the personalities of the adults. This is apparent when we observe two preschool teachers, each of whom is adept in encouraging children to enjoy music. Each teacher will have worked out her own method of guidance. Parents differ widely in the selections they present to their children. Most parents, for example, enjoy simple folk tunes and sea chanteys and feel comfortable in sharing this interest with children. A few parents rely entirely on semiclassical and classical melodies. Regardless of adult likes and dislikes, such a variety of music is available for listening, for dancing, and for singing that all grownups can find several types of music from which both they and the children with whom they work can derive pleasure and satisfaction.

Music at school should reflect the cultures of the children and develop a sense of pride in a musical heritage. Music from other lands and words in other languages provide a basis for understanding that everybody shares music in one form or another. Since adults are responsible for the choice of music experiences for children, careful thought should be devoted to the choice of materials and methods.

When Mrs. James was appointed a teacher in a preschool in an ethnically mixed area of New Jersey, she became aware that the children played in small groups that reflected their ethnic backgrounds and she felt unsuccessful in her attempts to structure a more integrated class environment. The parents appeared to reinforce the pattern of ethnic friendships when they called for their children at the end of class sessions.

Mrs. James decided to ask each of the mothers to contribute a children's song that reflected her cultural background so that the children could learn the songs during school.

As the children learned each song, a brief comment was made about the song's origin and meaning. Children helped each other with words in Spanish, Italian, Greek, and English and communication across ethnic lines began to occur. Later, the children prepared simple food treats to match the intercultural music experiences. Parents were pleased to hear the musical exchange of cultural backgrounds and the children had a valuable social studies lesson based on a common frame of reference, music.

In correlation with previous discussion, the following points may be helpful in evaluating music and guidance methods for young children.

1. The music of a song is more important than the words. Since children "feel" music, even the simplest song should have a pleasant melody.

2. The words of a song should relate to the child's interests. Preschool children are most interested in simple objects and everyday experiences. Besides, they can learn songs more easily if they understand them.

3. Songs for young children should contain rhythm and repetition of both melody and words. Rhythm is especially pleasant to children and will also aid in their learning and remembering.

4. Pitch and range of tones will determine whether children will be able to perform in singing. We should listen to children's voices and choose appropriate songs for them.

5. It is not specific vocal training that will encourage children in singing but rather the fun the experience affords and the opportunities offered for experimenting.

6. The teacher's attitude toward music is far more important than her skill in performance. The main purpose is to encourage preschool children to like music.

7. Not all children should be expected to participate in the same way nor to enjoy the same experiences in music. One child may be attracted to the rhythm of the music, a second child to the melody, and a third to the effect of the words accompanying the music.

8. Music and movement activities should reflect a variety of cultural backgrounds in the preschool to assure each child a sense of pride in his heritage.

9. Music should be geared to the present enjoyment of children. They should have the opportunity to hear and to take part in good music suited to their interests and to be allowed to respond to it freely. Although it is true that they cannot continue indefinitely to react spontaneously, such freedom should be permitted during preschool years. As stated when the purposes of preschool education were discussed, this is one period in which it is especially important that the environment and availability of learning experiences be planned, but that the child be encouraged to choose for himself those experiences that are of interest and importance to him. Our purpose is to establish good attitudes that will provide wise self-direction and selection as he matures.

SUGGESTED ASSIGNMENT

Part I

1. Choose twelve records that you think would be appropriate for the group of children to which you are assigned. Make an annotated list of these records and tell why you chose each of them.

2. Select and learn fifteen songs with a variety of mood and context that are appropriate for preschool children. Plan how you would introduce and use each song with a group of children.

Part II

1. Make an anecdotal record of one child's responses to experiences with rhythm.

2. List the records chosen by two children during free play periods. Include conversations or comments concerning these records. Why do you think each record was enjoyed by the child who chose it?

3. Describe the following kinds of musical experiences in the preschool and tell how each of two or three children participated in each kind of experience:
   a. Songs.
   b. Singing games or finger plays.
   c. Creative movement.

Part III

How is the preschool or day care center and its program planned to encourage a happy response by children to music? Be explicit.

Part IV

With a group of students, discuss how you would implement each of the following in a preschool program:
   a. Listening for pleasure.
   b. Music as an aesthetic experience.
   c. Music as a social studies experience.
   d. Movement and dance as a creative experience.

SELECTED READINGS

1. Cherry, Clare, *Creative Movement for the Developing Child*, Fearon Publishers, Palo Alto, California, 1968.

This book was designed to help adults work with children to develop and enhance a movement program for preschoolers. Included are many practical guidelines and suggestions to encourage movement and creative interaction between teacher and child. The discussion will be helpful to those adults who lack self-confidence in their abilities to work with children in music and movement.

2. Hess, Robert D., and Doreen J. Croft, *Teachers of Young Children*, Houghton-Mifflin, Boston, 1972.

Chapter 8 describes the arts in preschool programs in terms of goals and objectives. The authors show concern for all art forms including music, and the discussion of aesthetic appreciation and judgment is good.

3. Jaye, Mary T., *Making Music Your Own*, Silver Burdett Company, Morristown, New Jersey, 1971.

The author has compiled appropriate songs and suggested musical activities to enhance a music and movement program in the preschool classroom. This book will be helpful to teachers and aides.

4. Landeck, Beatrice, *Children and Music*, William Sloane Associates, New York, 1952.

Landeck emphasizes the importance of fostering pleasant attitudes toward all kinds of music experiences. She states that the joy of self-expression in music is possible in some measure for all people. Parents and teachers will gain confidence in free expression in music through this book.

5. Sheehy, Emma D., *Children Discover Music and Dance*, 4th printing, Teachers College Press, Columbia University, New York, 1974. Chapter 4 provides an excellent source of information about singing, songs, and how to use vocal music forms with children. Chapter 7 provides information about movement and dance that can help the reader plan movement and dance experiences for young children. This book can be helpful to those interested in creative music programs in group care centers.

6. Swanson, Bessie R., *Music in the Education of Children*, Wadsworth Publishing Company, Belmont, California, 1961.

Directions are presented for simple musical instruments that can be made by children and adults and suggestions for the sound purchase of rhythm instruments are included.

chapter 17

Science and Mathematics

Science and mathematics experiences are normal facets of young children's environmental learnings. During all their activities, they are learning about the world. Sometimes, teachers talk about their feelings of inability to teach in these subject matter areas but, at the same time, they probably are imparting to children the basic facts on which later knowledge will accumulate.

A major portion of the preschool program is planned with the idea of enriching children's experiences and thereby adding to their knowledge. As with other activities, science and mathematical experiences should be commensurate with the interests and understanding of each child. The natural curiosity of young children and the questions they ask indicate the problems that occur to them, and their trial-and-error methods of testing, trying, learning, and repeating are similar to those employed when hypotheses are tested in the scientific laboratory. The exploratory nature of preschool behavior is a simple form of scientific procedure.

Most activities at a preschool and in the home have their roots in some scientific or mathematical concept if the adult probes the situation carefully. Adults guide young children toward conceptual understanding through the introduction of appropriate language that they apply to what is occurring as well as by the kinds of resources and experiences they make available for use by children.

INDOOR ACTIVITIES

Concepts of bulk and weight constitute important knowledge for children. By handling blocks of different shapes and sizes, children learn the differences between small and large, light and heavy, thick and thin, tall and short, deep and shallow, and round, square, or triangular. They learn that hollow blocks and solid blocks of the same size are different in weight even if made of the same material and that two blocks of identical size weigh differently if one is cardboard and the other wood.

If children do not converse about these differences, an alert teacher can stimulate these learnings by her comments and, as questions are asked, her simple explanations will help the child to be aware of these properties in other objects. Children, in their egocentricity, are especially interested in linear measurements as they assess their body measurements. For this reason, a linear measuring device is a popular and educational piece of equipment.

Miss Betsy was sitting on the floor with a group of children who were involved with block building. Rudy came over to her and asked her to straighten her leg out. When she did so, he proceeded to measure her leg with one foot-long block. He discovered that her leg was three blocks long. He then measured his own leg with the block and concluded that he would have to be three Rudys to be as big as Miss Betsy.

A prerequisite to mathematical and scientific understanding is the ability to classify objects according to a specified set of criteria. Preschool children have many opportunities to experience this as they learn to place toys and blocks in appropriate places in the room or on shelves. Small groups of children often classify themselves by the kind or color of clothing they wear or by their ages.

Block building is a good source of knowledge concerning balance. Balance also is demonstrated on the seesaw and in a balance scale. Some preschool children may become especially interested in speculations concerning the relationship between weight and balance.

Mimi and Kathy were four-year-old friends. Both indoors and outdoors, they were almost constant companions. The first time they tried to use the seesaw, they were unsuccessful because Mimi's additional weight lifted Kathy high in the air and kept her there. Miss Schmidt suggested that Mimi move forward toward the center of the seesaw and perfect balance was achieved. Later, when Miss Schmidt weighed the children, Mimi and Kathy were delighted when she called their attention to the fact that moving the weights on the scale had a similar leveling effect.

Wooden planks, blocks, and other toys also provide children's early experiences not only with the force of gravity but also its effect on speed acceleration and momentum. The toy truck that is released from the top of an inclined plank teaches the child that rapid descent can be expected on an inclined plane. In block building, he learns that balance becomes more difficult as structures attain greater height.

Related learnings occur when children recognize that an inclined plank will make it easier to get the big toy truck up to the edge of the indoor sandpile. Frequently, a discussion of inclined driveways or the ramps in downtown parking areas will follow. Sometimes, simple explorations in the use of levers and pulleys can be demonstrated. These examples can be used by the teacher as a planned experience but, even better, she can improvise as individual children show interest.

Children four-to five-years-old are likely to be interested in the weights of household commodities such as "a pound of butter" or "an ounce of cheese." A small household scale in the housekeeping corner is a good suggestion for preschool equipment. Simple cooking experiences that involve children directly with measuring and simple counting opportunities are helpful when proper measuring tools are available.

Three-and-a-half-year-old Maria accused her teacher of fooling the children during a pudding-making experience. The simple experience chart that Mr. Thomas drew to illustrate the recipe showed two cups of milk but Mr. Thomas had employed one two-cup container to hold the milk. Maria had presented a good example as to how children learn.

Children under three years of age who have been exposed to concepts of measurement sometimes offer information as to how they perceive.

Ruth, age two years and nine months heard her mother call out, "I can't find the measuring cup I use to prepare the rice." Ruth ran to the desk, grabbed a ruler and came to her mother proudly saying, "You can use this measurer."

Magnets are valuable in a nursery school. By their use, children learn that magnets pick up some things but not everything, and the teacher can then explain that magnets attract objects that are made of some kinds of metal. Sometimes, play with magnets culminates in a child's curiosity about the nature of many objects and he learns to distinguish among many materials.

The youngest children at the nursery school sometimes show special interest in the light switches and fixtures. Although these children are not ready for more than a brief comment by adults, the wonder of electrical power is apparent on the face of the child who pulls a string or turns a switch and gazes toward the electric bulb to watch the result. These children can be encouraged in their interests by simple comments such as, "When you turn the switch, a pretty light comes on," or "When you pull the string, the light makes the room bright like the outdoors when the sun is shining." Stressing these phenomena by verbal description may help make them more meaningful and interesting to children. Moreover, children will realize that adults share their interests and when they are older and ready for factual explanations they are likely to express their questions.

Electricity is not merely an adjunct of lights and electrical appliances. Sometimes, sparks fly when we shuffle across a carpeted floor. Hair may crackle when it is combed. Some clothing clings to our bodies almost as if it were magnetized. All of these situations are within the experience level of young children. Teachers can provide simple demonstrations by rubbing a hard rubber comb with wool and then holding it near a piece of paper. The paper will cling to the comb.

Interest in diverse materials may create an opportunity to relate the child's pleasure in sounds to his understanding of physical matter. When we strike a drum a resonant noise results, but a triangle emits a bell-like sound. Graduated iron bars will enable the teacher to show that short bars make a high tone, long bars a low one. Water glasses filled with different quantities of water will produce different tones when we tap on them.

Very young children are often interested in the striking of a clock or the ticking of a watch. These experiences, of course, are related to sound and have no connotation of the passing of time. Time, however, is a concept in which all children become interested. Some writers state that conceptual learning in this area cannot be accurate during preschool years and, indeed, there seems to be little evidence that young children can learn the intricacies of measurements of time. This is exemplified by the child who arrived at school and asked the teacher, "Is this tomorrow?"

Nevertheless, young children are aware of the importance of time in their daily schedules. Time is emphasized in most homes by the pattern of family living. Frequently, parents say, "It's time for breakfast," or "It's time for me to go to work," or they state, "It's time to go to bed." Thus, some knowledge of time occurs before numerical hours become a part of the child's knowledge.

Probably, when children start to school, they become even more conscious of the importance of time in their own lives. They learn that school starts at a certain time each day and that they leave the school after a specific period of time. Children at home or at school gradually learn that days have different names and that one day succeeds another. Preschool children often converse about which days they come to school and which ones they stay at home.

Annual events such as birthdays and special holidays reinforce interest in measurements of time. Efforts to explain time to preschool children are usually futile, however. Occasionally, children in the primary grades demonstrate their misconceptions.

Janice, age six, sometimes displayed jealousy because she was three years younger than her brother Dale. Frequently, she stated, "Dale is older than me but in three more years I'll be nine, too."

Some children at the school probably will show interest in the movement of the hands of the clock and in the squares representing the days on the calendar. Simple descriptive statements by adults will provide a basis for future learning. These children are experiencing the importance of time in their lives simply by the schedules that dictate their routines.

Sometimes, older preschool children enjoy gauging their activities according to the location of the hands on a clock. Although many children do learn to tell time before they enter elementary school, it would seem that this ability indicates rote learning rather than real understanding. Obviously, preschools, unlike public schools, are geared toward more general learnings. Children need to experience time in its relation to their own lives before abstract thinking a out it will be possible.

Numerical concepts assume some importance when children are of preschool age. At first, children express these concepts by saying "lots of bricks" or "a few blocks." As adults comment concerning activities and equipment with such remarks as, "You've used two colors in your painting." or "We need three more glasses for the snack table," enumeration begins to seem sensible and useful to children. Preschoolers take great pride in the number of candles on a birthday cake. When they count more than three or four objects, however, their inaccuracy proves their lack of understanding.

Volume is a concept that even the youngest children in the school may begin to understand. Pouring milk from a bottle or pitcher into a glass at snack time may stimulate conversation concerning this physical measurement. Obviously, activities in this area are largely exploratory. Even adults are often unable to judge volume and capacity accurately.

At snack time, one of the aides sat at the table with the children. This person served the milk or juice by pouring it from a large pitcher into a smaller one that she presented to each child so that he might fill his own glass. Almost always, she misjudged the capacity of the small pitcher and so much was poured that the children's glasses would overflow. Several of the four-year-olds would remind her each day that she should be careful not to fill the small pitchers more than half-full.

An alert adult takes advantage of such comments and talks with the children concerning liquid measurements. Older preschool children are familiar, of course, with measurements such as a "pint of cream," a "quart of milk," or a "gallon of gasoline," and this knowledge can lead to interesting conversations between children and their teachers.

Air is everywhere although it cannot be seen. When soap bubbles are blown, they are filled with air. Inflated balloons and car tires contain air. Air lifts things and holds them up. This can be proved when we inflate a paper bag or a balloon and an object placed on top of it is elevated. Warm air from a register heats the playroom and the hot air goes up. This is proved when we place a sheet of paper on the register. Window fans bring cool air from outdoors into the playroom.

Probably the best means for demonstrating chemical changes can be provided if kitchen facilities in the school permit group projects planned by the teacher. Butter making and cookie baking are particularly interesting as group projects since the products can be used for snacks or lunch and thus have real value to the children. Gelatine desserts are interesting because the process from liquid to semisolid can be observed. Outside the kitchen, crystal gardens made from porous rocks or bricks over which specific amounts of certain household liquids are poured will show chemical changes quickly enough to promote continued interest by preschoolers.

Children like to plant seeds and watch them grow. Therefore, plants that grow rapidly are the best choices for the preschool. Sprouting seeds on damp blotters or a wet sponge will furnish information about how seeds start to grow. When grass seed planted in a wet sponge grows quickly but soon turns yellow and begins to die, children's questions will provide an opportunity to explain that most plants need soil as well as water and sun, that soil and water as food for plants are absorbed through their roots. If seeds are planted near the sides of a glass bowl, the root formation can be seen. Many experiments in planting and observing can be afforded by a terrarium. Sweet potato and carrot-top plants usually are fascinating because of their rapid growth.

Miss Morris placed a glass jar containing a sweet potato that had sprouted on a table near one of the playroom windows. Each morning, before they went to the playground, Bryce and Jan visited the playroom to see how much the vine had grown since the day before. As they went outdoors, they would illustrate, by gesturing with their hands, how much the stem had increased in length.

If playground facilities permit, outdoor gardening activities can be fun. Occasionally, in cool climates, children plant seeds indoors in planters that can be carried to the playground when weather permits. These activities usually are more interesting if plans are discussed by the teacher and children during quiet periods. Story books that describe similar projects stimulate interest.

PLAYGROUND EXPERIENCES

An outdoor environment presents many opportunities for casual science experiences. Children demonstrate their awareness of variety in soils and rocks as they prod in the gravel and sand in the play area and touch the muddy clay after flower beds have been watered. It is not unusual for a child to display a smooth-shaped rock proudly and to put it in his pocket for future examination.

Other examples of outdoor science experiences are: weather vanes and wind wheels; insects and worms; birds' nests, feeders, and houses; and evidences of seasonal changes such as sprouting leaves or blooming shrubs, colorful leaves and falling leaves, and rain or snow. Sometimes, a child's unique enthusiasm will make adults aware of scientific facts that are often unnoticed.

Randy, four-years-old, seemed to be interested in wheels and gears of all kinds. Indoors, his favorite play involved turning the toy trucks upside down and spinning the wheels. He displayed intense interest in the record player. The music seemed unimportant to him, but he asked many questions about the turntable, what caused it to spin, and why several speeds were possible.

On the playground, Randy enjoyed the wheel toys, not in the way in which other children enjoyed them but by turning the tricycles over and comparing the speeds of the small and large wheels. Almost every day, he discussed this phenomenon with some student or teacher.

Frequently, his conversations would also include discussion of the small windmill attached to a tree branch that overhung the playground. Thus, wind direction and velocity assumed importance to teachers and participating students. Even when Randy was absent from school, comments were often made concerning the speed or lack of movement of the windmill.

Changes in weather are usually noticed by young children and each change presents new lessons in science. Raindrops, rainbows, thunder, lightening, frost, snowflakes, and ice provide interesting subjects for conversation and explanation. These changes can furnish ideas for a variety of activities. For example, evaporation is a phenomenon that can be explained to preschoolers.

Sara, age three years, was disappointed when she was told that the children could not play outdoors in the early morning because of the rain. Miss Patton stood by Sara at the window and talked about the water puddles on the playground.

When lunch was over and the group went to the playground, Sara asked Miss Patton what had happened to the puddles. Several children stood nearby and they listened intently as the teacher explained that the puddles had evaporated.

As a follow-up activity the next day, Miss Patton placed a small pan of water on the burner of the stove and the children observed the steam rising from the pan and talked about the disappearance of the water. As a second demonstration, Miss Patton provided a small bottle of perfume that she left uncovered on a high shelf in the playroom. The children were greatly interested in the rapid disappearance of the liquid.

The foregoing examples indicate that teachers need not be trained scientists to provide science experiences for children. Teachers, students, and parents should not feel ashamed if they cannot answer children's questions. A scientific method of investigation is demonstrated when the adult answers as many questions as possible but is not reticent in saying, "I'll have to find out about that and we'll talk about it later." Sometimes, cooperative effort is possible when a teacher can suggest that she and the children refer to some book for information. Often, adults and children can learn together by watching and discussing some natural phenomenon.

OBSERVATION AND CARE OF ANIMALS

Animals furnish excellent opportunities for learning. Most adults remember, with nostalgia, childhood experiences with animals and will agree that all children deserve acquaintance with them. Students often recall how a dog awaited them at the end of the school day, how a stray kitten became a sweet, cuddly playmate, or how a baby bird that the rain washed from the nest became a cheerful backyard companion.

Some people, of course, grow up with almost no contact with animals. As children, they had no opportunities to become acquainted with pets. In fact, definite fears of certain kinds of animals may have been established. Since it probably will be difficult for those people to force themselves to have animals around the house, not all children will have pets at home.

Nursery rhymes and children's classics contain a preponderance of characters from the animal kingdom, and there appears to be general appeal in stories that tell about the experiences of children with animals. Therefore, since experiences should be chosen in accordance with children's interests, it follows that animals should be provided for them.

Moreover, the premise, "a child needs a pet," has scientific basis when we consider that children need feelings of independence and security. Feelings of independence can be fostered at a very early age if children are allowed to help care for animals. The two-year-old who helps minister to a pet gains rapidly in status in his own estimation. A pet is a creature less independent than the child himself and the child is no longer the weakest and most dependent member of the family—his comparative standing is elevated. Each additional task of pet care as children grow gives them the important knowledge that they are growing up, which is deeply satisfying to them.

Animals can also give children feelings of security. With pets, they usually demonstrate attitudes of love and gentleness. Pets are relaxing because they demand nothing but the attention that children are capable of giving. Pets supply simple satisfactions of affection, acceptance, and playfulness. For two reasons, a preschool should provide some experiences with animals: (1) as a means of supplementing home experiences in which there may be no contacts with pets, and (2) as a means of stimulating learning learning about nature.

A great deal has been written about the nature lessons provided by the observation of animals, lessons that describe the life cycle from birth through death. The gaining of such knowledge by preschoolers may possibly help ease the strain of meeting human emergencies later. There also is the opportunity to learn individual differences not only between species but between members of the same animal family and this information is interesting to children.

Hamsters, guinea pigs, white mice, rats, and rabbits are among the best-suited species for school observation since they are small, easily handled, clean, inexpensive, and friendly. In observing animals, children usually are interested in learning how they move, how and what they eat, what sounds they make, where they usually live, how they sleep, how they produce their young, and how they see, smell, and hear.

The kinds and numbers of animals that can be kept at school depend, of course, on the physical setting. Some private schools stress outdoor experiences and even provide farm animals for observation; some schools maintain cages for small animals and rodents; and others may possess only gold fish, a canary, or a parakeet. The personal feelings of the adults are also important in dictating how many animals and what kinds can be kept at a school. Animals require a great deal of care and attention that cannot be given by the children and, if no interested adult is employed by the school, it is probable that this area of experience should not be attempted. If facilities are not appropriate for pets, animals sometimes can be brought to the school for brief periods of time. Usually, the children will enjoy bringing their own pets to school to visit or young animals can be borrowed for half-day periods from nearby farms or households.

THE VALUE OF EXCURSIONS

Experiences outside the child care center also can be provided from time to time as a means of stimulating group interest, adding variety to the over-all program, and furnishing additional opportunities for students to observe children's behavior in different situations. Several factors should be considered before decisions are made concerning these excursions. Attending school sessions probably will be such an invigorating experience for the younger children that no excursions are needed to broaden their interests. Also, if one or two new children are in an older group, excursions may add further strain in their efforts to adjust to the school and the other children.

They should not be planned merely for the purpose of going somewhere away from the school. Programs are child-centered and such journeys should be considered with the children's needs in mind. Well-planned trips may be helpful to children, however, in several ways: (1) helping them develop a keener sense of observation, (2) providing them with experiences that may not otherwise be possible, (3) developing in them attitudes of pleasure in being a part of the group, (4) helping them develop a desire to seek information outside their immediate environment, (5) helping them acquire the ability to follow the directions necessary in group behavior, and (6) providing fun for them.

Excursions are often considered to be extensive and elaborate trips that must include the entire group. This is not true at the preschool level. An excursion may be a walk to the nearby grocery by a teacher and one or two children or a walk down the block to watch the tree trimmers at work in a park across the street. Such jaunts are often planned for the speial purpose of establishing rapport between teacher and child, to aid a timid child to gain feelings of acceptance or prestige, or to provide enriched experiences for a child or children who appear to need more stimulation than the usual school program offers. Occasionally, two or three children with similar interests may be chosen by a teacher for a specific kind of experience.

Whether the trip is a simple one for only a few children or an elaborate one for the entire group, excursions should be planned carefully.

As an assignment, the advanced college students were asked to plan an excursion for some or all of the children in the group to which they were assigned. Detailed plans were to be evaluated by the instructor before the excursion date was set and comprehensive reports were to be submitted following the experience.

Miss Parker planned to walk with Fred and Sally, both age four-and-one-half, to a nearby zoological museum. Her reason for choosing only two children was because "the displays in the museum would not be interesting to some of the children." She chose these specific children because "Fred is alert and interested in almost everything. His is talkative and curious and I am eager to know what he will say about the stuffed animals. Sally is shy and quiet, but I think she likes new experiences. I believe it will make her happy to be chosen to go on this trip with Fred and me."

When the three returned to the school, the children appeared to be tired but not unhappy. Miss Parker seemed unenthusiastic concerning the excursion. Later, her final report stated, "We had a pleasant walk to the museum. I told the children about the displays we would see, describing the way in which the cases illustrated the natural living conditions of the animals and birds. They were interested but they asked no questions. Fred stopped to watch a street-sweeping machine and asked several questions about it and the men who operated it. Sally listened intently to our conversation and seemed to be pleased to be with us.

"When we arrived at the museum, my troubles began. The first room contained a huge case showing a prairie scene with coyotes, prairie dogs, and owls. Fred was interested when I told them what each of the creatures was and commented on the grass and tree stumps in the case. Then he asked if the animals were alive. When I answered negatively, he wanted to know why, what killed them, why they looked like they were alive, and many other questions I didn't know how to answer. When I tried to satisfy his curiosity as best I could, he asked what made the animals die if I wasn't sure someone had killed them, and many other things. We walked on to other rooms, but he asked similar questions and I don't think he was satisfied with my answers. Perhaps his questions were unusual because his father is a physician.

"I think my excursion was not a good one. Both of the children were very quiet as we returned to school. I think Sally would have enjoyed being with us if the trip had been more satisfying for Fred. If I were planning another excursion, I would not choose to visit a museum. I might take the children to the tennis courts to watch a tennis match or to the edge of the highway to watch the road graders. In those situations, I would not feel so inadequate."

Parents always should be consulted before excursions are planned. Sometimes, parents prefer to share these experiences with their children or there may be reasons why they think their children should not make a particular trip. If teacher-child ratios do not provide enough adults for the contemplated excursion or if more cars are needed for transporting the children and adults, parents sometimes accompany the group. Obviously, it is wise to plan for the presence of at least one adult other than the driver in each car. These trips will be more meaningful to children, also, if there are enough adults to answer questions that may occur to them during the observation.

Appropriate excursions for groups of young children may be: a farm, a dairy barn or bottling firm, a bakery, the fire station, a football practice field, a greenhouse, and many others. Teachers should be acquainted with the facilities in the community.

Children should be prepared by being told where they are going and something about what they will see; follow-up activities will reinforce the learnings that result. When the excursion ends, older preschool children will enjoy a quiet time for discussing what they saw and did. Younger children probably will not participate in such discussions, but they will enjoy hearing the teacher tell about the experience in story form.

Important factors to be considered when planning group excursions are:

1. Decide what rules will be necessary and be certain that they are understood by the children.

2. Attempt to foresee some of the questions that may be asked. This means that you must have a knowledge of the place, objects, or situation that will be observed.

3. Estimate the length of time the excursion will take and set definite times for departure from and return to the school. Parents may desire this information.

4. If people are involved in the place you propose to visit, be certain that they have been consulted and that you have their cooperation.

5. Be sure there are enough adults for the safety of the group. If the adults are to be responsible for certain children, see that the children know to which one they have been assigned.

6. If not all children are to go on the excursion, be certain that there are enough adults left at the school for adequate supervision and that activities for the stay-at-school children are planned.

7. If parents are providing cars, it is wise to have a teacher and a parent together rather than two parents or two teachers.

8. Plan which children will ride in each car and choose the adults and children carefully. A shy child may need the support of an adult whom he knows.

9. Plan follow-up activities consisting of stories, music, or toys that may help children reproduce their experiences in their play.

ADULT RESPONSIBILITY

The choice of science experiences for children depends on the developmental level of the children, their interests as well as those of the teacher, and on the facilities of the particular school. Many of these activities require a great deal of adult and individual supervision. However, the scope and diversity of these learnings indicate that every adult can provide science experiences for children. Since children are imitators, they are likely to assume interest in objects and situations that interest the adults who guide them.

As in all adult-child experiences, adults are largely responsible not only for what children learn but for their attitudes toward future experiences. Children are free to observe and ask questions about things that have speial interest for them and a wise teacher is alert to these interests. She is ready to express questions or propose further investigations. She does not act as an authority by simply proffering information. She approaches problems as a co-worker with real interest in sharing experiences with the children. Because of this cooperative spirit, interests in nature and science are likely to provide splendid opportunities for establishing rapport with individual children and clues for their future guidance.

Sam was four-years-old when he entered nursery school. He was a quiet, serious child. Miss Barnard did not feel that she understood him nor that he was interested in school activities. He seldom spoke to adults or children.

Near the end of the second week of school, Sam was sitting on a small chair in front of the aquarium watching the gold fish. His facial expression was serious and he had remained in the same position for almost ten minutes. Finally, Miss Barnard pulled another small chair next to Sam's chair, sat down, and quietly commented, "The fish swim very fast." Sam said, "Yes," and he was silent for a few seconds. Then suddenly he began talking in an animated manner about the aquarium he and his father had acquired recently, the kinds of plants it contained, how many varieties of tropical fish his father had purchased, and how much fun it was to watch them. Apparently, by simply sitting down and demonstrating that she liked to watch the fish, Miss Barnard had made Sam feel that he could share his interests with her.

Preschool children benefit from casual as well as carefully planned experiences that provide insight into how our world works. Guidance in mathematic and science experiences, like guidance in other activities for young children, can be chosen wisely if we study children and attempt to look at the world as it must appear to them. In these areas, however, we must be especially certain that we are presenting information that is accurate as well as geared to the child's level of understanding. If we misrepresent or distort the concepts we present to the child, he will be required to unlearn those ideas before further learning can occur and this process often is more difficult than an intitial learning process. A skillful teacher will be alert to the many resources available in the local library and, in turn, she is certain to derive pleasure from sharing the basic facts of mathematics and science with the children whom she guides.

SUGGESTED ASSIGNMENTS

Part I

Accurately describe situations in which teachers in the child care center stimulated interest in or promoted children's understandings in any four of the following.

1. gravity	**5.** balance	**9.** cold
2. volume	**6.** electricity	**10.** time
3. weight	**7.** classification	**11.** numbers
4. size or shape	**8.** heat	**12.** seasons

Part II

Accurately describe situations in which the children at the preschool learned something about each of the following.

1. soils and rocks	**4.** animal life
2. chemical changes	**5.** plant life
3. conservation	**6.** outer space

Part III

Carefully plan an excursion for two or more children in the group to which you are assigned and describe each step of your planning. Answer the following questions about your plans.

1. Why did you choose this specific experience?
2. How is the experience related to the interests of the children?
3. How will you prepare the children for the excursion?
4. What follow-up activities do you recommend?

SELECTED READINGS

1. Carmichael, Viola S., *Science Experiences for Young Children,* Southern California Association for the Education of Young Children, Los Angeles, California, 1969.

The author has compiled a collection of scientific facts and information a teacher should know ranging from rocks to insects to rockets. She has suggested ways of presenting these materials to preschoolers. This book would be particularly helpful to those adults who need a background of accurate knowledge in order to offer science to young children.

2. Chambers, W. R., and John Murray, *Mathematics Begins,* Nuffield Foundation Mathematics Project, John Wiley, New York, 1967.

This first book in the Nuffield Mathematics Series offers the teacher a clear explanation of how mathematics concepts evolve in conjunction with the developmental process in children. Suggestions are presented to help identify where children are as well as ways to help children beginning in infancy to collect experiences, discuss them with adults, and acquire appropriate language skills.

3. Croft, Doreen J., and Robert D. Hess, *An Activities Handbook for Teachers of Young Children,* Houghton-Mifflin, Boston, 1972.

This book presents lesson plan ideas for introducing and extending premathematic experiences in preschool. It will he helpful to those people who have had some knowledge of the "new math." Experiences in mathematics based on Piaget's developmental theories are illustrated.

4. Goldberg, Lazer, *Children and Science,* Charles Scribner's Sons, New York, 1970.

The author expertly presents his views along with ideas of well known scientists about how experimentation and exploration of the environment can elevate the natural curiosity of children. He believes that direction can evolve under the guidance of a sensitive adult who respects a child's need to explore and play and who provides materials and a physical setting that stimulate children's imaginations.

5. McIntyre, Margaret, "Books Which Give Mathematical Concepts to Young Children: An Annotated Bibliography," *Young Children,* National Association for the Education of Young Children, Vol. 24, No. 5, May, 1969, Washington, D. C.

This is a comprehensive listing of books for young children that offer concepts in language appropriate for their developmental levels.

chapter 18

The Handicapped Child in the Child Care Center

There is growing interest and concern in the education and training of exceptional children and youth of all ages. Throughout history the child with a handicap has been a source of anxiety to his parents and his society, but until recently comparatively little was known about diagnosis, treatment, and training of these children. Now, awakening social conscience and modern medicine have developed the belief that the child with a handicap is first of all a human being, basically no different from other children, that his handicap may be corrected or improved, and that he may be helped to participate in a wide range of activities as an adult.

Social philosophy in the United States indicates a general thesis that all children should have equal opportunities, and it is an accepted opinion that, if handicaps are not severe, there is merit in free association between the handicapped child and so-called "normal" children. Many child care centers and preschools for handicapped children have been established in the last two decades and many people are taking training preparatory to specialized work in these schools. Also, an increasing number of ordinary preschool centers are welcoming a small percentage of handicapped children as enrollees in their programs either as full-time or part-time members of children's groups.

No definition of what characterizes a child with a handicap is universal but we may assume that the youngster with a physical, emotional, or mental problem that interferes with his normal growth and development is a handicapped child. The recognition that most of these children are normal in most respects has shifted the emphasis from the handicap to the child and the United States Department of Health, Education, and Welfare now is encouraging and stimulating state programs by providing financial aid, consultation services, and recommendations for programs for handicapped children. Organizations of parents and other people who are interested in various types of handicaps are becoming more numerous and are expanding their programs. Meanwhile, research is being undertaken at an accelerated rate.

No single program can be adapted to every child who is handicapped, but the emphasis of this chapter is devoted principally to those children who can be accomodated in a preschool for "normal" children. Handicapped children often can acquire skills, ideas, and attitudes for which motivation is lacking when they are isolated or are associated only with other handicapped children. Moreover, it is a good experience for "normal" children to learn to live with the handicapped child and to accept him. Actually, it may be difficult to define some of the traits that show differences between these groups of children. Children who are not handicapped may vary as markedly in abilities and potentialities as do (1) those with different kinds of handicaps, and (2) handicapped and "normal" children. Every child has unique problems and needs and each child is handicapped insofar as there are some things that may be difficult for him.

ORIENTATION OF THE HANDICAPPED CHILD

Criteria for enrollment of a handicapped child into a center for "normal" children may be based on chronological age, developmental stage, degree of physical disability, personality and adjustment traits, and level of self-help skills. Practices for the enrollment and admittance of handicapped children are the same as for other children. Application forms usually describe defects or weaknesses of the child and medical examination reports give details as to the severity and prognosis of the handicapping impairment. If the problem is structural, teachers probably will need to be prepared for immediate explanations to older preschool children. If the deficiency is functional, it may be that the other children can learn gradually of the child's problem. In either instance, specific plans for orientation should be discussed and chosen by staff members in cooperation with parents.

During all preenrollment interviews, administrators and group teachers seek specific information about the child's life history as well as parental attitudes and practices in child rearing that concern the child. For at least three reasons, this information is particularly important when a child is handicapped: (1) the child probably has had a more prolonged and concentrated dependency on his parents, and his separation from home is likely to cause severe pressures for both him and his parents; (2) the child probably is more dependent on habitual routines and certain methods of training and guidance than a "normal" child; and (3) physicians, psychologists, or psychiatrists have frequently recommended certain types of care that become, in some measure, the responsibility of the teacher. It is not unusual for these professional persons to have suggested school attendance.

As stated in a previous chapter, staff members sometimes can reassure parents about the behavior patterns of their children and their own feelings about this behavior. This is even more likely to be true when children are exceptional. Usually, these parents have been counseled by professionally trained people before their children reach school age. State health departments and mental health associations provide excellent materials for them. Staff members are not trained to suggest therapeutic measures. Rather it is their place to make referrals when they appear necessary and to cooperate in carrying out resultant instructions. Nevertheless, confidence that the teacher is interested in and accepting of this child is even more important for parents of a handicapped child than for other parents. Even before children are old enough to attend school, staff members can provide a helpful service in inviting parents to visit the school and to observe other handicapped children in a group situation.

Although orientation for a handicapped child in a preschool probably will be slower than for most children, this is not always true. Since good preschools allow children to set their unique patterns of adjustment to the situation, no unusual procedures are necessary. Parents are encouraged to stay at the school as long as their children want them to do so, and frequent discussions are especially important for parents and teahers during this period.

If sufficient staff is available and a handicapped child is expected for enrollment in the preschool, it often helps if one of the staff members can conduct serious study about the specific handicap, how the child is likely to be affected, and how the staff can best help the child and the parents. The following is a portion of a report made by a teacher who was asked to discuss the subject of blind children during an in-service meeting.

A teacher's first reaction to accepting a blind child is usually one of fear for the child's safety. Will the child be able to go up and down stairs without assistance, will she be able to manage outdoors, is there danger of her being bumped by a swing or of her falling from the jungle gym or the seesaw? A second concern is whether the school is sufficiently staffed to accept a child with very little or no vision. Also, there is always the common good of the group to be considered. Usually, the teacher considers the possible effect the presence of a blind child in the school might have on the others and how, when, or even if she should tell the other children that this child cannot see.

In introducing the school to the child, parents are encouraged to talk about school at home as a means of preparing the child for the new experience. The child's first visit to the school is of special significance because it gives her an opportunity to become acquainted with the teacher and to explore the physical surroundings before her formal arrival. Even with careful preparation, the first day at school can be exciting and terrifying for the blind child. She suddenly finds herself surrounded by new voices, often shrill and piercing, and by other unfamiliar sounds. Some children want to explore their new environment, whereas others prefer to sit in one place or to stay near their parents or the teacher whom they know.

The child who cannot see tends to be more sensitive to the teacher's tone of voice and to the manner in which she takes her hand or helps her. She cannot know the expression of approval in her smile but she can feel it in her actions and hear it in her tone. When she trusts her, she is willing to try out the new materials she offers and to participate in the various new experiences the school provides. The blind child should not be expected to take part in all the activities of the daily program any more than the child with vision. However, she always should be given the opportunity to participate in the various group activities and to explore and investigate the possibilities of creative materials. Sometimes, she must be encouraged to conform to the group activity because it would have been her normal behavior to imitate had she had vision. Nonconformance in such instances would make her stand out as being different and would not be helpful either to her or to the group.

In a singing game, the teacher might show her the appropriate actions with her hands or the right way to turn her body. At all times, the blind child must be expected to be as independent as possible. She should be encouraged to walk freely about the room or yard without assistance, to take off her coat, put it in her locker and to take her turn at various daily responsibilities. There are times, of course, when a helping hand is necessary.

Although there is great variation in individual performance, many blind children at this age show more interest in outdoor equipment and activity involving the use of large muscles than in materials such as beads or peg boards that require finer motor coordination. In many instances, it seems as if the blind child is more at ease outdoors in open spaces where she does not feel so strongly the impact of many voices and the pressure of activity closing in on her as in a small playroom.

The products of the child's efforts in creative activities are not always comparable in quality to that of the child with vision, particularly in the eyes of her peers. However, it might be good in terms of her effort and ability. The teacher should indicate that this is so and thus encourage acceptance by the group. Music is one activity most blind children like and in which they excel.

They quickly recognize familiar tunes and usually sing in clear, true tones. They also remember stories and repeat them.

Because the blind child needs more time for exploring and accquainting herself with the prossibilities of toys and equipment, it is important to guard against introducing too many new experiences to her during her early days at school. In most activities, she needs more practice before she attains the same degree of facility as the child with sight. She has to be shown rather than told. Her learning then proceeds somewhat by trial and error until she discovers cues that are helpful to her.

The baby who is born blind doesn't know what seeing is nor does she know that she is deprived of anything, that she is missing anything. And she won't for a long time. She doesn't realize that other people are different. By the time she realizes that she can't see, she can have grown into a happy person who is meeting life as well as any other child. We can help her to feel that she is loved and wanted and that she is an independent person.

Occasionally, another child will seek to participate in the orientation of a handicapped child to the preschool, apparently because of an emotional need to play the role of nurturer.

Luann was a quiet child, age four years and three months. She had no brothers or sisters. Luann seldom took part in vigorous play. Outdoors, she sat in the swings or walked around sedately on the playground. Indoors, she usually played quietly in the doll corner or listened to the record player.

At mid-term, Malcolm, a hydrocephalic child whose age was three years and four months, was admitted to the schoool. Malcolm had two older sisters who were "normal." His medical records stated that his handicap was not severe but that some retardation was apparent mentally and physically. It was apparent from his physical appearance and his facial expression that he probably was afflicted in some manner, but his appearnace was not so indicative of hydrocephaly that one would classify him at first sight. His parents, in talking to staff members, speculated that some social retardation probably existed due to the aforesaid areas of deficiency.

From the first day, Luann became Malcolm's guardian. He was her constant companion both outdoors and in the playroom. She would clasp his hand in hers and talk to him in adult fashion as they walked together. Frequently, Luann would caution other children to be careful of Malcolm's safety.

GUIDANCE OF THE HANDICAPPED CHILD IN THE PRESCHOOL

The principal objectives in guiding handicapped children in the center are like those of child guidance for all children. Briefly, they are: (1) to help children achieve the optimal level of their capacities; (2) to arrange experiences for them that will promote their skills, knowledge, and satisfaction; (3) to provide opportunities for association with other people as a basis for social confidence and eventual social reciprocity; and (4) to promote feelings of acceptance, achievement, and worthiness. The preschool handicapped child has the same physical, emotional, and social needs as any growing child. He wants to be active and to have fun doing things and being with people. Adults who work with children need to determine each child's capabilities or limitations and design their guidance of his learning and behavior to help him develop his strengths and minimize his weaknesses.

As stated, handicaps may be either structural or functional. They also may be of the body, mind, behavior, or a mixture of these conditions. Sometimes, a physical defect is accompanied by a mental impairment, or mental retardation may be accompanied by interference with motor skills. For example, a speech impediment may be caused by low mental ability, phyiscal abnormality, or emotional maladjustment. A deaf child may be mentally retarded or he may not be. Physically deficient children have as wide a range of mental ability as "normal" children. It is important that teachers know the status of a child's problem. Children with severe personality disturbances should not be placed in an ordinary school. They require special training.

The choice of good techniques for guiding handicapped children presents an interesting challenge in the school. What appears to be noncooperation or even rebellion by a handicapped child may be due to the extra attention he has received at home, his lack of experience, his inability to understand what we desire, or frustration resulting from his impairment. It is necessary to strike a balance between recognizing the needs of the child and realizing that all children need to develop an ability to accept controls and regulations.

Some handicapped children are cautious in trying to do things because people have had a tendency to protect them. One of the greatest contributions that schools can offer such children is to expect them to try a variety of things and to accept their failures just as "normal" children are expected to accept theirs. Gauging the readiness of handicapped children is more difficult since their backgrounds of experience probably are more limited and their interests and abilities may be more difficult to evaluate. Although the safety of handicapped children is important, it' is wise to recognize that we are less likely to accept minor falls and accidents as casually as we do with other children.

Hesitancy to explain the child's problem to other children sometimes is a reflection of a tendency by adults to consider handicapped children as different from other children. Unless staff members can accept these children as they do all children, it probably is better if they are not admitted to the particular school. Generally, young children react to handicapped children as if they were not at all unusual.

Claire, a child with a severe impairment of vision, was three years and four months of age when she was admitted to the school at the beginning of the term. Her only sibling, a two-year-old sister, who was "normal" did not attend the school. Although Claire's verbal skills were almost completely undeveloped, she was accustomed to being with other people and she indicated willingness to have her mother leave the school early on the second day.

The school director recommended to Claire's parents that they consult a speech clinician about help for her in language skills. Probably because of her lack of verbal skill and her retarded motor abilities, Clair seldom was included in group play, but she was always busy with some of the school equipment. She particularly enjoyed the outdoor sandpile, finger painting, music activities, and story period. During the first few weeks, an advanced student was assigned to the responsibility of attending Claire. Within a month, she was capable of walking from one room or one activity to another without verbal or physical guidance. In order that other children would be cautious of tripping her or becoming vexed when she was in the way, the teachers explained to them that Claire could not see and that they should tell her when they wanted her to move aside.

Because of difficulties in scheduling, no meeting of all staff members and all parents was planned until school had been in session for almost three months. At that meeting, Mrs. Duncan said, "Mr. Duncan and I are very grateful that our little blind child can attend school." In the conversation that followed, all parents who had not had occasion to visit the school during the term expressed their surprise that Claire was handicapped. They stated that their children had talked about Claire as they had about other children but had not mentioned that she was unusual.

The friendships of handicapped children are similar to those of other children.

Clay, a new child at school, was a totally deaf four-year-old. He was the youngest of three boys in his family and his siblings were "normal." Jerry, age four years and two months, was a "normal" child. He was a "middle" child in his family. He had two older sisters and a younger brother and sister.

Jerry had attended the school since he was two-and-one-half years old. He was a quiet child. One of his school records described him as "lethargic." He followed the routines easily and appeared to be interested in school although he was not enthusiastic.

On the first day of school, Jerry and Clay seemed to like each other. On successive days, they played follow-the-leader on the tricylces and sat together on the barrel swing. Indoors, they played together with the wooden trains and in the block corner. Apparently, words were unnecessary in this friendship.

We might speculate that Clay was fortunate to have found a child who was glad to play with him at his level and without talking. Jerry was a quiet child in disposition, but it also is possible that his home situation, with his four siblings, was invigorating enough that he sought quiet activities and children at school. Both of these children seemed happy in their companionship.

Occasionally, handicapped children are not accepted by their age mates. The rejection of "normal" children in the group usually arouses the pity and concern of teachers and ways of encouraging their acceptance are sought eagerly. These adult attitudes are even more pronounced when the rejected child is handicapped.

Bob, age three-and-one-half, was a cretin. His deficiency had been somewhat arrested by treatments beginning when he was only a few weeks old. He was a very attractive child. His complexion was surprisingly ruddy and his thick, glossy hair was especially beautiful. It was difficult for staff members to believe he was the same child as the subject shown in the pictures taken in his infancy and displayed to the teachers by his parents. His four siblings were of high school age and were "normal."

Bob's facial expression seldom was alert and his motor skills were poor in comparison to those of other children in his group. He spoke slowly and with a slight lisp. Bob seemed to desire an unusual amount of attention from both adults and children. His most frequent remarks were: "Look, Teacher," or "I want to play with you." Perhaps it was partially this habit of soliciting attention that caused the other children to refuse Bob's companionship. Also, his inability to perform at the level of the other children no doubt fostered his lack of popularity.

Situations of this kind are likely to trouble teachers and they often feel powerless to intercede beyond indirect encouragement. Perhaps they can be consoled by thinking that this child possibly will have similar experiences when he attends public school and that his having been at the preschool with its high ratio of adults to children may tend to "cushion" later attitudes when only one teacher is in charge of twenty to thirty children.

Obviously, the guidance of preschool children, handicapped or "normal," should be planned on the basis of the child as a unique individual and no two children, school groups, nor situations will be alike. This does not mean, however, that there are not certain standards by which guidance should be chosen. It is wise to remember the purposes of guidance: the optimal and happy adjustment of children to the present demands of their environment and the eventual development of well-adjusted adults.

It is all too easy for adults to squelch the self-confidence of the disabled child by overprotection or too much help. We may do this through pity, in order to maintain group conformity, or because it seems the easiest way to order the child's day. We must remember that he probably has a greater need to become self-sufficient, to develop self-determination, and to engender self-esteem than the "normal" child.

TYPES OF HANDICAPS

Obviously, those children with severe impairments or with multiple handicaps cannot be accomodated in most day care centers. These children, depending on the severity of disability and the prognosis, can be placed in special preschools for children with similar handicaps or they may need to be institutionalized. Selected readings listed at the end of this chapter will enable the reader to obtain information about where help and advice may be obtained. Only those handicaps affecting the greatest number of children and those that may not inhibit group activities will be described here.

Children with major speech disorders constitute one of the largest groups of seriously handicapped children. Estimates of the numbers of children in this category average approximatley five percent with another five percent reported as having minor speech difficulties. Speech is a complex function involving the neurological system, the throat, nose, lungs, trachea, larnyx, respiratory muscles, auditory organs, vocal chords, tongue, palate, teeth, and dependent on the mental status of the individual. As discussed in the chapter on language development, speech patterns also depend on the social milieu that surrounds the child. Children copy the speech patterns of those people around them.

As with other handicaps, these disabled children often feel insecure due to the pressures exerted by their caretakers to correct errors in speech or by the attitudes of their playmates, ranging from teasing to actual rejection. Sometimes, parents are unaware of what may actually be speech defects simply because they have become so accustomed to their child's way of speaking that they understand what he says. Continuous contact and good rapport with parents will permit referral to a pediatrician and/or a speech clinician according to the apparent nature of the problem. Such action should provide the basis for a therapist-parent-teacher program of treatment and guidance that will help the child.

Hearing is as important to speech as vision is to reading. As stated earlier in this text, speech develops by interaction with other people and if a child is born deaf he will not learn to speak until he is trained to do so by special methods.

Deaf infants make all baby noises including cooing and babbling but they usually begin to lose vocal quality and progress by about the age of nine months because they lack auditory stimulation. This often is the first sign that the child is handicapped. Moderate hearing deficits are not always easily detected.

When Rita's parents filled in the preenrollment information at the laboratory nursery school, they indicated that their main reason for enrolling Rita was the fact that she refused to listen to direction, that when they attempted to talk with her she often would ignore them and simply walk away. They wondered if she might be mentally retarded.

During the initial interview, Mrs. Lewerenz talked about her child's short attention span. She said the child seemed to "flit" from one thing to another.

At school, Rita seemed to enjoy most of the activities. She watched the other children closely and joined in their play as much as could be expected for a child new to the school. However, at story time Rita was the source of incessant disturbance. All of the children in her group were eager listeners and participants, but Rita would sit on her rug briefly, then tug at the arm of a nearby child. When the child did not respond, she would run into a nearby room for a brief time, and then return and ask another child to come and play.

After a few days, Rita's teacher discovered that if he would place his hand on Rita's shoulder to gain her attention and speak directly to her, Rita would follow the story for a short time only to lose interest when various children around the circle made comments to which the teacher would respond.

Mr. Dunstand, the teacher, described these circumstances in a staff meeting and a parent-director-teacher conference was scheduled. As a result, Rita's parents sought medical help and it was discovered that she had a rather severe hearing loss. In reviewing her behavior, it seemed evident that, in some way, Rita had become adept at lip reading if her attention was directed to the speaker but that when she was distracted continuity of communication ceased.

Rita's handicap was corrected by a hearing aid and, by the end of the term, she had made amazing progress in social interaction with adults and children in all activities.

The child with moderate hearing loss will hear only extremely loud noises and only by means of amplification will he be able to function normally. If the loss is not too severe, the child probably will develop normal speech by imitation but often he will produce some sounds incorrectly unless he receives special training by a speech therapist.

The behavior of deaf children varies according to severity, age, intelligence and environment. Sometimes, the child may seem to hear but if he (1) looks at the speaker's mouth instead of into his eyes, (2) responds to signs and gestures more readily than to spoken words, (3) fails to respond when the speaker cannot be seen, (4) tends to develop gestures instead of using speech, or (5) usually carries his head to one side, we may suspect that he has a hearing loss.

The orthopedically handicapped child is the least difficult to absorb within a regular preschool group because of the wide variation in motor skills in most groups Of course, the crippling defect must be minor or special provision needs to be made. Adults in the center should avoid overprotection. We must remember that the child needs to become as independent as possible through the use of his own resources.

Spastic children may or may not show evidence of mental retardation depending on the presence or absence of neuron damage. It is not uncommon for a child to be highly intelligent despite cerebral palsy. Most spastic children do not have hearing problems but they may have difficulty in speaking because of their motor impairment. Adults should not assume that the child is retarded or hard of hearing on the basis of his slow reactions.

Mental retardation is not mental illness. Mental retardation probably is present at birth or at a very early age unless it results from disease or accident in childhood whereas mental illness generally is not present, or is seldom diagnosed, until the child reaches elementary school age. The mentally retarded youngster usually behaves like a younger child, is friendly, and craves attention.

So far, no treatment has been discovered that can cure retardation and enable the child to acquire the abilities of "normal" children of his age. There are a few diseases such as cretinism and phenylketonuria which, if not treated early, can cause progressive mental retardation. Statistics show that fifteen times as many children are mentally retarded as compared with cerebral palsied. Most authorities agree that two to three percent of our population are mentally retarded.

Of course, there are many levels of mental retardation ranging from children who need nursing care to those who appear to function almost normally except for noticeable delays in motor development, speech, and reasoning. Recognition of mental retardation may be difficult because not only mental ability but also motivation, personality, and other traits influence the child's adjustment to his world. Most mildly retarded children enventually will learn to be self-sufficient and will be able to master reading, arithmetic, and writing skills at the third or fourth grade level.

The severely mentally retarded child probably will be institutionalized, and mentally retarded children with physical handicaps will need nursing care, but most mildly retarded children are not physically handicapped and will appear quite normal. Most public schools at present provide special classes for these children and many schools also maintain classrooms for children of somewhat less mental ability who are considered trainable as contrasted to educable. The National Institute for Mental Health has provided interest and support for such programs, and impetus was promoted by the National Association for Retarded Children, which is composed of thousands of parents of retarded children. The N.A.R.C. now coordinates nearly one thousand groups in communities across the country. Membership includes parents, physicians, teachers, other professional workers, and citizens interested in mental retardation.

A retarded child learns in the same way as a normal child, and methods for stimulating him to learn are the same although sometimes more patience and individual attention are necessary. We know that children develop best when they are guided by understanding adults who are alert to their developing interests and who attempt to meet their emotional needs. This is true of all children whatever their unique traits may be.

Hyperactivity usually is listed as a major characteristic of the brain-injured child. If his handicap is not recognized, it is not unusual for him to be treated in a punitive manner because of his behavior. It is important for the preschool staff to be alert to the child with a short attention span who is easily distracted and who demonstrates unusually poor memory or the inability to think logically in comparison to other children. Obviously, any one of these characteristics may appear in all children from time to time but when such patterns persist parents should be encouraged to consult their family doctor for possible referral to a neurologist or psychologist. Some children may progress well with one type of therapy, others with another, and a team approach often is warranted.

It has been stated throughout this book that it is important that the child becomes familiar with his world. This is our primary purpose in the education of the young and it is accomplished by perceptual learning. The great majority of brain-injured children have difficulty in making adequate observations that insure that kind of learning. The ability to perceive through the senses requires numerous skills that must develop in coordination and in the brain-injured child such coordination often cannot occur.

Controversy concerning the nature of learning disorders, their cause, and extent is a major educational dilemma today. Extensive research efforts are underway to categorize and curtail these learning deficits and it is generally an accepted opinion that learning disabilities may be based on psychological, sociological, emotional, or motivational factors as well as on actual brain damage. Children with learning disabilities may be described as having brain damage, perceptual motor deficits, dyslexia, minimal brain dysfunction. None have all of these. Children with severe learning disorders cannot be classified and they may tend to shift from one category to another.

Learning disabilities are experienced by every individual. If the most competent physicist in the world were asked to function as an airline pilot, it is probable that his area of dysfunction might be evident. Everyone has learning disabilities, greater in some areas than in others. Moreover, growth and development are uneven in rate and often unpredictable. It is vital, however, that parents and teachers know what is a normal area of weakness in learning or a serious developmental deficit in some area of the child's brain.

Cultural expectations define the relative importance of such disabilities. In some societies, our concern about learning deficits would be unwarranted. It may be possible for the individual to learn manual skills that make him a productive and happy adult even if he is unable to master the skills of reading, writing, or computing.

In our modern world, however, with the necessity to master communicative skills; to read about what is happening in our community, our country, and the world; and the increasing need to compute prices, living costs, and income tax figures; it is almost incomprehensible to imagine a self-sufficient, self-directing adult who has not achieved some competence in these basic skills.

Among school children with learning disabilities, one child may be able to work his math problems but he cannot read the instructions for doing them, another child may be able to speak fluently but unable to write a sentence, and a third child may be able to write down what he is told to write but unable to read what he has written. Most children with learning problems have many areas where they function well.

Carol was a child in the preschool who appeared to be shy but whose frequent smiles enhanced her personality. Her teacher noticed that, following an activity, she did not pick up materials and put them away. When the teacher asked her to put her paper scraps in the wastebasket, she would only smile. At first, the teacher became irritated, but after several weeks of careful observation it was apparent that Carol lacked space orientation. She simply did not know where toys belonged once they were removed from storage. She did not know where to find the wastebasket although she had been directed to it previously. Her sweet smile and shy manner had usually resulted in her getting the help she needed and had served to cover up her own confusion and anxiety.

In the preschool, teachers can best help the child by concentrating on the child's competencies and by helping him to accept himself and to assume a comfortable position with his peers. If the problem is a minor one that has not caused behavior discrepancies, it is probable that he has not experienced the crippling failures that so often occur in later school years. Therefore, adults in the preschool can work toward encouraging the child's sense of self-confidence, a trait that may be of inestimable worth as he grows up.

Emotionally maladjusted children are difficult to categorize. All children have conflicts but most youngsters develop the ability to resolve their problems in socially approved ways, and careful guidance by the teacher may be all that is needed. If problems are serious and continuous, however, teachers and parents must cooperate in working with the child if he is to be retained in the preschool group.

SELECTED READINGS

1. Braun, Samuel J., and Miriam G. Lasher, *Preparing Teachers To Work With Disturbed Preschoolers,* Tufts University, Medford, Massachusetts, 1970.

This is a description of one of four pilot projects funded by the National Institute for Mental Health. Parts Two and Three of the book will particularly interest those people who are considering work with emotionally disturbed children. Contacts with community agencies and communication with parents are stressed. Methods of working with these children are presented.

2. Bryant, John E., *Helping Your Child Speak Correctly,* Public Affairs Pamphlet No. 445, New York, 1970.

The author has written succintly concerning the causes of speech disorders, their detection, and what role parents can play in recognition and treatment, Evaluations by speech therapists are explained. This booklet should be valuable to all parents who suspect their children may be encountering speech difficulties.

3. Dashe, Marilyn, ed., *Children With Special Problems: A Manual for Day Care Mothers,* Greater Minneapolis Day Care Association, 1972.

This pamphlet presents specific problem descriptions and suggests methods of helping handicapped children. It would be especially valuable for day care centers that need guidelines for selecting and placing handicapped children into centers for "normal" children.

4. Day Care and Child Development Council of America, *For Handicapped*

Preschoolers-Early Childhood Education, Child Care Reprints, Vol. III, Washington, D. C., 1972.

This folder of reprints includes a description of model centers for handicapped children and discusses the early detection and remediation of learning disabilities. The articles present the current status of day care for the handicapped.

5. *Directory for Exceptional Children,* 7th ed., Porter Sargent, Boston, 1972.

As an addition to a community library, this book would be an excellent choice. Private and public facilities in the United States and Canada are classified according to the problems of children whom they serve, and federal and state agencies as well as associations and societies that may be able to offer assistance are listed.

6. Finnie, Nancie R., *Handling the Young Cerebral Palsied Child At Home,* E. P. Dutton, New York, 1970.

This book pertains to the cerebral palsied child of preschool age. It presents detailed descriptions of various levels and kinds of cerebral palsy, prescribing attitudes and training methods that parents should employ. The careful choice and importance of professional therapists is stressed. Advice on handling routine situations is given so that parents can be helped in training the child toward a maximum of self-sufficiency. Line drawings illustrating how to control the child's movements make the book particularly helpful. Appropriate toys to promote self-control are described.

7. Francis-Williams, Jessie, *Children With Specific Learning Difficulties,* Pergamon Press, Elmsford, New York, 1973.

The basis for this book is a report of research concerning the early identification of children of normal intelligence who have learning difficulties. Teaching experiments designed to help such children are described.

8. Fraser, Louise Whitbeck, *A Cup of Kindness,* Bernie Straub Publishing Company, Seattle, 1973.

As the mother of a handicapped child and the director of a school for the mentally retarded, Mrs. Fraser describes methods she has found most successful in guiding handicapped, children toward self-determination. She discusses various kinds of retardation and recommends to parents and teachers ways of helping children afflicted in specific areas.

9. Furman, Robert A., and Anny Katan, eds., *The Therapeutic Nursery School,* International Universities Press, New York, 1969.

This book is a report of a nursery school in Cleveland, Ohio. The premise is that children who are diagnosed as maladjusted can be helped through and by their parents. Chapter 4, "Case Reports," will be interesting to students and parents. The emphasis of the book is Freudian.

10. Heisler, Verda, *A Handicapped Child in the Family: A Guide for Parents,* Grune and Stratton, New York, 1972.

Parents will find this description of group meetings of parents of handicapped children valuable. It should provide a vicarious sharing of feelings and information with other parents who have similar problems.

11. Hellmuth, Jerome, ed., *Learning Disorders,* Vol. 3, Bernie Straub Publishing Company, Seattle, 1968.

Contributors to this book offer a comprehensive presentation of types of learning disorders. Probable learning potentials of children are discussed and appropriate teacher training is described.

12. Hill, Margaret, *The Retarded Child Gets Ready for School,* Public Affairs Pamphelt No. 349, New York, 1963.

Despite the length of time since publication of this pamphlet, the materials provide an excellent explanation as to how preschool teachers and parents should work together. Lists of skills and habits that should be encouraged in retarded children are of special importance.

13. Hurley, Rodger, *Poverty and Mental Retardation,* Vantage Books, New York, 1969.

Hurley proposes a causal relationship between proverty and mental retardation. Descriptive emphasis is placed on children from the ghetto and children of migrant workers. People who are interested in working with underprivileged children will find this book well worth reading.

14. Kirk, Samuel A., *Educating Exceptional Children,* Houghton Mifflin, Boston, 1972.

Kirk provides a comprehensive survey of exceptionality and presents ways in which extra equipment and well trained teachers can enable many handicapped children to be placed in regular classrooms.

15. Kvaraceus, William C., and E. Nelson Hayes, eds., *If Your Child Is Handicapped,* Porter Sargent, Boston, 1972.

Forty six stories of parents who have handicapped children comprise this text. Parents will gain insight as they read about how other parents have reacted to this problem and students and teachers will be made aware of problems faced by parents.

16. Lewis, Eleanore Grater, "The Case for Special Children," *Young Children,* Washing, D. C., August, 1973.

The author describes the assimilation of handicapped children into a nursery and kindergarten school for "normal" children. Staff members, observers, and parents who are interested in reading about an actual situation will enjoy this article.

17. Owen, Freya Weaver, et al., *Learning Disorders In Children: Sibling Studies,* Monograph, Vol. 36, No. 4, Society for Research in Child Development, University of Chicago Press, 1971.

This booklet is a good example of research being conducted to examine possible causes of and characteristics of learning disorders. Summaries at the end of each chapter will be meaningful to interested readers and source materials suggested in the bibliography will be helpful to teachers and parents.

18. Smith, Bert Kruger, *Your Nonlearning Child,* Beacon Press, Boston, 1968.

Mrs. Smith has written a comprehensive, easily read book that will be helpful to parents who have discovered that their child is brain-injured or has learning disability. Her use of descriptions of specific children enhances the interest of the reader. Teachers will gain understanding from this book. Chapter 11, "How the Damaged Child Views Himself," will be especially valuable. A final section of the book furnishes names and addresses of groups and organizations involved in research about and treatment of children with learning disorders.

19. Wender, Paul H., *The Handicapped Child,* Crown Publishers, New York, 1973.

This is an easily read book that will be helpful to parents and teachers who seek information about hyperactive children. Characteristics and causes of hyperactivity are discussed and the reader is guided toward an understanding of the problems that occur to the child and his family as a result of this handicap.

INDEX